EDUCATION LIBRARY

15 Norham Gardens, Oxford OX2 6PY

01865 274028 (enquiries and renewals)
education.library@bodleian.ox.ac.uk
www.bodleian.ox.ac.uk/education

This is a NORMAL LOAN item.
We will email you a reminder before this item is due.

Please visit our website for details of:
• how many books you can borrow and for how long
• how to check when your books are due back
• how to renew your books; items may be renewed if
not reserved by another reader
• level of fines; fines are charged on overdue books

BODLEIAN
LIBRARIES
UNIVERSITY OF OXFORD

THE WOBURN EDUCATION SERIES
General Series Editor: Professor Peter Gordon

EDUCATIONAL RECONSTRUCTION

The 1944 Education Act and the Twenty-first Century

GARY McCULLOCH

THE WOBURN PRESS

First published in 1994 in Great Britain by
THE WOBURN PRESS
Newbury House, 900 Eastern Avenue, Newbury Park,
Ilford, Essex IG2 7HH, England

and in the United States of America by
THE WOBURN PRESS
c/o International Specialized Book Services, Inc.
5602 N.E. Hassalo Street, Portland, Oregon 97213-3644

British Library Cataloguing in Publication Data

McCulloch, Gary
    Educational Reconstruction: 1944
    Eductional Act and the Twenty-first
    Century. – (Woburn Education Series)
    I. Title II. Series
    370.941

            ISBN 0-7130-0191-7 (cloth)
            ISBN 0-7130-4019-X (paper)

Library of Congress Cataloging-in-Publication Data

McCulloch, Gary.
    Educational reconstruction: the 1944 Education Act and the twenty-
first century/Gary McCulloch.
        p.   cm.—(The Woburn education series)
    Includes bibliographical references and index.
    1. Education and state—England—History—20th century.
2. Education and state—Wales—History—20th century. 3. Education—
Law and Legislation—England—History—20th century. 4. Education—
Law and Legislation—Wales—History—20th century. 5. School
management and organization—England—History—20th century.
6. School management and organization—Wales—History—20th century.
I. Title. II. Series.
LC93.G7M33 1994
379.41′09′044—dc20   94-21265
                                                           CIP

Typeset by Vitaset, Paddock Wood, Kent
Printed in Great Britain by Bookcraft (Bath) Ltd, Midsomer Norton

For my parents – graduates of the 'class of 1944' – and for my son

Contents

Acknowledgements

I must first of all thank everyone who has helped me, knowingly or otherwise, in the writing of this book. Peter Gordon, as editor of the Woburn Education Series, gave strong support for the project and much wise advice. Ivor Goodson, Peter Gordon, Anthony Hartnett, Roy Lowe, Brian Simon and Penny Tinkler made helpful comments on draft chapters of the work. Thanks also to members of the various conferences and seminars where I developed the ideas put forward in this book, and to my colleagues and students at the University of Auckland and Lancaster University. As always, all errors of fact and interpretations are mine alone.

Some of the general issues that are developed in detail in the book are outlined in my inaugural lecture at Lancaster University, *Lessons From The Class Of 1944? History As Education*. I would also like to acknowledge the following journals which have published earlier work in particular areas: *Education Research And Perspectives* (especially for Chapter 2), *History Of Education* (Chapter 7), and *International Studies in Sociology of Education* (Chapter 8).

May I also take this opportunity to acknowledge the support of the Leverhulme Trust for the research project 'Education and the working class: history, theory, policy and practice', on which some of the research for this book (especially Chapter 5) is based. Also the Economic and Social Research Council for its support for the research project 'The professional culture of teachers and the secondary school curriculum', which helped to formulate some of the ideas especially for Chapter 8. The research committees of Lancaster University and the University of Auckland also assisted with travel funds to visit archives helpful for this study.

The work is dedicated to my parents, who went to school in the 1940s, and also to my son Edward, whose schooling is to begin in 1994 and will continue well into the twenty-first century. As always, my deepest debt is to my wife Sarah, for her unstinting support and the inspiration she provides.

1

Introduction

'Upon the education of the people of this country the fate of this country depends.' With these famous words of Benjamin Disraeli, the White Paper *Educational Reconstruction*, published in July 1943, opened its case for reform. During the half-century that has elapsed since then, ideas about the most suitable ways of 'educating the people' have changed appreciably. In spite of such changes, the basic contention about the central role of education in determining the 'fate of the country' remains strong, and continues to be used to justify far-reaching and systematic educational reform.

This book focuses on the cycle of educational reform of the 1940s that was advanced so eloquently through the 1943 White Paper and reached its culmination in the Education Act of 1944. In this specific sense, it seems particularly apt for the title of the work to evoke the ideal of 'educational reconstruction'. In a broader spirit, too, such a note is apposite in suggesting the general theme of educational reform and renewal that runs throughout this book. While giving extended and detailed treatment to the reforms of the 1940s, it also explores their relationship to recent and contemporary changes in education.

This more general notion of 'educational reconstruction', related both to the past and to the present, echoes the American historian Michael Katz who has tried to show 'how the reconstruction of America's educational past can be used as a framework for thinking about the present'.[1] Katz reminds us that the 'historical products' created over time were generally contested between different groups during their formation, among a number of discrete alternatives. Moreover, he adds, they should be seen as 'neither inevitable nor immutable', and perhaps may 'no longer even be appropriate'.[2] In a profound sense, Katz would argue, thinking about the past can help us to rethink our ideas not only about the present, but also about the future. In Britain also, the educational historian Brian Simon captures such an aspiration most trenchantly when he insists: 'There is, perhaps, no more liberating influence than the knowledge that things have not always been as they are and need not remain so.'[3]

Establishing the dynamic connections between past, present

and future that are suggested here implies first an approach to educational history that is explicitly 'present-minded'. The history seeks to provide explanatory leverage towards a greater understanding of the problems and possibilities of the present. It is also, of course, 'futures-minded', evoking the unresolved dilemmas and potential frameworks of development that may help to inform our ideas about education in the years that lie ahead. This latter theme is particularly resonant in the final decade of the twentieth century. 'Preparing for the twenty-first century', to make use of Paul Kennedy's phrase, has become a common objective that is likely to become especially widespread as we approach the millennium.[4] Education is already proving to be popular territory for such plans and prognostications.

In academic discourse relating to education, the promise of the future symbolised in the dawn of a new century has helped to encourage discussion of how education should respond to the changing needs of what is often described as a 'post-modern' society.[5] Educational policies have also given much attention to this idea, if only as a rhetorical device to rationalise the need for reform. In Britain, the approach of the twenty-first century has been used to help justify a new cycle of radical reconstruction of the education system. According to Kenneth Baker, who as Education Secretary was chiefly responsible for the Education Reform Act of 1988, it was especially important at this time not to be 'baulked' by disagreements on how to tackle the problems afflicting education: 'For a variety of reasons the education system needed radical change if it was to match the needs of twenty-first-century Britain. If this meant foregoing the usual snail's pace at which reform in education was conducted, then so be it.'[6]

The idea of planning for a new century also seemed to encourage the design of blueprints for the future that were intended to cast aside 'out-of-date' barriers and distinctions. In 1991, a Government White Paper entitled *Education and Training for the 21st Century* sought to establish not only a new set of institutions, but also fresh thinking about how they should be envisaged.[7] The following year, the White Paper *Choice and Diversity* began with the idea of 'Schools into a new century', and emphasised the need to articulate a 'vision for education in the 21st century'.[8] Indeed, the 1992 White Paper concludes with a chapter, albeit of less than one page in length, that envisages 'A New Century of Excellence'. Plans being developed in the early 1990s, it reminds us, 'will take at least a decade to work through: a child tested at the age of 7 this year will not be taking GCSE [examinations] until 2001'.[9] As a result of these changes, it hopes, 'The education system of the 21st century will be neither divisive nor based on some lowest common denominator. Diversity, choice and excellence will be its hallmarks, with each child having an opportunity to realise his or her full potential, liberating and developing his or her talents.'[10] Another recent report, that of the independent National Commission on Education in 1993, is no less enthusiastic in thrusting its ideals forward into the twenty-first century, for example in its notion of 'twenty-first century teachers': 'In our vision, a teacher in the twenty-first century will be an authority and enthusiast in the knowledge, ideas, skills, understanding and values to be presented to pupils.'[11] Such idealisations of education in the twenty-first century again underline the imperfect state of the current education system to encourage radical reform.

Much of this literature focusing on the assumed needs of the twenty-first century tends to disregard or play down the importance of understanding the nature of education as it has developed over the past hundred years. In recent policy initiatives, in particular, there has been a general emphasis on a technical or managerial approach to problems that fails to address more profound or long-term cultural, social, and historical issues. Sometimes, it appears that the history is despised or overshadowed because it represents the 'problem', whereas the future represents the 'solution'. In these circumstances, it is especially crucial to develop a greater awareness of the relevance of the historical dimension in understanding contemporary dilemmas. The reforms of the 1940s would appear to be at least potentially an important example in demonstrating such links.

In what ways may one conceptualise such 'relevance'? It is important, first of all, to develop frameworks for understanding. In Chapter 2, some general issues involved in this process are discussed in detail, especially in relation to the kinds of problems that may be encountered, and some specific approaches to establishing long-term historical frameworks. Chapter 3 seeks to locate the reforms of the 1940s within the context of successive waves or cycles of educational reform, relating them to the institutions that had been introduced in the nineteenth century, and also to the changes that were later to be promoted in the 1960s and in the 1980s/1990s. Chapter 4 then examines the continuing influence of the 1944 'settlement' over the following half-century, and the changing visions of what 1944 represented, to suggest an important 'historical' dimension in even the most ahistorical of education policies.

The following chapters proceed to discuss particular aspects of the reforms of the 1940s within a broader historical framework. In Chapter 5, the 'tripartite' nature of the reforms, their emphasis on identifying three different types of child, is explored. Chapter 6 investigates the civic idealism that helped to motivate and justify the reforms, and which gave them so much of their lasting authority. Chapter 7 highlights conflicting notions of the secondary school curriculum that underlay the reforms of the 1940s, and which continued to exert a lasting influence. Chapter 8 discusses the position of school teachers in these reforms, especially in relation to assessment and examinations. Chapter 9 then examines the influence of the reforms that took place in Britain, upon those 12,000 miles away in New Zealand. The concluding chapter attempts to draw some provisional 'lessons' from this historical study, and again looks forward to assess the prospects for the current cycle of educational reform in the 1990s and beyond.

It should be emphasised, perhaps, that this work does not seek to give the 'final word' on the 1944 Act and its relationship with present and future change. Nor does it attempt to work towards closure on the many issues involved. Rather, it envisages open and continuing debate. Many themes other than those developed in this book also deserve exploration in much greater depth, and it is hoped further research will begin to do so in the years ahead. If we approach the 1944 Act not simply as a fixed and finished piece of legislation, nor even in terms of its unresolved issues and ambiguities, but in a thematic fashion that highlights its multiple realities as is the case in the present work, we must expect no less.

NOTES

1. Michael Katz, *Reconstructing American Education* (London: Harvard University Press, London, 1987), p.1.
2. Ibid.
3. Brian Simon, 'The history of education', in J.W. Tibble (ed.), *The Study of Education* (London: Routledge & Kegan Paul, 1966), p.92.
4. Paul Kennedy, *Preparing for the Twenty-First Century* (London: Harper Collins, 1993).
5. E.g. P. Schlechty, *Schools for the Twenty-First Century* (San Francisco: Jossey-Bass, 1990), p.39.
6. Kenneth Baker, *The Turbulent Years: My Life in Politics* (London: Faber & Faber, 1993), p.169.
7. Department of Education and Science, *Education and Training for the 21st Century*, 2 vols. (London: HMSO, 1991).

8. Department for Education, *Choice and Diversity* (London: HMSO, 1992), paragraph 1.21.
9. Ibid., paragraph 15.1.
10. Ibid., paragraph 15.7.
11. Report of the National Commission on Education, *Learning to Succeed: A Radical Look At Education Today and a Strategy for the Future* (London: Heinemann, 1993), pp.196–7.

2

Lessons from the Class of 1944?

The passage of the 1944 Education Act accompanied some of the most dramatic events of the Second World War. The debate on its Second Reading in the House of Commons coincided with D-Day, as Allied troops invaded occupied France. The Committee stage began soon after a major strike by a flying bomb in West London. Delayed over the summer, the Bill did not receive Royal Assent until 3 August.[1] And yet it was by no means a mere sideshow to the main drama. On the contrary, understanding the hopes that were attached to the 1944 Education Act gives us a vital clue to the vigour of the British war effort. And when the dust of war had settled, the Education Act remained, a lasting monument to sacrifice and a foundation stone for a society at peace.

Fifty years on, in the midst of a new set of reforms designed to replace those of the 1940s, it seems very suitable for us to revisit the 'class of 1944'. As we do so, it may be possible to understand the aims of the educational reforms that culminated in the Education Act of 1944. These represented a remarkable cycle of reforms that affected every aspect of education in England and Wales. At the same time, they helped to consolidate many features of educational provision that had already become characteristic. They attracted broad support for their main principles from across the political spectrum, and established a settlement in education that endured for a generation. It is crucial to understand the vision of reform that underlay these developments.

Interpreting the 1944 Act

The present work interprets the Education Act of 1944 not simply in terms of the final, carefully negotiated text that became law in August 1944, but in a way that encompasses the processes and aspirations that contributed to its formation. This involves a multi-dimensional approach to the problem. It demands a detailed examination of the Act and of its contribution to educational change. It also entails understanding how the Act was constructed, and the role of key individuals and groups in its formation. Further to this, it requires investigation into how the Act related to the several major education reports that surrounded it. These included the Spens Report on secondary education (1938), the so-called 'Green Book' of 1941, the McNair Report on the training of teachers (1944), and the Fleming Report on public schools (1944). In particular, however, the importance of two documents that immediately preceded the Act of 1944 needs to be emphasised. Both of these were published in July 1943: the White Paper on *Educational Reconstruction*, followed by the Norwood Report on the secondary school curriculum and examinations. The general intention of the current work is to address the aims and aspirations that underlay the reforms, and at the same time to develop an awareness of their problems, limitations, and contradictions.

In pursuing these aims, the current work adopts a thematic approach, inquiring into how particular issues and problems were worked out. It may thus be contrasted with a chronological approach, which would give a detailed, blow-by-blow account of the background to the Education Act. The latter method has its uses, although it can easily lead to a dry narrative of what has been aptly styled as 'Acts and facts'.[2] It is not intended here to provide a detailed discussion of the negotiations that paved the way for the Education Act of 1944, nor of educational politics in the Second World War. A magisterial account of this type has already been produced in Peter Gosden's work *Education in the Second World War*.[3] The earlier work of Harold Dent is also unrivalled in the field for its detailed knowledge and incisive analysis of the text of the Act itself.[4]

Recovering the reforming vision that informed the 1944 Act means also to try to understand it in its wider contexts and relationships. To do this, it is important to locate it in relation to the social, political, cultural, and other developments of the 1940s. The role of the Second World War, the importance of wartime politics and of hopes for post-war planning, the involvement of social inequalities and of religious, civic, and industrial values – these are all fundamental to a broader interpretation of the 1944 Act. The international, indeed global context also seems highly significant in this regard. Roy Lowe has recently demonstrated the differences and the similarities in national responses to the general crisis of education in the Second World War.[5] And it is helpful, too, to establish some notion of the microcontext: the relationship of schools, teachers, pupils, families, and individual lives to the public drama that reached its dénouement in 1944. For example, it is clear that the working lives and responsibilities of individual teachers were directly affected by the wider educational changes that were taking place around them.[6] The local dimensions of the national policy process, including the changing relationship between local education authorities and the central education department, are equally worthy of detailed inquiry.[7]

It is important at the same time to establish a longer-term historical framework for our study. The Education Act of 1944 represented what seemed, and still seems, to be a key moment in educational reform. Assessing its historical importance entails asking how it related to trends that have taken decades, generations, or even the entire modern era of schooling to work themselves out. The surface appearance of rapid change and activity can often be deceptive unless we appreciate the long-term patterns and continuities within which they occurred, and which in turn they influenced or reinforced. Again, this historical framework may be conceived as both national and international in its scope. When it is viewed in terms that emphasise the development of English social institutions, for example, we may relate the Act to the rise of the so-called 'Welfare State'.[8] It has been argued that the 1944 Act, with the Education Act of 1918, are 'of interest to the English social or education historian as major signposts along the road to the English welfare state'.[9] Some historians, especially Correlli Barnett, have sought to link it to a protracted decline in Britain's economic competitiveness.[10] Still others have emphasised how it left social and gender differences relatively unscathed.[11] Equally, when interpreted within a global framework it might be seen as characteristic of the 'liberal era', which involved what has been described as a 'sense of optimism and faith about the notion of the school as an agency of social redemption'.[12]

The further intention behind suggesting longer-term historical frameworks is to begin to develop clearer links between the Education Act of 1944, and the cycle of reform of which it was part, and the current set of educational reforms in the 1990s. The cycle of reforms that has been going on for at least the past decade, and which at present shows no sign of coming to an end, has often been described as the most radical set of reforms since those of the 1940s. Fifty years on, what lessons have been learned from what happened then? And how can we compare the current generation of education reform with that of the 1944 Education Act?

This aspect of interpreting the 1944 Act offers opportunities to highlight contrasts between the past and the present no less than their similarities. Both continuity and change are explicitly represented in this comparison between these cycles of reform half a century apart. But it does not only suggest a means of interpreting the Act of 1944; it also suggests that we can use an understanding of the reforms that took place in the 1940s to inform a clearer awareness of educational issues and policies in the 1990s. The question becomes, to what extent are current policies an attempt to reform, or reconstitute, or adapt, the vision of the 1940s? Is there a comparable aim that underlies the educational reforms of the 1990s, and if so how can we explain the changes, the differences, the continuities, in relation to those of fifty years ago?

History and education policy

In seeking to relate the reforms of the 1940s with those of the 1990s, it is important to be aware of the complex and problematic relationship between history and education policy. On the one hand, education policy has commonly appeared to be lacking in historical perspective. The events and problems of the past tend to be treated as an irrelevant distraction to the issues at hand. In a profound sense, however, history continues to impinge on even those most historically unaware of educational policies. Elisabeth Hansot and David Tyack, in the United States, argue that 'The issue is not *whether* people use a sense of the past in shaping their lives but how accurate that historical map is. Present actions and plans for the future flow ineluctably from beliefs about what went before. Whether individual or collective, whether haphazard or methodical, a sense of history clearly has an impact on educational policy.'[13] To some extent, recent policies in the British context have been drawn from historical interpretations of educational problems, such as those of Martin Wiener and Correlli Barnett.[14] At other times, for example under the Labour Prime Minister James Callaghan, they are based more upon lessons derived from personal experience.[15]

Often, in order to have a tangible and clear 'lesson' for the present, the complex relationships of historical change are selected and simplified. This process can exert a major influence upon the nature of educational policies. In Scotland, for example, as R.D. Anderson has documented, the notion of a distinctively democratic and egalitarian 'Scottish tradition' has developed to become a potent factor that itself influences reform. Anderson describes this Scottish tradition as a 'powerful historical myth', not in order to signify that it is untrue or false, but to suggest its role as 'an idealization and distillation of a complex reality'. It takes on ideological and political force as it informs change – 'interacting with other forces and pressures, ruling out some developments as inconsistent with the national tradition, and shaping the form in which the institutions inherited from the past are allowed to change'.[16] In New Zealand, too, as the former Director of Education, C.E. Beeby, has commented, educational change in that country during the twentieth century has been based on three successive 'educational myths', each of which has been especially potent for about twenty-five years before giving way to the next.[17]

Notions of an 'English tradition' in education have been similarly employed to inform and justify specific forms of outlook, planning, or policy. In the nineteenth century, as Eric Hobsbawm has well shown, the 'invention of tradition' was a means of establishing or reinforcing the status of particular social institutions, and of defining the ways they were to develop.[18] Public schools and universities were notable in taking advantage of this method of sustaining their own authority, which in turn defined the role of other institutions in relation to them.

Perhaps the clearest twentieth century example of this kind of process in the English context is the attempt by Cyril Norwood in the 1920s to articulate and defend an 'English tradition of education'. Norwood, who was at that time Head of Harrow School, and later chaired the committee that produced the Report on curriculum and examinations in secondary schools (1943), perceived a strong line of historical continuity that justified the values and the continued existence of the public schools. The English tradition of education, he argued, was 'not in its origin based on a logical theory', nor was it 'the creation of any inspired educational reformer'. Rather, it had 'merely grown out of the life of the nation', and had eventually been 'taken to be something which everybody knows'.[19] He drew on the ideal of knighthood, chivalry, and the English gentleman, and related this to the ethos of the public schools. It was, he maintained, an 'education which trains a generation through mind and discipline, through culture of the mind and perfection of the body, to a conscious end of service to the community'.[20] According to Norwood, it was therefore this 'highest English tradition' that should be preserved and extended into the future.

In developing such a notion of relevance, there is some danger that this potential contribution of historical perspectives in understanding, and even influencing, current policies may be portrayed as in some way obvious and unproblematic. Gerald Grace, for example, in a comparative analysis of schooling in England and New Zealand, argues that a full understanding of contemporary changes must be based on an understanding of historical 'roots' and 'lessons': 'Contemporary policy discussion dismisses history at its peril. The surface structure of contemporary social and educational problems is constituted and patterned by the deep structure of historical principles and of historical struggles.'[21] Moreover, he claims, 'The danger for policy-makers of ignoring history is that the analysis of policy issues becomes literally superficial and key elements in the situation are missed out.'[22] Similarly, N. Ray Hiner, in his presidential address to the History of Education Society in the United States, has declared confidently that historians of education 'should contribute much more to the discussion and formulation of educational policy, broadly defined', because 'as historians of education, we have special skills, insights, and perspectives that are indispensable to sound educational policy'.[23] In promoting links between 'history' and 'policy', however, it is important to go beyond such broad affirmations, and to recognise clearly the problems involved.[24]

The important work of Hansot and Tyack develops the notion of establishing a historical framework within which to locate and judge current educational policies. In their article 'A usable past: using history in educational policy', they make the point that history can show the ways in which public education has served, and can still serve, a 'common good'. Further to this, they argue, it can also contribute to enlarging the range of those who define and benefit from that common good, in particular by communicating a critical appreciation of the problems and limitations of those past traditions. Thus they are looking for history to help provide what they describe as an 'integrative sense of the shared beliefs that hold the parts together, such as the ideology of equality and democratic participation,'[25] as an antidote to the fragmented politics of recent years. In fact, they argue, 'without sound notions of equality and civicism it is hard to see how citizens can weather a time of scarcity without resorting to a narrow privatism, a possessive individualism'.[26] On this view, history provides a means by which to stabilise and rationalise current attitudes towards the education system, and also to reform the system towards an enlarged sense of the 'common good'.

Another American historian, Donald Warren, has suggested that educational history should not merely seek to illuminate selected policies, but should address the role of specific agencies which often operate at some distance from educational institutions, but which, even so, influence the character of educational policy and practice. Such agencies would include the Treasury, and also professional and industrial organisations with their own vested interests and traditions. Warren argues that such history, rather than being conducted on traditional lines, should be 'rigorously interdisciplinary', encouraging dialogue and engagement with economics, planning, administration, and law. Warren also contends that in its approach to policy, history introduces a 'longitudinal' dimension, evoking the experience of past initiatives, as an antidote to the more usual 'linear' tendency. At the same time, according to this view, it gives a greater prospect of developing comparative policy studies, and accords the humanities a greater role in a research area dominated by social and behavioural sciences.[27]

In Britain, Harold Silver has been especially prominent in advancing historical interpretations of recent and contemporary education policy. In his recent work *Education, Change And The Policy Process* he argues that historical tools can help to penetrate 'current debate and policy, the processes, practices and vocabularies in which they are embodied, and which they reflect and engender.'[28] Like Warren, Silver emphasises the need to relate closely to and be more involved in work in other disciplines, such as politics and social policy. Silver is especially interested in showing the policy process as it takes form over time, to explain how the assumptions, ideologies, opinions and interests that are involved in policy formation interact and change. Moreover, he is also acutely conscious of the problematic aspects of relating history to policy, and of the likely effects of such an emphasis on historians themselves: 'In determining a proper role for themselves historians will be inevitably and usefully compelled to review their own organising concepts and assumptions, to learn from evaluators, ethnographers and others grappling from different directions with the same complex sequences and processes.'[29]

Historical frameworks of understanding

Such approaches begin to hint at possible historical frameworks for understanding the Education Act of 1944 that will have purchase or leverage on the present and the future. One may indeed be able to go beyond the familiar trends and landmarks that are usually associated with 1944. This is especially important since the 'familiar' has been rendered problematic in the light of changing contemporary problems since the 1940s. The idea that the reforms of the 1940s formed part of a long-term process of gradual progress towards the future, a common liberal framework of interpretation, has been widely discredited over the past twenty years. It has become more usual to take the opposite view and to regard the reforms of the past, including the 1940s, as leading ineluctably towards malaise and social crisis. Both of these possible frameworks of interpretation, however, seem grossly simplistic, and need themselves to be challenged.

An alternative framework for understanding the 1944 Act would interpret it as the apogee of a century of educational development, a characteristic flowering of an era of educational reform that is already becoming a distant memory. On such a view, it is especially important for us to understand that this *was* a different era from our own, and that many of the assumptions and values that were then widely shared may now appear peculiar, alien, or even novel. On the other hand, it is necessary to explore the ways in which such assumptions and values were contested and discussed among the various interests involved in developing the reforms of the 1940s. Another key issue would be the extent to which the ideas and policies that were established in different areas in the 1940s have continued to exert an influence that continues to this day. In other words, such a framework would attempt to locate the Education Act of 1944 in terms of *change, contestation* and *continuity*, from the vantage point of our rapidly changing situation in the 1990s.

This kind of project would also have important implications for our understanding of education in the 21st century. We would not be seeking to extrapolate a continuing trend into the future, as in the more rigid liberal and marxist models. Nor would we be aspiring to match the changing needs of education to the supposed new needs of the twenty-first century, as in the somewhat functionalist rhetoric that has become fashionable. It does mean that we would expect the twenty-first century not to offer a clean break from the past, and that the 1940s will continue to echo and reverberate, sometimes in surprising and perhaps unwelcome ways. The projects of the past, mutilated, disfigured and dismembered, will be strewn across new projects even at the same time that these lean eagerly forwards towards the future.

Contesting the educational State

An area of particular concern in the present work is the character of what has come to be called the 'educational State'. As a focus of interest, this offers immense opportunities to study the processes of change, continuity, and contestation between different interests and ideologies. It is especially important for an historical study to emphasise this domain, because such works have tended to depict the State in rather crude and deterministic terms. In England, the notion of an 'educational Establishment' often serves to convey the sense of a self-serving elite group in ultimate control of education policy, imbued with common values arising from their public school education, and with common class interests in restricting and manipulating educational reform. From this premise, the State is generally portrayed, if not as entirely opaque, then as monolithic in nature and uniform in its effects.

Recent research in the 'policy sociology' of education, on the other hand, has emphasised the competition of ideologies and interests that goes on inside the educational State. It also warns against assuming the role and character of the State to be either fixed or monolithic. According to Stephen Ball, the educational State constitutes 'that conglomeration of sites and agencies concerned with the regulation of the education system'. Such sites and agencies, Ball continues, 'contain and represent contesting interests in policy formation and policy debate,' which generate in turn 'conflict and incoherence within the state and within and across the various sites which make up the state.' He suggests that these conflicts take the form of 'general and particular disputes over and struggles for control of the meaning and definition of education', for instance in arguments over pedagogy, curriculum and assessment.[30] The work of McPherson and Raab also indicates incoherence and competing interests within what they call the 'policy community', with particular reference to Scottish education since 1945. They define this policy community as 'the community of individuals who mattered', and 'also the forum in which the interests of groups were represented, reconciled or rebuffed'.[31] Such analyses suggest that a more problematic and complex set of processes is at work, within and around the educational State, than is evident in historical discussions of English educational policy that are dependent on a simple model of the 'educational Establishment'.

Some historians have also begun to develop a more theorised view of the character and role of the educational State. Andy

Green's work on the growth of public education systems in the nineteenth century indicates a close relationship between these systems and the rise of the 'liberal state'. According to Green, 'the development of education can only be understood as part of the wider process of state formation that led to the emergence of the modern capitalist state.'[32] In a similar vein, Pavla Miller contends that during the nineteenth century mass education systems became 'one of the arenas where competing social groups attempted to allay their fears and realize their dreams and aspirations.' In this process, she affirms, 'the state has never been a simple executive of the ruling class', but has been 'the site of continuous struggle between powerful interests over the way decisions are made and institutions are shaped to deal with common problems'.[33] There is clearly a need for more historical research to understand the processes, values and interests involved in contesting the educational State. In particular, it seems important to develop such work in relation to the first half of the twentieth century, in order to bridge the gap between the nineteenth-century ferment detected by historians such as Green and Miller, and the contemporary patterns of power relationships highlighted in the policy sociology literature. Such a project should help us to determine the extent to which such patterns were already in place by the end of the nineteenth century, and the parameters within which contestation has persisted since that time, especially during periods of relatively sudden or rapid social and educational change such as the 1940s.

The present work tends, therefore, to concentrate on different facets of the struggles that went on within and around the educational State during the reform cycle of the 1940s. Such tensions are especially significant when addressing the contested character of the 'settlement' of 1944, and the alternative possibilities that it tended to obscure. They also carry more long-term implications in relation to the nature of the modern 'educational State'. These are often not reflected at all, or else only partially, in the public, written texts that are produced; in the official Reports, for example, or in the legislation. It is therefore crucial to inspect the processes at work in the production of such texts, and the nature of the negotiations and conflicts involved. Silences on particular issues are also worthwhile to contemplate. Whether signifying reverence, as was often the case with the public schools, or incomprehension as with the secondary moderns, the failure to address a topic may belie its longer term significance.

Another aspect of this general project concerns the deciphering and untangling of the sources of particular policies or trends, both in the short term and over a longer period. Related to this is a struggle with the shorthand by which reforms are conventionally associated with particular names or influences. 'Norwood', for example, may mean the Norwood Report, or the Norwood Committee, or Sir Cyril Norwood himself, in different contexts, and each of these entities may have quite different or even opposing types of significance in relation to particular themes. Then again, if one of these entities is clearly identified for a specific purpose, it is useful to know the particular stage or period to which the analysis refers. Such considerations begin to bring out the complexities of the interactions in and around such committees that tend to be obscured by convenient labels.

A still wider issue that requires attention concerns the familiar images of reforms and how they are usually assumed to relate to each other: the landscape or scenery of major Acts, Reports, and personalities by which cycles of educational reform tend to be depicted. A major purpose in revisiting such scenes must be to approach them from routes and directions that are less familiar, or to wander from the beaten track into the untamed bush to discover what has hitherto lain unnoticed. It may be possible even to shift the scenery around and observe the relationship of different features that are usually seen separately, or to embark on land-scape gardening that will open up new vistas, or certainly to view the surroundings in different shades of light. Each of these approaches will in turn affect the ways in which the reforms of the 1940s are seen to relate to those of our own day; that is, they will exert a different kind of leverage as we seek to understand the changes and continuities that have combined to produce our con-temporary sets of problems and solutions.

In terms of the contestation involved, a further key issue is to decide which were the winners, and which the losers, of the major and important conflicts of the time. If we conceive the Education Act of 1944 as symbolising a 'settlement' of a debate between competing values and interests, with specific alternatives at stake in the contest, it is necessary to determine which were confirmed and which were rejected. Some will have enjoyed a 'good war', to be followed by a generation of entrenched and unchallenged supremacy. Others will have been debated openly, perhaps for the first time, only to be relegated once more to the margins. Still others will have seen a long-term decline accelerate into speedy oblivion. In this sphere, then, one is concerned with the politics of educational reform, and with the eventual outcomes as the heat of the debate begins to subside.

In still more general terms, what is being suggested here is the importance of a social history of educational policy. This needs to resist the temptation to 'raid' the past for easy answers to current issues. Nevertheless, it will face both ways, towards the past and towards the future. Such an approach is likely to highlight cultural depth and the longevity of issues that may on the surface appear to be novel. By the same token, it is unlikely to appeal to those who are seeking a quick fix of an administrative or technical kind to the problems of today. It should convey a sense of the complexity of past dilemmas, as well as of their relationship to wider social, political, economic and cultural changes. Stephen Ball has argued that a 'sociology of education policy' should examine in a critical way the social and ideological bases of the policy process.[34] A social history of education policy might be conceived in terms of helping us to understand the sources of today's problems, the underlying issues concealed in contemporary nostrums. A major part of the purpose of the current work, then, is to explore the potential of a social history of education policy by revisiting the scene of a familiar set of reforms to seek fresh insights, both on the past and on a changing present.

NOTES

1. F.A. Cavenagh, 'The Education Bill in the House of Lords', *Journal of Education*, No.901, Aug. 1944, pp.385–6.
2. See e.g. Ivor Goodson, *The Making Of Curriculum* (London: Falmer, 1988), Ch.4 for a discussion of the problems of this kind of approach.
3. P. Gosden, *Education in the Second World War: A Study in Policy and Administration* (London: Methuen, 1976).
4. See especially Harold Dent, *The Education Act, 1944: Provisions, Possibilities and Some Problems* (London: University of London Press, 1944).
5. Roy Lowe (ed.), *Education and the Second World War: Studies in Schooling and Social Change* (London: Falmer, 1992).
6. Martin Lawn, 'What is the teacher's job? Work and welfare in elementary teaching, 1940–1945', in M. Lawn, G. Grace (eds), *Teachers: The Culture And Politics of Work* (London: Falmer, 1987), pp.50–64.
7. See e.g. Gareth Elwyn Jones, '1944 and all that', *History of Education*, 19/3 (1990), pp.235–50.
8. Derek Fraser, *The Evolution of the British Welfare State* (London: Macmillan, 1973), esp. pp.205–6.
9. D.H. Akenson, 'Patterns of English educational change: the Fisher and the Butler Acts', *History Of Education Quarterly*, 11 (1971), p.143.
10. Correlli Barnett, *The Audit of War: The Illusion and Reality of Britain as a Great Nation* (London: Macmillan, 1986), esp. Ch.11, 'Education for industrial decline'.
11. e.g. Deborah Thom, 'The 1944 Education Act: the "art of the possible"', in Harold Smith

(ed.), *War and Social Change: British Society in the Second World War* (Manchester: Manchester University Press, 1986), pp.101–28.

12. Thomas Fleming, 'Canadian school policy in liberal and post-liberal eras: historical perspectives on the changing social context of schooling, 1846–1990', *Journal of Education Policy*, 6/2 (1991), p.183.

13. Elisabeth Hansot and David Tyack, 'A usable past: using history in educational policy', in A. Lieberman and M.W. McLaughlin (eds.), *Policy-Making In Education* (Chicago: National Society for the Study of Education, 1982), p.21.

14. Ibid.

15. Lord Callaghan of Cardiff, 'The Education Debate – I', in M. Williams, R. Dougherty and F. Banks (eds.), *Continuing The Education Debate* (London: Cassell, 1992), p.16.

16. R.D. Anderson, *Education And Opportunity In Victorian Scotland: Schools And Universities* (Edinburgh: Edinburgh University Press, 1983), p.1.

17. See A. Jones, G. McCulloch, J. Marshall, G. Smith and L. Smith, *Myths And Realities: Schooling In New Zealand* (Palmerston North: Dunmore Press, 1990), for further discussion of the 'myth of equality' in New Zealand education; also C.E. Beeby, 'The place of myth in educational change', *New Zealand Listener*, 8 November 1986.

18. Eric Hobsbawm, 'Introduction: inventing traditions', in E. Hobsbawm, T. Ranger (eds.), *The Invention Of Tradition* (Cambridge: CUP, 1983).

19. Cyril Norwood, *The English Tradition Of Education* (London: John Murray, 1929), p.x.

20. Ibid., p.244.

21. Gerald Grace, 'Notes on the schooling of the English working class: what lessons for New Zealand? A comparative briefing paper', in Hugh Lauder and Cathy Wylie (eds.), *Towards Successful Schooling* (London: Falmer, 1990), p.107.

22. Ibid., p.116.

23. N. Ray Hiner, 'History of education for the 1990s and beyond: the case for academic imperialism', *History of Education Quarterly*, 30/2 (1990), pp.151–2.

24. See also Gary McCulloch, 'Usable past or inexcusable present? History and education policy', *Education Research and Perspectives*, 18/1 (1991), pp.3–13, and Gary McCulloch, *The Secondary Technical School: A Usable Past?* (London: Falmer, 1989), esp. Ch.2, for further discussion of such issues.

25. Hansot and Tyack, 'A usable past', p.21.

26. Ibid., p.22.

27. Donald Warren, 'A past for the present', in Donald Warren (ed.), *History, Education and Public Policy: Recovering the American Educational Past* (Berkeley: McCutchan, 1978).

28. Harold Silver, *Education, Change and the Policy Process* (London: Falmer, 1990).

29. Ibid., p.30.

30. Stephen Ball, *Politics and Policy Making in Education: Explorations in Policy Sociology* (London: Routledge, 1990), pp.20–21. See also e.g. Roger Dale, *The State And Education Policy* (Milton Keynes: Open University Press, 1989).

31. Andrew McPherson, Charles Raab, *Governing Education: A Sociology of Policy Since 1945* (Edinburgh: Edinburgh University Press, 1988), p.133.

32. Andy Green, *Education and State Formation: The Rise of Education Systems in England, France and the USA* (London: Routledge, 1990), p.212.

33. Pavla Miller, 'Historiography of compulsory schooling: what is the problem?', *History of Education*, 18/2 (1989), p.135.

34. See especially Ball, *Politics and Policy-Making in Education* (1990); and Richard Bowe and Stephen Ball, *Reforming Education and Changing Schools: Case Studies in Policy Sociology* (London: Routledge, 1992).

3

Cycles of Reform

The cycle of reform associated with the Education Act of 1944 needs to be understood in relation to the long-term development of modern educational institutions. The characteristic features of schooling developed in England and Wales, as elsewhere in the world, during the nineteenth century. The reforms of the 1940s were a major attempt to develop these agencies further in order to adapt to perceived changes in society. The initiatives of the 1960s, and of the 1980s/1990s, were similarly concerned to relate education more effectively to wider changes. This chapter will attempt to locate each of these cycles of reform within a broad historical framework, in order to provide a panoramic overview. It will also highlight the key reforms that were proposed, and issues of contestation, continuity and change that relate to these.

The rise of modern schooling

The general features of education systems that have tended to be taken for granted during the twentieth century are comparatively recent in their origin. It was in the nineteenth century that the fundamental principles underpinning such systems came to be accepted and enforced, not only in England and Wales but around the world in societies of different kinds. Schools as discrete institutions, catering for different types of children as pupils, have a very long history that dates back to the ancient world. Several historians have also emphasised basic underlying continuities between the educational practices and curricula of the fourteenth, fifteenth and sixteenth centuries, and those of recent and contemporary times. Hamilton, for example, suggests that schooling 'began to take its present shape in the Middle Ages, and it has been repeatedly reformed since that time'. As 'a malleable instrument of the political state', according to Hamilton, schooling was 'conceived by christianity and raised by capitalism'.[1] And yet it is the emergence of national systems of schooling in the nineteenth century that is especially striking. Such systems were provided by the State, 'free' (that is, paid for out of public funds), age-related, secular, compulsory, and standardised to ensure so far as possible similar conditions in different schools of the same type. As Pavla Miller notes, 'Sometimes earlier, sometimes later, but above all in the last third of the 19th century, systems of mass compulsory schooling were established in most countries of the Western world.'[2] She continues:

> . . . what was significant was an international acceptance of the rational, compulsory-schooling model, a commitment of substantial proportions of public funds to the schooling enterprise and, over three or four decades (a brief period in historical terms), irreversible break-throughs in the actual enforcement of what came to be understood as the one model of efficient schooling.[3]

It was a process that transformed the role of schools in society as a whole, just as much as their influence on individual lives and families. Miller's account also emphasises the way in which particular practices and assumptions became entrenched through this general development:

> . . . the attempted standardisation of curricula, school architecture, teaching practices and school behaviour; the regularisation and enforcement of school attendance of all children of what came to be understood as school age, and the enforced non-attendance of those deemed too young; the undermining of parents' custodial role over their offspring; the gradual loss of control by local communities, individual parents – and eventually the teachers themselves – over what went on in the school; and a considerable expansion of social space controlled (in theory at least) by the state.[4]

Mary Jo Maynes, surveying the rise of schooling in western Europe, also points to the nineteenth century as its key formative phase. In that period, she suggests, 'far from being the sporadic and casual experience that it had been early in the nineteenth century, schooling was changing in character – becoming more ritualised, formalised, regular, and longer in duration'.[5] In the United States, too, Michael Katz observes similar processes taking place:

> . . . by the latter part of the nineteenth century the organization, scope, and role of schooling had been transformed. In place of a few casual schools dotted about town and country, in most cities there existed true educational systems: carefully articulated, age graded, hierarchically structured groupings of schools, primarily free and often compulsory, administered by full-time experts and progressively taught

by specially trained staff. No longer casual adjuncts to the home or apprenticeship, schools had become formal institutions designed to play a critical role in the socialization of the young, the maintenance of social order, and the promotion of social development.[6]

The reasons for this sudden and rapid invention of schooling in different societies continue to be debated,[7] but it is important at least to recognise twentieth-century developments as being strongly marked and influenced by the institutional origins of schooling in the nineteenth century.

Located within this general phenomenon, schooling in England and Wales possessed several distinctive characteristics during this formative period. First, in relation to many other nations mass schooling developed somewhat late and rather grudgingly in this country. As Andy Green notes: 'The development of a national public system of education in England and Wales lagged behind the continental states by a good half century.'[8] Until the 1870s it was based mainly on various forms of local and voluntary provision, and in many quarters there was strong and enduring resistance both to the expansion of popular education, and to any systematic intervention on the part of the State.[9] According to Green, indeed, the patterns that emerged at this time left a permanent legacy: 'The decisive feature of English education was the relative weakness of state or public forms.'[10] This tardy and reluctant patronage was in spite of the fact that industrialisation and urbanisation had developed on a major scale well before other countries. Several historians have noted the long-term significance of this difficult beginning. Richard Johnson, for example, argues that it set the tone for a particularly strong version of 'educational conservatism', closely related to 'a broader pattern of social and cultural conservatism which had much to do with the class and gender strategies of ruling groups'.[11]

A second feature of the English pattern of schooling that emerged in the nineteenth century was its clear differentiation in terms of social class. Working-class children were to be confined to elementary forms of instruction, while secondary and higher education were reserved for the middle class. Such social distinctions were an explicit and integral aspect of nineteenth century educational provision. As Robert Lowe, a leading educational administrator, explained in 1867:

> The lower classes ought to be educated to discharge the duties cast upon them. They should also be educated that they may appreciate

and defer to a higher cultivation when they meet it; and the higher classes ought to be educated in a very different manner, in order that they may exhibit to the lower classes that higher education to which, if it were shown to them, they would bow down and defer.[12]

From the monitorial schools of the early nineteenth century to the Board schools created in the 1870s, mass schooling was recognised to be class-specific. Meanwhile, the 'public' (independent) schools, many of which such as Eton and Winchester had existed for centuries, were revived and reinvigorated during the nineteenth century with a renewed conviction of their purposes as a vital form of elite provision. Local endowed grammar schools varied in their fortunes, and related to different kinds of middle-class market, but could generally also demonstrate clear differences between their own role and that of the elementary schools.[13] It is true that ambiguities and complexities often belied straightforward categories. There were, for example, many schools intended for the 'respectable' working class that rivalled the familiar institutions of the middle class.[14] But in general terms the framework of provision reflected the differing terms of the three separate education commissions that reported in the 1860s: the Newcastle Commission on mass education, the Taunton Commission on secondary education, and the Clarendon Commission on the nine 'great' public schools.

A third key feature of English educational provision was the deep divide between liberal-academic forms of education and more practical, technical, and vocational approaches. This basic distinction was closely related to and also tended to reinforce the social class differences in educational provision. Moreover, it echoed the hierarchy of different forms of knowledge evoked by the philosopher Plato in classical Greece. The public schools were associated with liberal education rooted in the classics. The elementary schools were intended to focus on a limited range of instrumentary areas of instruction. There were many attempts to develop distinctive kinds of technical or practical education, usually with disappointing esults over the longer term. Other initiatives such as the Bryce Report of 1895 tried to reconcile the 'liberal' and the 'vocational', or to identify a compromise approach.[15] However, the liberal/vocational divide tended to resist such interventions, and remained a prominent aspect of educational provision in the twentieth century.

The major Education Acts of 1870 and 1902 consolidated the general system of education that developed in England and Wales at this time, and the characteristic tensions between local and central control. Under the Elementary Education Act of 1870, School Boards were set up in local areas where it was found necessary to 'fill the gaps' left by voluntary provision for elementary schooling. Even if the State did not as yet accept a full role in providing a national system of elementary education, this provision meant that such a development was highly probable.[16] Voluntary schools were left in existence, often competing for pupils with the secular Board schools. The Education Act of 1902 extended the authority of the State into secondary education, under the auspices of the Board of Education which had been established in 1899. School Boards were replaced by local education authorities (LEAs) with powers to co-ordinate elementary and higher education. The measures of 1870 and 1902 were both surrounded by debate and controversy, and both created new tensions in the system and in society at large.[17] Together, they provided a basis for a national system of elementary and secondary education in England and Wales.

Reforming the system

If the developments of the nineteenth century were crucial in establishing and consolidating the modern system of schooling, those of the twentieth century aspired towards further expansion, both in terms of the numbers involved and in relation to the age range of pupils. They were also intended to *reform* the system, to adapt it to what were perceived to be the changing social and economic needs of Britain in the new century. But although such reforms did have some effect, the structures and cultures of schooling proved to be highly resilient to fundamental change.

One major focus for reforming initiatives was in the harsh provisions of elementary education. A broad and incoherent movement in favour of a 'New Education' challenged the methods and curriculum of the Victorian elementary schools.[18] At the same time, the demands of 'national efficiency' inspired opposition in many quarters to the apparently outmoded classics-based curriculum of the public schools, and a growing emphasis on the promotion of health, welfare and science.[19] Moreover, the early decades of the twentieth century witnessed increasing clamour for equality of opportunity through education. Although scholarships and 'free places' provided a narrow educational ladder by which able scholars could proceed from elementary schools into secondary education, by the 1920s and 1930s pressure for some form of 'secondary education for all' had become a potent demand.[20]

The Education Act of 1918, which became law on 8 August, only a few months before the end of the First World War, may therefore be interpreted as a measure intended to rectify the problems that had been widely identified in the education system, and to satisfy the diverse aspirations for change. H.A.L. Fisher, President of the Board of Education from December 1916, was responsible for guiding the Education Bill towards the statute book. The Act extended the powers of LEAs, giving them authority, for example, to provide nursery schools for children from the age of two years old. It also encouraged a broader, more advanced, and more practical curriculum in elementary schools, extended medical inspection to all children in all schools, and provided for day continuation schools for young persons of between sixteen and eighteen.[21] Even so, it reflected at the same time an essential continuity in relation to pre-war education, although the war itself had helped to focus attention upon the urgency of reform. Sherington argues that the Act was merely 'an uncertain half-way house', by which 'some advances were made, but much was left undone; others were not attempted or only partly developed'.[22] The continuation schools were a failure, and the financial rigours of the 1920s stifled many of the initiatives that the Act had sought to encourage. The central ambiguity of the 1918 Act, the extent to which it promoted change or continuity, was to be a recurring feature of educational reforms in the twentieth century.

In particular, three major cycles of reform are especially notable: those of the 1940s, the 1960s, and the 1980s/1990s. The reforms of the 1940s culminated in the Education Act of 1944. Those of the 1960s were associated chiefly with comprehensive schools, with 'progressive' education, and with curriculum change. The reforms of the 1980s/1990s were characterised by 'conservative' no less than by 'modernising' intentions, by an emphasis on 'choice and diversity', and by a reconstruction of central authority over the system. The key themes of these cycles of reform serve to remind us both of the elusive nature of radical change, and of the importance of understanding the particular context and problems to which reforms relate.

The 1940s

The major cycle of reform associated with the 1944 Education Act took place during the Second World War, and owed much of its vigour to high expectations for a post-war society. Many of the proposals that had been developed in the 1920s and 1930s became part of these new plans for the future. The Board of Education developed a general scheme of reform from as early as 1941 with its 'Green Book', *Education after the War*. A White Paper, *Educational Reconstruction*, was published in July 1943, followed by an Education Bill in December 1943. The Act itself did not become law until 3 August the following year.

During the 1930s, the Board of Education had tended to resist initiatives to reform the education system. The Spens committee on secondary education, which was set up in 1933 and reported at the end of 1938, recommended several important changes including the elevation of what were then 'junior technical schools' to the status of secondary schools.[23] But its financial implications, and fears that it would endanger the academic and liberal traditions of the existing secondary grammar schools, meant that it was more or less shelved even before the outbreak of war in September 1939.[24] The war itself disrupted educational provision especially as pupils and schools were evacuated from areas in high risk from air raids, and as many teachers were called up for military service.[25] Educational reform quickly gained a prominent place on the political agenda, stimulated by radical hopes and discontent with the existing structures that had failed to prevent war. In many ways, these pressures echoed those that had led to the 1918 Education Act during the First World War. The Dunkirk crisis of 1940 and the change of government to a Coalition, led by Winston Churchill and including the Labour Party, were powerful factors that reinforced this trend. Towards the end of 1940 and in the early months of 1941, Board of Education officials prepared and circulated a 'Green Book' as a discussion document. As has been noted, 'In many ways it amounted to an updating and adopting of immediate prewar policies and aims to meet the growing political demand for a more radical approach.' Among these officials, Gosden suggests, there were 'traditionalists who were above all anxious to preserve what they believed to be essentially sound', and 'others who saw a need – and an opportunity – for radical change'.[26]

These moves were further supported by a new President of the Board of Education, R.A. Butler, who was appointed to the post on 20 July 1941. Butler, a young Conservative MP who had been associated with the pre-war 'appeasement' policies of Neville Chamberlain's National Government, was not appointed by Churchill with the aim of promoting reform; indeed Churchill was concerned mainly with the war effort itself and tended to resist what he regarded as distractions on the 'home front'.[27] A product of Marlborough College and Pembroke College, Cambridge, Butler was an unlikely crusader on behalf of educational reform. Kevin Jeffreys goes so far as to suggest that Butler was 'chosen primarily because on his past record, at the India Office and Foreign Office, he seemed less likely to depart from Churchill's injunction that the education department should stick to the task at hand – evacuation and its attendant problems for schoolchildren'.[28] His background contrasted starkly with that of his Parliamentary Secretary, James Chuter Ede, who had been appointed the previous year. Chuter Ede, an experienced Labour MP and former elementary school teacher, nevertheless joined forces with Butler to negotiate a major initiative.

Two years after Butler's arrival at the Board, these efforts led to the publication of the White Paper *Educational Reconstruction*. This document announced the government's intention to 'recast the national education service' with a 'new layout' that was 'based on a recognition that education is a continuous process conducted in successive stages'.[29] There should be a 'sufficient supply' of nursery schools for children below the compulsory school age of five. The school leaving age would be raised from fourteen to fifteen immediately, and to sixteen 'as soon as circumstances permit'. There would be two stages of education up to this leaving age: primary, from five to eleven, and secondary, above eleven. The White Paper envisaged that 'At the primary stage the large classes and bad conditions which at present are a reproach to many elementary schools will be systematically eliminated; at the secondary stage the standard of accommodation and amenities will be steadily raised to the level of the best examples.'[30] All schools would provide school meals and milk for their pupils. After the school leaving age, there would be provision either for continued full-time attendance at a secondary school, or for part-time day attendance at a young person's college. It was planned also to develop 'an effective system of inspection and registration of schools outside the public system; new financial and administrative arrangements for the voluntary schools, and the recognition of the special place of religious instruction in school life'.[31]

The White Paper placed responsibility for providing primary education, secondary education, and further education upon the LEAs. Each LEA would make a comprehensive survey of existing provision and likely needs for their area, and submit development plans for the Board to consider. The scope of powers of LEAs would be adjusted to meet the new layout, including through abolishing the anomalies of 'Part III Authorities' which were confined to 'elementary education' under the terms of the 1902 Education Act. The duty of parents would also be extended from ensuring instruction in reading, writing and arithmetic, to ensuring 'efficient full-time education suitable to the child's age and abilities'.[32] Three main types of secondary schools would be developed, to be known as grammar, technical, and modern schools. Direct grant schools, funded directly from the Board rather than through the LEAs, would continue at least for the time being. Provision would be made 'for the school day in all primary and secondary schools to begin with a corporate act of worship',[33] although it would still be open for parents to withdraw their children from religious worship or instruction. Voluntary schools would be offered further financial assistance, 'accompanied by a corresponding extension of public control which will ensure the effective and economical organisation and development of both primary and secondary education'.[34] The aims of the Education Act of 1918 in relation to day continuation schools would be adapted 'to meet the requirements of the post-war world' through the development of what the White Paper called 'young people's colleges'.[35] All young persons from 15 to 18 would be required to attend an appropriate centre on a part-time basis (see Appendix I for further details on the provisions of the 1943 White Paper).

Ten days after the publication of the White Paper, the Norwood Report on the curriculum and examinations in secondary schools provided more details on the substance of the reforms. This report was produced by a sub-committee of the Secondary School Examinations Council (SSEC), which was chaired by Sir Cyril Norwood, President of St John's College, Oxford, and a former Master of Marlborough College and Head of Harrow. Norwood himself had strong ideas on reform in relation to the secondary school curriculum and examinations. At the same time, as has already been noted above, he was steadfast in his defence of an 'English tradition' in education that he associated with the public and grammar schools.[36] Many of these views were reflected in the final report of the committee. Part One of the report concerned the general layout of secondary education, and proposed what it saw as a suitable typology of three different types of schools and curricula related to different 'types of mind'. Like the White Paper that preceded it, it therefore encouraged the development of separate grammar schools, secondary technical schools, and secondary modern schools, or what became known as a 'tripartite system' of secondary education. Part Two dealt with examinations, arguing that secondary school examinations should shift from being externally administered by university examining bodies, to being internally administered – 'that is to say, conducted by the teachers at the school on syllabuses and papers framed by themselves'.[37] In Part Three, the report moved on to consider possible developments in the grammar school curriculum (see Appendix II for details of the Norwood Report).

The 1944 Education Act

The education proposals were debated in the House of Commons and the House of Lords, and were then included in the King's Speech as legislation to be drafted and passed in the coming year.[38] In December 1943, an Education Bill was introduced, based on the White Paper, as 'a self-contained measure which replaces and reforms the existing law of education'.[39] This in turn was debated by Parliament in the early months of 1944. The Bill was arranged in five parts. The first Part (Sections One to Five of the Act) was concerned with central administration of the education system, with the aim of redefining the 'powers and duties of the Central Authority'.[40] In the Act itself, the Board of Education was changed to a Ministry, and the President of the Board became the Minister of Education. The Consultative Committee of the Board, which had provided several major reports on different issues since its inception in 1899, was replaced by two Central Advisory Councils, one for England and one for Wales, to 'advise' the Minister 'upon such matters connected with educational theory and practice as they think fit and upon any questions referred to them by him'. The Ministry was to ensure that LEAs executed national education policy in an effective way.

Part Two, which encompassed Sections Six to 69, occupied the bulk of the Act. It established the new statutory system of education. Section Six abolished the Part III LEAs created under the 1902 Act, that is, 169 of the existing 315 LEAs which were responsible for elementary education only. Section Seven recast the system of public education from a division into two fields – 'elementary' and 'higher' – into 'three progressive stages to be known as primary education, secondary education, and further education'. LEAs in each area would be expected to 'contribute towards the spiritual, moral, mental and physical development of the community by securing that efficient education throughout those stages shall be available to meet the needs of the population of their area'.[41]

The following sections spelled out in detail the new responsibilities of the LEAs. Under Section 11, it was stipulated that every LEA would prepare a 'development plan' for their area, and submit this to the Minister for approval. Voluntary schools were classified under Section 15 as controlled schools, aided schools, or special agreement schools. Detailed provision was made for the 'management' of primary schools and the 'government' of secondary schools – a distinction in terminology based on the old division between elementary and higher education.[42] Section 25 provided for the school day to begin with 'collective worship on the part of all pupils in attendance at the school', and for religious instruction to be given – the first time that these had been made statutory obligations for schools. The education of pupils needing 'special educational treatment' was provided for under Sections 33 and 34. Section 35 defined 'compulsory school age' as being from five to 15 years, and made provision for the future raising of the school leaving age to 16. Under Section 36, parents' duties were extended to the securing for their children of 'efficient full-time education suitable to his age, ability, and aptitude, either by regular attendance at school or otherwise'. The enforcement of school attendance was also detailed.

Sections 41 to 47 of the Act focused on further education, including the provision under clause 43 of 'county colleges' to provide part-time education for young persons. Section 48 extended the duty of all schools to provide not only medical inspection but also free medical treatment for their pupils. LEAs were also to provide, under Section 49, 'milk, meals and other refreshment for pupils', and 'adequate facilities for recreation and social and physical training' (Section 53). Free transport where necessary was also to be provided by LEAs (Section 55). It was emphasised in Section 61 that no fees were to be charged 'in respect of admission to any school maintained by a local education authority, or to any county college, or in respect of the education provided in any county college'. Lastly, the Minister was given powers, under Section 68, to intervene where any LEA or the managers or governors of any county or voluntary school were acting or proposed to act 'unreasonably'.

The third part of the Act (Sections 70 to 75) dealt with independent schools. In particular, it provided under Section 70 for a register of independent schools to be open for public inspection, and for legal sanctions and procedures for complaint. Part Four (Sections 76 to 107) was a general section. It began with a very important 'general principle' to be observed by the Minister and LEAs, that 'so far as is compatible with the provision of efficient instruction and training and the avoidance of unreasonable public expenditure, pupils are to be educated in accordance with the wishes of their parents' (Section 76). Section 81 provided for LEAs to be empowered to assist pupils with fees and scholarships. LEAs were also allowed to conduct or assist research (Section 82), to organise or participate in conferences (Section 83), and to make grants to universities or university colleges to improve facilities for further education. Under Section 88, LEAs had a duty to appoint a chief education officer. The financial arrangements shared between the Minister and LEAs were detailed in Section 100. Lastly, Part Five of the Act (Sections 108–22) made 'supplemental' provisions for the working of the Act.

These, then, were the main provisions of the Education Act of 1944 (see Appendix 3 for further details of some of the key sections). It was accompanied by two further official Reports on specific areas of education. The McNair Committee had been appointed by Butler in March 1942 to consider the supply, recruitment and training of teachers and youth leaders. It reported in 1944 with proposals to improve the recruitment and conditions of service of teachers.[43] Meanwhile, the Fleming Committee, also set up by the President of the Board in 1942, was concerned with public schools and their relationship to the education system as a whole. This Report argued that public schools should be continued, but that recruitment should be widened to include pupils of different social classes.[44]

These major reforming proposals were broadly supported by the two main political parties, Conservative and Labour, and by 'public opinion' in general. There were areas of controversy, but little of the heat that the reforms of 1870 and 1902 had generated. Religious interest groups were suspicious of the possible implications of reform, and much of the detailed negotiation that preceded the Act involved them. The Catholic Church in particular remained hostile. In March 1944, too, the government was defeated on a vote in the House of Commons for the only time during the war (117 votes to 116), on the issue of equal pay for women teachers.[45] Churchill treated the issue as one of confidence in the government as a whole, and the amendment was struck out. At the same time there were many, especially in the Labour Party, who advocated

the development of 'multilateral' secondary schools of a composite
type for all abilities and aptitudes, rather than the tripartite system
that was officially favoured.[46] Even so, on the whole a bipartisan
political consensus in favour of the reforms was maintained throughout the passage of the Act.

Underlying this consensus there was a range of differing hopes
and calculations. Butler himself was acutely conscious of why his
reforms were generally acceptable to the Conservative Party and to
the government as a whole. 'Education', he noted, was 'a subject
suiting the composition of the National Government'.[47] Certainly
this was true in comparison with other proposals such as those of
the Beveridge Report on social insurance, or the Uthwatt Report
on town and country planning, both of which had been published
towards the end of 1942. Conservative Party resistance was much
stronger on both of these aspects than on education; in the case of
Beveridge because of the financial implications, and in respect to
Uthwatt because of fears over property rights.[48] By contrast, as
Butler shrewdly observed:

> Their reasons for plumping for an Education Bill are fortunately clothed
> in considerable forgetfulness of the revolutionary nature of educational
> change. They have been prompted to come the way of education because
> it has been very difficult to obtain agreement between the Parties on any
> matters which involve property or the pocket, whereas, on religious
> questions, there is a feeling that it is out-of-date to wrangle. This is a
> further example of how political interest is shifting from the soul of
> man to his economic position, which all seems very unhealthy.[49]

Despite Churchill's initial reservations about educational reform,
later recorded at length in Butler's autobiography,[50] the Prime
Minister could also appreciate the advantages of an Education Bill.
Again according to Butler's diary,

> The Prime Minister, I know from his views faithfully recorded to me,
> feels it will be possible to treat controversial parts of this Bill as non-
> political, and thus prevent a split between the major Parties. On the
> other hand, were the Government to press ahead with the Uthwatt
> Report, they would find the question of Betterment coming to the
> front and, as it is, the new Minister of Planning is finding himself in
> very deep water.[51]

The Government Whips were also content with discussion of
educational reform, because 'The beauty of the Bill, as they saw
it, was that it provided endless opportunity for debate on issues

which in their view were not vital to the war and which would keep Members thoroughly occupied without breaking up the Government'.[52]

On the Labour side, there were other considerations that also encouraged support for the Education Bill.[53] Chuter Ede was able to show that the White Paper met most of the 17 points raised at the Labour Party Conference earlier in the year: 'I detailed this first to the Committee dealing with the extent to which the Paper met the specific demand . . . I claimed that we had substantially met the Labour Party's requirements. This was generally agreed.'[54] George Ridley, another Labour Party veteran and Chairman of the Party's National Executive Committee, was 'very eulogistic' of the White Paper: 'He said he hoped to lay a wreath on the grave of the word "Elementary". Ours was a fine scheme, and the document was worthy of it.'[55] The abolition of such nineteenth-century class distinctions was indeed a powerful inducement. Chuter Ede himself had no doubt of its significance as he responded to continued criticisms from W.G. Cove, another Labour MP and a representative of the National Union of Teachers: 'I said the White Paper was the greatest State document ever issued on education.'[56]

Further grounds for support on the Labour side were expressed by R.H. Tawney, a highly influential figure who had been largely responsible for drafting and developing the Labour Party's policy on 'secondary education for all' in the 1920s. Tawney was uncomfortably aware of the failure to promote effective reform at the end of the First World War, and was anxious that this time it should be pushed through during the war itself. He insisted to Butler that there was 'no such thing as post-war reconstruction' in relation to education, since:

> Once the war ends, there will be a new situation. The Government will have on its hands a mass of problems, from demobilisation to rebuilding towns, which cannot be postponed. It will do, whatever its political colour, what it must do, not what it should do. Educational reform will be regarded as a luxury which can wait.[57]

To this feeling of urgency, Tawney also added suspicion of the Conservatives, and he was consistently alert to the possibilities of the 'reactionaries' conspiring to delay and frustrate the Bill. He complained that 'The obstinacy of the resistance to quite simple reforms surprises me. The Conservative elements in the country seem to me even more unregenerate than they were in the last war.'[58] After the publication of the White Paper, he remained convinced that 'the Tories will do their best to crab the government's policy as a whole'.[59] It was in this context that he saw the proposals of the White Paper as 'on the whole, a long step forward', and considered that 'If Butler sticks to his guns, the Act will be a really important one.'[60]

Thus, a number of contradictory interests and ideals across the conventional political divide helped to forge an effective alliance, and to marginalise dissent on the Labour and Conservative benches and within the religious interest groups. It was this that paved the way for the Education Act to be passed well before the end of the war, and before a Labour government came to power in July 1945.

The 1960s

In beginning to assess the importance of the reforms of the 1940s, it is helpful also to compare the thrust of the 1944 Act with the general aims of the two more recent major cycles of reform in the 1960s and the 1980s/1990s. Both of these latter sets of initiatives were intended to abolish what were seen as the outmoded practices and structures of the past, and also to set the tone for the education system for the next generation.

The reforms of the 1960s did not involve major legislation of the stature of the 1944 Act. However, they did seek to promote aspects that had been either overlooked or delayed in the 1940s, especially in the areas of secondary school organisation, 'progressive' education in primary schools, curriculum reform, and higher education. From 1964 the Ministry of Education, created in 1944, became the Department of Education and Science. Its initiatives were not always consistent with each other, ideologically or politically, but overall during this period there was a dominant emphasis on egalitarian reform and social justice. Even so, as with earlier cycles of reform, it is not at all clear that the aims of the reformers were achieved, and there is again an important ambiguity in terms of continuity and change.

The Education Act of 1944 had not laid down national guidelines for the organisation of secondary education, although the White Paper and the Norwood Report of the previous year had made it clear that the 'tripartite system' of grammar, technical and modern schools was the favoured policy. Technical schools were never popular, and secondary moderns were widely regarded as a 'second-rate' alternative to the grammar schools. Although the new Ministry of Education strove to defend the grammar schools, by the early

1960s many LEAs were beginning to prefer comprehensive schools which would cater for all abilities and aptitudes.[61] This trend was confirmed by the new Labour government that was elected on a slim majority after 13 years of Conservative rule in 1964. Circular 10/65 declared the government's objective as being 'to end selection at eleven plus and to eliminate separatism in secondary education'.[62] It therefore requested LEAs to prepare plans to reorganise secondary education in their areas on comprehensive lines.

In the primary schools, the reaction against the traditions of the old elementary schools, already evident in the inter-war years, intensified during this period, and this led to the promotion of more child-centred and 'progressive' methods of teaching. The Plowden Report of 1967, produced by the Central Advisory Council on Education that had been introduced in 1944, endorsed this general trend.[63] It also sought to encourage 'positive discrimination' for schools in deprived areas, and to discourage streaming of classes by ability. 'Open plan' primary schools were also intended to mark the shift away from the narrow and restrictive approach of the Victorian elementary schools.

In the area of curriculum reform, too, the 1960s was a phase of hectic activity. The 1944 Act had left the curriculum (except religious education) to the schools and the LEAs, but by the 1960s there was a wide range of agencies competing for influence.[64] In the late 1950s, Sir David Eccles as Minister of Education had begun to declare an interest in the State becoming directly involved in what he described as the 'secret garden of the curriculum'. The short-lived Curriculum Study Group gave way in 1964 to the Schools Council for Curriculum and Examinations, which sponsored many curriculum initiatives of different kinds.[65]

The reformers of the 1940s, like those of earlier generations, had regarded universities as beyond the bounds of State activity, but in this area too there were important initiatives in the 1960s. The Robbins Report on higher education, published in 1963, argued for considerable expansion in the university sector to respond to the 'extension of educational opportunity in the schools and the widening of the desire for higher education on the part of young people'.[66] It was hoped that this would permit greater numbers of working class people to go into higher education after leaving school. A perceived need for more technological skills led at the same time to the development of polytechnics, which would be controlled by the central Department.

On the other hand, despite all of this activity there were many underlying continuities. Ball has pointed out that the 'noise' of educational reform was rarely matched by 'real' changes in educational practices.[67] The spread of the comprehensives did not in the main challenge the dominance of the 'grammar school curriculum'. According to Goodson:

> Within the comprehensive schools, a clear hierarchy of school subjects developed. The hierarchy was based on the primacy of grammar school subjects which were naturally given priority by the grammar school staff who largely took over the headships and head of department posts.[68]

This means, he argues, that 'As in the tripartite system, so in the comprehensive system, academic subjects for able pupils are accorded the highest status and resources. The triple alliance between academic subjects, academic examinations and able pupils ensures that comprehensive schools provide similar patterns of success and failure to previous school systems.'[69] Similarly at the primary school level, existing methods and assumptions were maintained in practice in spite of calls for a 'primary school revolution'.[70]

The problem of curriculum change was often regarded at this time as a technical or organisational one, requiring good management and planning. New ideas competently produced and thoroughly implemented would, it was assumed, succeed in overhauling school curricula very quickly. According to *The Times Educational Supplement* in October 1965, 'for all the ink and vitriol spilt over the organisation of education, this decade is more likely to be remembered for the quiet revolution in the field of the school curriculum'.[71] As late as 1967, Professor J.F. Kerr, one of the early curriculum pioneers in the United Kingdom, remained confident that 'At the practical and organisational levels, the new curricula promise to revolutionise English education.'[72] It soon became clear, however, that in most cases the 'new curricula' were for some reason not being taken up by schools, or were being interpreted by teachers in ways contrary to the intentions of the reformers. The co-ordinators of Schools Council curriculum projects, despite the extensive resources at their disposal, often became frustrated by the task of national curriculum development. Within a few years confident plans had given way to disenchantment, especially with declining financial resources in the 1970s.[73]

Similar trends were evident in the area of higher education in spite of the expansion and diversification of the 1960s. The existing universities maintained a higher status than the new polytechnics, while the proportion of working-class students failed to rise appreciably. In other areas where reforms were not followed through, it was also clear that traditional patterns were relatively undisturbed. Issues relating to the public schools, for example, were referred to a separate committee, as they had been in the 1940s, and again came to little.[74] Overall, it soon appeared that the appearance of rapid change had been deceptive and that further reforms would become necessary. The bounds of reform had been greatly widened, especially in the school curriculum and higher education, which would legitimise later attempts to consolidate change. At the same time, few groups could approve of the outcomes of reforms. On the left, existing inequalities still seemed all too acute. On the right, resentment was stirred by the challenge to such institutions as grammar schools, and by perceived threats to established standards and values.

Towards the 1993 Education Act

The cycle of reform that culminated in the Education Act of 1993 might be said to have begun with the speech by the Labour Prime Minister, James Callaghan, at Ruskin College in October 1976 that launched the so-called 'Great Debate'.[75] It gained momentum after the election of the Conservative Party to government under Margaret Thatcher in 1979. Under a succession of Secretaries of State for Education, radical reform became a dominant aim, leading first to the Education Reform Act in 1988 and then to the White Paper *Choice And Diversity* in 1992 and the subsequent Education Act of 1993.

As with the cycle of reform in the 1960s, initiatives during this period were by no means fully consistent or coherent in their approach. Even so, they attracted the label 'New Right', as much as anything else to evoke the fresh potency of what were often familiar goals. In some ways it has represented a period of reform that is unprecedented since the rise of modern schooling in the nineteenth century, both for its trenchant criticisms of established institutions and values, and for its concern to change the entire culture of schooling towards new ends. There is, however, an important tension between the economic-libertarian right, concerned to open up schooling to the whims of the marketplace, and the moral-authoritarian right which seeks to enforce and uphold particular standards and ideals of morality in the schools. The 'New Right' may be only a temporary phenomenon, both unstable

BLACKWELL'S
51 Broad Street
Oxford
OX1 3BQ
Tel: 01865 792792
VAT No.: 532585539

SALE
365 13 9682   30 Oct 2003 15:38

CASHIER: PS
X1009   SECONDHAND SALE   4.00

TOTAL   ITEMS   1   4.00

CASH   4.00
CHANGE   0.00

VAT INCLUDED IN ABOVE TOTAL AMOUNT

RATE   0.00%   0.00 IN   4.00

Thank you for shopping at
Blackwell's

and contradictory, but for the present at least it constitutes a major assault on the institutions of schooling and the assumed values of education.

The reforms of the 1980s and 1990s have tended to follow from disillusionment with the familiar liberal ideals and aims of schooling. They have exploited public and parental concerns about the quality of schooling to mount a frontal assault on what is described as the 'educational Establishment'. Teachers, schools, administrators and liberal curricula have become common targets of criticism, and in an important sense have been turned into scapegoats for the failures of the schooling project and of society at large. The reforms have attempted to reduce the role of the established educational bureaucracies such as the LEAs and the central administration and to enhance that of the local communities. In practice, they have usually served to increase the political power of the State while implicating local parents in responsibility for the problems of the schools.

Many of these features were evident in the Education Reform Act of 1988. At the Conservative Party Conference in October 1987, Margaret Thatcher as Prime Minister emphasised the need to establish a 'national curriculum for basic subjects', but also the importance of encouraging 'parental choice' by promoting competition between schools and the development of 'independent state schools' outside the control of the LEAs.[76] These aims were carried through by the Secretary of State for Education, Kenneth Baker. The Education Reform Act of 1988 provided for a National Curriculum in schools, delegated management and budgeting to schools, established a basis for grant-maintained schools and city technology colleges (CTCs), abolished the Inner London Education Authority, and reorganised the structure and funding of further and higher education. The powers of the LEAs, emphasised in 1944, were now undermined. The authority of teachers in relation to the school curriculum was also diminished. The Act correspondingly enhanced the supposed rights of parents in choosing between schools, and encouraged the growth of particular types of school, thus potentially endangering the comprehensives. At the same time, it went well beyond the 1944 Act into the territory of higher education, ground carefully cultivated in the 1960s.

The 1988 Act was promoted as the climax to this cycle of reform. And yet even after it became law, and after the departure of Margaret Thatcher as Prime Minister, a new wave of initiatives gathered force. Thatcher's replacement, John Major, identified education as a key area of policy for the general election that was eventually held in the spring of 1992.[77] The Conservatives' narrow victory in this election, their fourth consecutive win, signalled the launch of a further attempt to overhaul the education system. This was reflected first in the important White Paper *Choice and Diversity*, published in July 1992. What it called the 'five great themes' of educational reform in the 1980s were set out for further development: quality, diversity, parental choice, greater school autonomy, and greater accountability.[78] In order to build on these themes, it was argued, further changes were now necessary. John Patten, the Secretary of State for Education, sought to encourage more schools to apply to 'opt out' from local authority control and secure grant-maintained status. He proposed further steps towards selection and specialisation, and also promised a fresh initiative against truancy, new procedures to review religious education, and an emphasis on morality.[79]

The Education Bill based on the proposals of *Choice and Diversity* was published at the end of October 1992. It was the longest in history, running to 200 pages and 255 clauses, and much of it was concerned with the legal position of grant-maintained schools and their relationship to LEAs. It envisaged a new Funding Agency for Schools that would gradually take over from LEAs when schools opted out from their control.[80] After nine months of debate, at the end of July 1993, the Bill eventually received its Royal Assent. It now contained 308 clauses (now 'sections'), almost three times the number of the 1944 Act.[81]

Beneath the rhetoric and the impetus of change, it is possible once again to identify continuities from the past embodied in the reform cycle of the 1980s and 1990s. In some cases these involve strong echoes of earlier policies and practices. Several historians have noted the parallels between the National Curriculum of the late 1980s and the Secondary School Regulations of 1904.[82] Others have detected the potential revival of 'tripartite' divisions in secondary education through the growth of a separate sector of 'opted out' or grant-maintained schools.[83] It is possible, therefore, to interpret recent and current changes not as 'breaking the mould', but as 'confirming the pattern'.[84] In order to evaluate such claims and to explore the issues that they raise, it is necessary to relate or compare current developments with those of the past; to develop an explicit framework through which to assess both 'novelty' and 'tradition'.

Contextualising the Act

This chapter has sought briefly to depict what the general outlines of such a framework might look like. It has placed the reforms of the 1940s at the centre of the picture in order to suggest the key role occupied by the 1944 Education Act, both as an instrument for redressing earlier problems and as a reference point for later cycles of reform. In many ways, fifty years on, the Education Act of 1944 can be seen as occupying a central place in the history of twentieth century educational reform.

Three further themes present themselves from this account. First is the continuing importance of the origins of the modern system of schooling in the nineteenth century for an understanding of twentieth century reforms. The problems and limitations of schooling in those formative years have been repeatedly addressed, but have in many cases survived relatively unscathed, or have been expunged to reappear elsewhere in a new guise. The status divisions between the 'liberal' and the 'vocational' provide one such case. Social inequalities based on class are another, and other sources of inequality such as gender, religion, geography, and latterly ethnicity have made what Tawney regarded as a 'hereditary curse', more complex and wide-ranging.[85] The relationship between the central authority and local services has been another structural issue dating from the nineteenth century which succeeding generations of reformers have attempted to resolve.

A second theme is the importance of the wider social and political relationships of educational reform. Each of the major cycles of reform discussed above has been informed by contemporary problems and trends, and has in turn contributed to them. Thus in the case of the 1940s, the wartime context is clearly crucial for an understanding of what the reforms were about, as are the politics of the Coalition and social aspirations for an improved post-war society. In the 1960s and the 1980s/1890s, too, an awareness of this wider context is fundamental to analysis of the aims and limitations of reform.

Lastly, the continual tension between change and continuity becomes apparent as the central ambiguity of educational reform. Often, in retrospect, programmes of reform have appeared less impressive than the imposing edifice that they have sought to challenge. What has been novel in principle or policy has tended to be interpreted in practice along more familiar lines. And yet change does occur, sometimes rapidly and unexpectedly, and enough to dispel temptations to succumb to a blanket fatalism. Some historical perspective is a basic part of assessing how far particular reforms represent continuity, and how far they represent change. This becomes especially clear when we come to inspect how succeeding generations have interpreted the 1944 Act for their own purposes, and it is to this issue that we now turn.

NOTES

1. David Hamilton, *Towards a Theory of Schooling* (London: Falmer Press, 1989), p.vii.
2. Pavla Miller, 'Historiography of compulsory schooling: what is the problem?', *History of Education*, 18/2 (1989), p.123.
3. Ibid.
4. Ibid., pp.123–4.
5. Mary Jo Maynes, *Schooling in Western Europe: A Social History* (Albany: State University of New York Press, 1985), pp.133–4.
6. Michael Katz, *Reconstructing American Education* (Cambridge, MA: Harvard University Press, 1987), p.6.
7. e.g. Francisco Ramirez and John Boli, 'The political construction of mass schooling: European origins and worldwide institutionalization', *Sociology of Education*, 60/1 (1987), pp.2–18; and Yasemin Soysal and David Strang, 'Construction of the first mass education systems in nineteenth century Europe', *Sociology of Education*, 62/4 (1989), pp.277–88.
8. Andy Green, *Education and State Formation: The Rise of Education Systems in England, France and the USA* (London: Macmillan, 1990), p.6.
9. Carl Kaestle, '"Between the Scylla of Brutal Ignorance and the Charybdis of a Literary Education": elite attitudes towards mass schooling in early industrial England and America', in L. Stone (ed.), *Schooling and Society: Studies in the History of Education* (London: Johns Hopkins University Press, 1976), pp.177–91.
10. Green, op. cit., p.313.
11. Richard Johnson, 'Thatcherism and English education: breaking the mould, or confirming the pattern?', *History of Education*, 18/2 (1989), pp.103–4.
12. Robert Lowe, 'Primary and classical education', in David A. Reeder (ed.), *Educating our Masters* (1980), pp.125–6.
13. See e.g. Hilary Steedman, 'Defining institutions: the endowed grammar schools and the systematisation of English secondary education', in Detlef Muller, Fritz Ringer and Brian Simon (eds.), *The Rise of the Modern Educational System* (Cambridge: Cambridge University Press, 1987), pp.111–34; and David Reeder, 'The reconstruction of secondary education in England, 1869–1920', in Muller and Ringer, Simon (eds.), op. cit., pp.135–50.
14. See e.g. W.E. Marsden, *Educating the Respectable: A Study of Fleet Road Board School, Hampstead, 1870–1903* (London: Woburn Press, 1990); and Meriel Vlaeminke, 'The subordination of technical education in secondary schooling, 1870–1914', in Penny Summerfield and Eric Evans (eds.), *Technical Education and the State Since 1850: Historical and Contemporary Perspectives* (Manchester: Manchester University Press, 1990), pp.55–76.
15. e.g. Harold Silver, 'The liberal and the vocational', in his *Education As History* (London: Methuen, 1983), pp.151–72.
16. James Murphy, *The Education Act 1870: Text and Commentary* (Newton Abbot: David & Charles, 1972).
17. See e.g. Harold Silver, 'Education, opinion and the 1870s', in his *Education As History* (1983), pp.81–99; and Brian Simon, *Education and the Labour Movement, 1870–1920* (London: Lawrence & Wishart, 1965).
18. See R.J.W. Selleck, *The New Education, 1870–1914* (London: Pitman, 1968); and R.J.W. Selleck, *English Primary Education and the Progressives, 1914–1939* (London: Pitman, 1972).

19. e.g. E.J.T. Brennan (ed.), *Education for National Efficiency: The Contribution of Sidney and Beatrice Webb* (London: Athlone Press, 1975).
20. e.g. Rodney Barker, *Education and Politics 1900–1951: A Study of the Labour Party* (Oxford: Clarendon Press, 1972); Brian Simon, *The Politics Of Educational Reform 1920–1940* (London: Lawrence & Wishart, 1974).
21. Details of the provisions of the 1918 Act are in Arthur A. Thomas, *The Education Act, 1918* (London: P.S. King and Son, Ltd, 1919), which includes the full text of the Act, and Lawrence Andrews, *The Education Act, 1918* (London: Routledge & Kegan Paul, 1976).
22. Geoffrey Sherington, *English Education, Social Change and War, 1911–20* (Manchester: Manchester University Press, 1981), p.182; also Geoffrey Sherington, 'The 1918 Education Act: origins, aims and development', *British Journal of Educational Studies*, 24/1 (1976), pp.66–85.
23. Board of Education, *Report of the Consultative Committee On Secondary Education with Special Reference to Grammar Schools and Technical High Schools* (London: HMSO, 1938) (Spens Report).
24. Bill Bailey, 'The development of technical education, 1934–1939', *History of Education*, 16/1 (1987), pp. 49–65; Gary McCulloch, *The Secondary Technical School: A Usable Past?* (London: Falmer, 1989), Ch.3.
25. See A.M. Preston, 'The evacuation of schoolchildren from Newcastle upon Tyne, 1939–1942', *History of Education*, 18/3 (1989), pp. 231–41; Roy Lowe, 'Education in England during the Second World War', in Roy Lowe (ed.), *Education and the Second World War* (London: London, 1992), pp.4–16; John Macnicol, 'The evacuation of schoolchildren', in Harold L. Smith (ed.), *War and Social Change: British Society in the Second World War* (Manchester: Manchester University Press, 1986), pp.3–31.
26. Peter Gosden, *Education in the Second World War: A Study in Policy and Administration* (London: Methuen, 1976), p.239.
27. See Paul Addison, *The Road to 1945: British Politics in the Second World War* (London: Jonathan Cape, 1975).
28. Kevin Jefferys, *The Churchill Coalition and Wartime Politics, 1940–1945* (Manchester: Manchester University Press, 1991), p.115.
29. *Educational Reconstruction*, paragraph 2.
30. Ibid.
31. Ibid., paragraph 4.
32. Ibid., paragraph 24.
33. Ibid., paragraph 51.
34. Ibid.
35. Ibid., paragraph 67.
36. See Gary McCulloch, *Philosophers and Kings: Education for Leadership in Modern England* (Cambridge: Cambridge University Press, 1991), Ch.4.
37. Norwood Report, p.140.
38. House of Commons Debates.
39. Board of Education, *Education Bill: Explanatory Memorandum by the President of the Board of Education* (London: HMSO, December 1943: Cmd 6492), p.2.
40. Ibid.
41. Education Act, 1944, Section 7.
42. See H.C. Dent, *The Education Act, 1944* (London: University of London Press Ltd. 1944), p.30.
43. Board of Education, *The Supply, Recruitment and Training of Teachers and Youth Leaders* (London: HMSO, 1944) (McNair Report).
44. Board of Education, *The Public Schools and the General Educational System* (London: HMSO, 1944) (Fleming Report).
45. House of Commons Debates, 28 March 1944.
46. See Brian Simon, 'The politics of comprehensive reorganization: a retrospective analysis', *History of Education*, 21/4 (1992), pp.355–62.
47. R.A. Butler, diary, 9 September 1943 (Butler papers, Trinity College, Cambridge, G15).
48. See Addison, *The Road to 1945*, esp. Chs.6, 8.
49. Butler, diary, 9 September 1943 (Butler papers).
50. R.A. Butler, *The Art of the Possible* (London: Hamish Hamilton, 1971).
51. Butler, diary, 9 September 1943 (Butler papers).

52. R.A. Butler, diary, December 1943 (Butler papers).
53. J. Chuter Ede, diary, 20 July 1943 (Chuter Ede unpublished diary, British Museum, Add.Mss. 59696, Vol.VII).
54. Ibid.
55. Ibid.
56. Ibid., 21 July 1943.
57. R.H. Tawney to W.P. Crozier, 7 September 1941 (*Manchester Guardian* papers, Manchester University Library, B/T18/40).
58. Tawney to Crozier, 19 February 1943 (*Manchester Guardian* papers, B/T18/70).
59. Tawney to Crozier, 18 July 1943 (*Manchester Guardian* papers, B/T18/54).
60. Ibid.
61. See Gary McCulloch, *The Secondary Technical School: A Usable Past?* (London: Falmer, 1989) on technical schools and the changing attitudes of LEAs.
62. Department of Education and Science, 'The organisation of secondary education' (Circular 10/65, 12 July 1965).
63. Central Advisory Council for Education, *Children and their Primary Schools* (London: HMSO, 1967).
64. See e.g. Gary McCulloch, Edgar Jenkins and David Layton, *Technological Revolution?* (London: Falmer, 1985).
65. See e.g. C. Chitty, 'Central control of the school curriculum, 1944-87', *History of Education*, 17/4 (1988), pp.321–34.
66. Committee on Higher Education, *Higher Education* (London: HMSO, 1963) (Robbins Report), pp.4–5.
67. Stephen Ball, 'Introduction: comprehensives in crisis?', in S. Ball (ed.), *Comprehensive Schooling: A Reader* (London: Falmer, 1984).
68. Ivor Goodson, 'Defining a subject for the comprehensive school', in I. Goodson (ed.), *The Making of Curriculum: Collected Essays* (London: Falmer, 1988), p.139.
69. Ibid., pp.140–41.
70. See e.g. Brian Simon, *Education and the Social Order 1940–1990* (London: Lawrence and Wishart, 1991).
71. *Times Educational Supplement*, 8 October 1965, 'Comment'.
72. J.F. Kerr, *Changing The Curriculum* (London: University of London Press, 1968), p.15. See also e.g. Peter Gordon, 'A unity of purpose': some reflections on the school curriculum, 1945–70', in W.E. Marsden (ed.), *Post-War Curriculum Development: An Historical Appraisal* (Leicester: History of Education Society, 1979), pp.1–8.
73. See e.g. Barry MacDonald, Rob Walker, *Changing the Curriculum* (London: Open Books, 1976).
74. Public Schools Commission, *First Report* (London: HMSO, 1968).
75. On the background of this speech, see Clyde Chitty, *Towards a New Education System: The Victory of the New Right?* (London: Falmer Press, 1989), Ch.3.
76. *TES*, 16 October 1987, report, 'Dramatic steps that will carry Britain forward'.
77. *The Sunday Times*, 10 February 1991, report, 'Major puts schools at the top of his agenda'; *The Independent*, 18 March 1992, report, 'PM pledges school "revolution"'.
78. Department for Education, *Choice And Diversity: A New Framework for Schools* (Cm 2021) (London: HMSO, 1992), paragraph 1.9 – paragraph 1.20.
79. *The Times*, 29 July 1992, report, 'Patten seizes control of state education in school reform'; *TES*, reports on the White Paper, 31 July 1992.
80. *The Independent*, 31 October 1992, report, 'School agency to take on crucial role'; *TES*, 6 November 1992, report, 'Backbench Tories poised to attack Bill'.
81. *TES*, 30 July 1993, report, 'The longest Act draws to a close'.
82. E.g. Goodson, *The Making Of Curriculum*, foreword; and Richard Aldrich, 'Educational legislation of the 1980s in England: an historical analysis', in *History of Education*, 21/1 (1992), p.68.
83. E.g. Roy Lowe, 'Secondary education since the Second World War', in Roy Lowe (ed.), *The Changing Secondary School* (London: Falmer, 1989), pp.4–19.
84. Richard Johnson, 'Thatcherism and English education: breaking the mould, or confirming the pattern?', *History of Education*, 18/2 (1989), pp.91–121.
85. R.H. Tawney, *Equality* (1935; revised edn 1964, London: Unwin Books), p.142.

4

Visions of 1944

Sir Bernard Partridge's famous cartoon on the 1944 Education Act, published in *Punch* as the Act became law in April 1945, portrayed R.A. Butler as the proud father taking his son to school for the first time. Butler reassures the 'New Boy' that 'It may not be very easy at first, but you'll soon settle down.' This proved to be an accurate prediction, as the Act was to last longer than any of its major predecessors. Its powerful and continuing influence on educational change has developed significantly in the half-century since its introduction, as its dominant image has changed over that time. There have been three general views adopted in relation to the Act, and they have tended to succeed each other. The first was *celebration* – an uncritical endorsement of the contribution made by the Act towards educational and social progress. The second, which developed mainly in the 1960s and 1970s, tended to be more *critical*, emphasising the shortcomings in both the planning and the outcomes of the Act. In the 1980s and 1990s a third image, based on *nostalgia*, became increasingly evident. Each of these visions of 1944 had an important impact on views about the contemporary development of education, and about national priorities. They have thus helped to influence the nature of education policies over the longer term in a manner that is often overlooked.

Since the Second World War, there have been few sustained attempts to develop a broad and overarching image of an 'English tradition' which would help to justify particular policies or reforms. The 1944 Education Act has, on the other hand, exerted strong influence on educational reform as a symbol of certain qualities that are regarded as innately English. At other times, defects in the Act have also been taken to represent characteristic evils in the English tradition which justify urgent reforms. Initially, its dominant image was one that stressed its role in a progressive liberal tradition that had gradually ensured the development of equality of educational opportunity within a democratic welfare society. By contrast critics, especially in the 1960s and 1970s, were aware mainly of the underlying social inequalities that the Act had left unscathed, and which were vividly apparent in the Norwood Report of 1943. Lastly, as new reforms were developed in the

THE NEW BOY

Mr. R. A. Butler: "It may not be very easy at first, but you'll soon settle down."

[The New Education Act came into force on April 1st.]

1980s and 1990s, the Act of 1944 came to assume an increasingly rose-tinted hue, both for the political and social consensus that it represented and for the durable nature of its achievements.

Celebrating the Act

Harold Dent, editor of *The Times Educational Supplement* in the 1940s, was among the most prominent and notable propagandists on behalf of the 1944 Act. Through the *TES* and in a succession of his own publications, he supported the principles that underpinned the Act and the further developments that he argued should arise from it.[1] As soon as the Act had been passed, Dent expressed a strongly held view that it was 'a very great Act, which makes possible as important and substantial an advance in public education as this country has ever known'.[2] His writings were intended to help ensure the approval and understanding of the public which would be needed to make the legislation a success.

Dent regarded the Act as the culmination of the planning of a 'new order' in education that had been a 'main preoccupation' of English educationists since the end of 1940.[3] This had involved the emergence of 'a broader and deeper conception of the meaning, the purpose and the scope of education'.[4] He stressed as an example of this development the ideas that underpinned the Norwood Report of 1943: '. . . by far the most interesting and significant feature of the report was the fact that all the recommendations were based upon and derived from a reasoned philosophy of education. The committee went right back to the ultimate question of purpose, and defined clearly their position in respect of education as a whole and secondary education in particular.'[5] The implementation of the Act he saw as nothing less than a 'great adventure', in which LEAs, teachers, and parents all had new and important opportunities. Dent was also optimistic that the different types of secondary school would be given parity of esteem, as the White Paper of 1943 had envisaged: 'Ex-elementary school teachers, fortified by their increased salaries and by the new status of their schools, will set out with renewed vigour to prove that these schools are as good as any.'[6] Overall, Dent was a strong and persuasive advocate of the advances achieved in the Act, and of the social opportunities that it represented.

In the years that followed, Dent continued to defend the principles of the 1944 Act. He emphasised the progress that had been made in promoting public education since the eighteenth century, and put the provisions of the 1944 Act in this long-term historical context to demonstrate the 'almost unbelievable change' that had come about in that time.[7] Moreover, he pointed out, it provided a systematic and coherent structure for national needs which could be developed further through the co-operation of the Ministry of Education, LEAs, and teachers.[8] He recognised that economic difficulties were preventing rapid expansion of facilities for public education, but was steadfast in defending the 1944 Act against what he called the 'Jeremiahs': 'Even if – as will not happen – the country never took another step towards fully implementing that Act, the impetus it gave to educational reform and the material advances it made possible during the first eight years after its passing, endowed it with a vitality which nothing short of national collapse could extinguish.'[9] Reform in education as envisaged in the Act was, he contended, of more importance than 'material progress': 'What matters above all to our country is the extent and, even more, the quality of the educational *reform* set in motion by the passing of the 1944 Act. Re-organization and re-equipment are but means to that end.'[10]

By the 1970s, Dent remained a doughty apologist of what the Act had tried to achieve: 'Today, a quarter of a century later, there is a tendency in some sophisticated quarters to look down the nose at the Education Act, 1944, to regard it as a rather feeble middle-class compromise which has not altered anything very much. Nothing could be farther from the truth.'[11] He was by now willing to concede that it contained some flaws, but it was the historic progress represented in the Act that he sought to defend, as he argued that 'Time has, of course, revealed weaknesses in the Act, but these do not alter the fact that it made possible great advances all along the line.'[12] He was concerned also to relate the Act to the gradual evolution of public education since the nineteenth century, showing the progress that had been made during that time while acknowledging that there remained 'plenty to be done in the coming century'.[13]

The image of the 1944 Act that was invoked by Harold Dent may be readily categorised as a liberal-evolutionary view of educational reform. It saw changes in the education system as progressing steadily towards improvement for the benefit of all, providing greater individual opportunities and enhancing national prosperity. This long-term development had been achieved through rational agreement and political consensus. The 1944 Act was itself a symbol of this achievement and a staging-point towards further growth and improvement in the future. Where such improvements were possible, however, it would be on the basis of the principles that underpinned that Act.

This liberal model of educational change had clear implications for the development of policy. It meant that a sound foundation for further progress could be assumed, and that future changes would be in the nature of fine-tuning the system as particular problems became evident. No radical or extensive structural reforms were therefore to be expected. It implied also that any such changes would have to justify themselves as being consistent with the provisions and ideals of the 1944 Act. In the 1940s and 1950s, these provisions and ideals were often equated with an underlying mission of the education system, to which teachers, LEAs, the Ministry, and the public at large should aspire. It was an image that also encouraged self-satisfaction and even complacency, a view that even if some problems were still to be resolved, the education system had already created an educated democracy and was an integral aspect of the welfare state.

Several other works adopted a similar line to that of Dent during this period. In the 1960s, G.A.N. Lowndes, a former educational administrator, portrayed the Act as the culmination of what he called a 'silent social revolution'. He emphasised the bipartisan political agreement that facilitated its passage into law, and also the strong support of 'public opinion' for the measure. The thinking of officials at the Board of Education in drafting the Act he described as having been 'imaginative, logical, and purposeful'.[14] In general, he praised the Act for extending educational opportunities, and for providing a basis for further expansion of the system.[15] The historian S.J. Curtis also stressed the wide support for the 1944 Act: 'Its main principles were accepted by all parties and criticisms were largely directed to administrative matters. It was an agreed measure in so far as anything in this world can be agreed.'[16] He argued that the 'overhaul of the national system of education' achieved in 1944 represented the "logical outcome of the lines of thought which had been expressed in the Hadow and the Spens Reports"'.[17] This was presented in complimentary terms as part of the progressive evolution of the system.

These images of the 1944 Act were vividly reflected in Ministry of Education reports produced in the later 1940s and 1950s. The Ministry's pamphlet *The New Secondary Education*, published in 1947, declared that the Act embodied a 'new conception of Secondary Education' that would make 'a revolutionary change in

education in England and Wales'.[18] This would indeed amount to
'the creation, for the majority of children, of a completely new
educational service'.[19] Such extensive changes would of course take
time, and circumstances were difficult, but it was confident that
'the plan for the future is established, and it will be carried out'.[20]
Further developments in the 1950s were presented as building on
the foundations of the 1944 Act. In 1958, for example, the White
Paper *Secondary Education For All: A New Drive* related its own
plans to the provisions and ideals of 1944. It noted that the 1944
Act 'provided that all children of secondary school age throughout
England and Wales, not just the selected few, should have a
secondary education in accordance with their age, ability, and
aptitude'.[21] It recorded the 'impressive' record of 'progress and
achievement' that had been made since 1944, and announced that
it now planned to make a 'further big advance' on the same lines.[22]

The oracle crumbles

These achievements began to appear less impressive from the
1960s, as the disappointments and failures of the 1944 Act came to
be stressed for the first time. By the 1970s, there were calls for a
new major Education Act to replace that of 1944. Increasingly,
also, radical critiques of the reforms of the 1940s became prominent.
Left-wing critics tended to emphasise their role in maintaining and
even reinforcing social inequalities rather than alleviating them.
At the same time, right-wingers began to point to the failure of the
1944 Act to improve economic and industrial competitiveness.

Controversy over the influence of the 1944 Education Act
developed in the 1960s as debate over educational policy became
increasingly polarised between the Labour Party and the Conservative Party. The 'partnership' between teachers, LEAs, and the
Ministry that had been celebrated during the 1950s as being at the
heart of the 1944 Act was also visibly damaged. To some extent,
the position of the 1944 Act was not affected by the reorganisation
of secondary education that was encouraged by the Labour government. On the other hand, the gaps and silences in its provisions
became more glaring, more a source of weakness than of strength
as they had previously seemed to be. Some of the provisions of the
Act themselves were interpreted in differing and incompatible
ways, and even openly challenged. The supply of free school milk
was abandoned due to the costs involved. Section 76 of the Act on
'parental wishes' became a focus of contention. Meanwhile, other

Sections began to be used more heavily and in unforeseen ways that brought them into question. In the early 1970s, for example, Margaret Thatcher as Education Secretary made novel use of Sections 13 and 68 to challenge LEAs that were attempting to reorganise schools in their areas.[23] At the same time, major sections of the 1944 legislation fell into abeyance. The Plowden Report on primary education, in 1967, was the last of the major Reports to be produced by the Central Advisory Council on Education set up in 1944, which was effectively wound up and not replaced.

In this changing context, even sympathetic appraisals of the 1944 Act were more keenly aware of its shortcomings than hitherto. Middleton and Weitzman, for example, described the Act as 'the greatest advance which could have been achieved in the time and circumstances', conceived 'in an era redolent with resounding phrases about equality and greater opportunity'.[24] Even so, they noted, 'The 1944 Act was basically a measure repairing a run-down system and it is difficult to find one area of innovation in its many clauses. It originated in a civil service study group which above all aimed at being safe, so the educational aspects of the schools system were probably the least considered. Policies were framed to suit the administrators and not for the benefit of the majority of children.'[25] The continuities represented in the Act also appeared no less evident than the changes that it helped to bring about. Middleton and Weitzman acknowledged that 'The 1944 Act has radically changed the face of Britain by opening up opportunity largely for the lower-middle class and skilled manual workers' children.'[26] On the other hand, they balanced this with the view that 'there was surprising life in the rearguard action of the old regime'.[27] Butler himself, in his memoirs entitled *The Art of the Possible*, published in the early 1970s, accepted that although 'many of the opportunities for progress offered by the Act of 1944 have been profitably seized', with 'great quantitative growth and much qualitative improvement to education', it remained true that 'not all the promises of the original Act had yet been fulfilled'.[28]

In this changing context, pressures to replace the 1944 Act with another general educational measure designed for the new generation began to increase. Edward Short, Labour Education Secretary in the late 1960s, attempted to have a new Bill designed to compel LEAs to reorganise their secondary schools as comprehensives approved by Parliament, but the Labour government fell from power before this could be achieved. Sir William Alexander, the influential secretary of the Association of Education Committees, declared in 1969 that 'There is fairly general agreement that very soon there will be need for a new major Education Act.'[29] Such a measure should be 'an agreed political measure, as the 1944 Act was', and so he argued that there should be 'adequate discussion of the problems that are involved and broad consensus of opinion established'.[30] Alexander pointed out that whereas the 1918 and 1944 Acts had followed wars, there was now the opportunity to devise major changes in peace time, 'shaping the education service for the remainder of this century'.[31] In particular, Alexander stressed the need to focus attention on further and higher education, since, as he suggested, the 1944 Act 'concentrated so heavily on the creation of secondary education for all children that it did not perhaps anticipate the growth which was to take place in further and higher education'.[32] The relative powers of central government and local government in education and the changing functions of teachers were also identified as important issues that needed re-examination. Overall, he urged, a new general framework should be put in place 'which enables the education service to meet the needs of the nation and the proper claims of the individual within limits of cost which the nation can afford'.[33]

In this kind of demand there was often an idealised notion of what the process of reform involved, influenced by the example of the 1944 Act itself. Such demands tended also to involve an assumption that the outcomes of any new general measure would improve upon the provisions, if not the general ideals, of the 1944 Act, and that they would therefore regenerate the basic principles that underlay it, for the benefit of a rapidly changing society. At the same time, it was argued, such a measure could satisfy the claims of the many different interest groups that were now becoming so restless. Thus, within the more critical appraisals of the 1944 Act that were fostered in the 1960s and 1970s, there remained ample scope for a liberal model of educational change that emphasised social progress and shared values.

This continued to be true in the 1980s, as the education system came under increasingly close scrutiny from Margaret Thatcher's Conservative government. By 1984, the Act had survived forty years of social and political change, but was associated with a Welfare State that for many in the Conservative Party seemed to belong to a former age. At the same time, hopes persisted that if a new Education Act could be brought about, it might rescue the principles of 1944 that now appeared to be under threat, and thus form the basis for another lasting settlement. Such a measure might even improve and broaden these principles, as *The Times Educational Supplement* reflected on the fortieth anniversary of the Act, that a fresh framework might help to 'enshrine', for the first time, 'legally enforceable rights for parents and children'.[34]

Above all, however, it was the perceived deficiencies and problems in the 1944 Act that were now providing the major incentive for a new radical measure of reform. Aldrich and Leighton, for example, recognised the Act as 'a monumental piece of legislation',[35] but were strongly critical of its structure, implementation and ultimate effects. They concluded that 'The deficiencies of the 1944 Act lie at the root of many of today's problems – the nature of secondary schooling, the powers of parents, teachers, governing bodies, and children, and the direction of the curriculum with particular reference to the relationship between schooling and employment.'[36] It was also in their view thoroughly outdated, reflecting 'the social and educational assumptions of an age when frustrations about such issues were regulated by custom and rarely brought to court'.[37] This kind of historical perspective, and the hopes for improvement that it implied, helped to encourage agitation for more radical educational policies. It was fondly anticipated that such reforms would not only attend to the neglected problems of the past, but would also be more suited to the changing conditions of the future.

An Establishment conspiracy?

Dissatisfaction with the 1944 Act was further encouraged by the development of radical critiques that portrayed it in terms of a conspiracy on the part of an 'educational Establishment'. According to this general viewpoint, the Board of Education and its advisers constituted a self-serving elite group in ultimate control of education policy, imbued with common values arising from their public school education, and with common class interests in restricting and manipulating educational reform. The survival of the public schools despite their general unpopularity during the war becomes an important indicator of such a conspiracy, and the Fleming Committee on the public schools an example of the kind of mechanism employed to ensure the maintenance of social stability.

The Norwood Report of 1943 also plays a key role in this interpretation. It is portrayed as a device that was intended to channel the heightened expectations for reform that existed during the war into socially conservative outcomes. In particular, its preference for three different types of secondary school is criticised as socially divisive and elitist. Its elaborate rationale in favour of what became known as the 'tripartite system' became the focus of critical attention especially when the grammar schools continued their dominance in the years after the war. Because of the strategic position of the Norwood Report, published as it was ten days after the 1943 White Paper and a year before the Act itself was passed, it could be portrayed as the darker side of the 1944 settlement, the handbrake on a generally progressive reform. While the 1944 Act itself made no reference to different types of secondary school, the quasi-official support given to the idea in the Norwood Report appeared to provide justification for a tripartite system. The prominence of its position made it especially vulnerable to critics of this system and to supporters of multilateral or comprehensive schools, more so indeed than were other advocates of tripartism such as the Spens Report of 1938.

The chairman of the Norwood Committee, Sir Cyril Norwood, was himself a convenient target for criticism which tended to strengthen the view that the Report was reactionary and socially divisive. Norwood was much more attuned to the traditions, problems and possibilities of public schools and grammar schools than he was to the prospects of technical schools or modern schools. His idealisation of an 'English tradition of education' was strongly reflected in the Norwood Report. His position in the charmed circle of advisers to the Board of Education, no less than his general background and advancing years, made it no difficult task to label him as a bastion of conservative forces determined to prevent wholesale or radical reforms in education. It was concluded that Norwood controlled the agenda of his committee, and that the final Report had a widespread influence in persuading the Ministry of Education and LEAs to favour a tripartite system rather than to adopt the pattern of a common secondary school for all.

The notion of education policy and reform implied in this critique of the 1944 Act was quite different from that embodied in the orthodox liberal model. Far from being based on consensus and shared values, with social progress and equality of opportunity as its general aspirations, on this view policy was the outcome of a small governing clique intent to preserve its own privileges at the expense of the population as a whole. It was therefore based on social antagonisms and the maintenance of inequality.

Contemporary critics such as G.C.T. Giles of the National

Union of Teachers were quick to express scepticism at the promises of the 1944 Act. While supportive of its general aims, Giles himself called attention to its 'weaknesses, compromises and evasions', and its failure to address the issue of the public schools. He also asserted the importance of developing multilateral schools rather than three different types of secondary school because of the entrenched nature of the 'caste system of education'.[38] In later years, the left-wing historian Brian Simon has also been highly influential in developing this view of the Act and relating it to the deeply rooted inequalities of English education. He was especially critical of the role of the Norwood Report. In the 1950s, he criticised its 'entirely arbitrary division of children into three disparate types, and the formulation of educational objectives in line with the supposed needs of these three types'. Simon argued that this was central to an understanding of post-war education: 'The Ministry of Education . . . has consistently referred to it as its authority in support of its educational policy, which has been based entirely on the Norwood typology. It has, therefore, been accorded a seminal influence in the development of secondary education.'[39]

According to Simon, the politics of the Norwood committee itself were 'devious and multifarious' and 'shrouded in a certain amount of mystery'.[40] But its establishment was a 'master-stroke' because it provided 'an ideological underpinning for the tripartite system'.[41] It thus 'appeared to lay down a clear pattern (and rationale) for a divided system of secondary education following whatever reforms were to be brought about by legislation'.[42] The 'devious practice' that it involved led directly to the defeat of the multilateral schools and the strengthening of 'selection and an elitist structure'.[43] Simon concludes that as a result of this kind of 'manipulation and control' during the formulation of the 1944 Act, 'after all the discussion and legislation, the country emerged with an hierarchical educational structure almost precisely as planned and developed in the mid-late nineteenth century'.[44] In short, the 1944 Act itself could be regarded as a 'Conservative measure', through which 'The "New Order" in English education, celebrated by Dent and many others, turned out to be the old order in a new disguise.'[45]

By the 1960s and 1970s, the notion of a reform that had effectively maintained rather than diminished social inequalities had become a widely accepted interpretation of the developments of the 1940s. The Norwood Report became a scapegoat for the failures and disappointments of educational reform in a way that indirectly affected perceptions of the 1944 Act itself. Thus, for the historian Angus Calder, the 'notorious' Norwood Committee, 'besides establishing the principles of a division at "eleven plus", forecast and influenced the entire shape of British education which emerged, mouselike, from the mountains of blather which preceded the Education Act of 1944'.[46] Other historians have also been scornful of the Norwood Report for its 'unscientific and unsupportable statements'.[47] Lawson and Silver were particularly stern in their judgement: 'The Spens Committee, in 1938, may have had to rely on overconfident psychological evidence; the Norwood Report of 1943 was concerned not with evidence but with assertion. It had less of a basis in discriminating analysis and concern for data than any other modern report on education.'[48] Despite these flaws, the influence of the Report remained impressive. According to Roy Lowe:

> The 1943 Norwood Report had claimed that it was possible to identify three kinds of child, and the years from 1945 to 1951 may be seen as marking the high point of the 'Norwood philosophy', a period when a thoroughgoing attempt was made by the Ministry of Education and many local education authorities to establish a tripartite secondary system of grammar, technical and modern schools.[49]

Felicity Hunt also emphasised the Norwood Report's 'profound effect on post-war education', this time in relation not only to social class but also to gender differences, especially the way in which 'it reiterated and emphasised existing social and ideological arguments for a differentiated curriculum and paved the way for its continuation and development in the post-war secondary schools'.[50]

Such criticisms, while focusing specifically on ancillary processes such as those involved in the Norwood and Fleming Reports, nevertheless influenced perceptions of the character of the 1944 Education Act itself, and of the overall 'settlement' with which it was associated. They tend moreover to illustrate the rise of a revisionist view of the 1944 Act that was predicated on the notion of something akin to an Establishment conspiracy, dedicated to the maintenance of social inequality through tripartite divisions in education.[51] This view had important implications for the development of educational reform. It exploded the notion that further reform could build upon the principles of the 1944 settlement; 1944 instead symbolised in a new form the historic class-based flaws of the 'English tradition' of which Tawney had complained before the war. It therefore underlined the urgency of more radical and thorough reform to bring about a greater degree of social equality. No less important, it cast into doubt the role of those involved in educational reform for their vested interests and prejudice, and thus suggested that the processes of reform would need to be more democratic in future than they had been in the 1940s.

It also had important though problematic interactions with policy formation in education, especially in the 1970s. This was particularly evident following the Ruskin College speech by the Labour Prime Minister James Callaghan in October 1976. The Cabinet Minister Tony Benn protested against the implications of Callaghan's speech by emphasising the need to defend the gains made by the comprehensive schools. He argued: 'There are certain dangers to face: [for example] the danger of divisiveness engendered by the 1944 Education Act with all its nonsense about different types of minds requiring different types of schools.'[52] Benn was advised on this intervention by his wife Caroline, who had collaborated with Brian Simon on an earlier work supporting the further development of comprehensive school reform.[53] But this was also the moment when policy trends began to move markedly against such perceptions and priorities.

The emergence of a right-wing critique of the 1944 Act directly challenged the former emphasis on redressing social inequalities, but at the same time shared many of the assumptions of what might be termed the radical left-wing stance. During the 1980s, as the Conservative government struggled with the consequences of economic decline and industrial conflict, the view gained ground that such problems were rooted in the character of the education system. Martin Wiener's highly influential work *English Culture and the Decline of the Industrial Spirit, 1850–1980*, published in 1981, emphasised the importance of the Victorian public schools in the 'shaping of a gentleman'. Wiener suggests that the nine ancient public schools examined by the Clarendon Commission of the 1860s became established, 'more or less as they were, as *the* model of secondary education for all who aspired to rise in English society'.[54] This encouraged a detachment from business, commerce and industry that 'continued to shape British attitudes and values in the twentieth century'.[55] Wiener's argument was highly attractive as an explanation for Britain's relative economic decline, and reinforced criticisms of the education system. It also implied that those responsible for running the education system, and where necessary for its reform, were themselves imbued with a public school-based set of interests and values that was counter-productive to fundamental change. There was again an implicit Establishment conspiracy against educational reform, but in this version of history the ultimate result was to reduce not social equality, but economic productivity.

This right-wing revisionism also carried with it important implications for an understanding of the 1944 Act. The reforms of the 1940s could be represented as being based on a social idealism and extravagance that were wholly misplaced in a nation facing economic ruin. They therefore ignored the realities of Britain's changing place in the world. Such a view was argued in forthright fashion by the military historian Correlli Barnett, most notably in his book *The Audit of War* (1986). According to Barnett, 'Britain's post-war decline began in wartime British dreams, illusions and realities'.[56] Barnett claims that the cultural and political elite were directly responsible for accommodating and even encouraging this mood of 'New Jerusalemism', and that underlying this was the pervasive influence of the public school ethos. The historic achievement of Thomas Arnold in the early nineteenth century, and Sir Robert Morant in the early twentieth century, was to consolidate 'education for industrial decline'.

The 1944 Act is linked to this tradition, and again it is the Norwood Report of 1943 that becomes the most prominent target for criticism. Educational reform in the Second World War, Barnett complains, was 'in little sense related to manpower policy or to the future industrial and export prospects so depressingly debated in other corners of Whitehall'.[57] He points out by way of illustration that the Norwood Report was mainly concerned with grammar schools, rather than with technical education. Indeed, he reserves his most withering attack for the Christian and platonic 'prejudices' displayed by Cyril Norwood and his committee's Report. Barnett dismisses the Norwood Report as 'an exercise in hypocrisy, if not actual deception'. He continues:

> Norwood steered his willing committee towards his own cherished objective with no less pertinacity than Beveridge; and that objective was to preserve the domination of the grammar school and its academic values at the cost of other kinds of secondary school and of any type of education inspired by purposes related to life and work in the modern world.[57]

Barnett finds the Norwood Report an 'amazing document' that 'publicly affirmed in uncompromising language the prevailing outlook and beliefs of the British educational establishment, and in particular of those who controlled, and would control, the levers of the educational system'.[58] The conspiracy of the 'educational Establishment' is here rendered explicit as an explanation for the failures of reform. The Norwood Report is held responsible not only for social inequality but also for economic and industrial decline, an ideal scapegoat for the failures and disappointments of post-war Britain.

As a result of this betrayal, Barnett concludes:

> Not until 1965 was there launched a fresh attempt to break the dominance of the grammar school over secondary education, this time by merging the 1944 Act's three types of school over a single 'comprehensive' establishment; and even then grammar-school values, as manifested by an obsession with results in academic examinations set by university boards, were still to triumph.[59]

Finally, he observes the attempts to break through this 'obsession' in the 1980s through such reforms as the Technical and Vocational Education Initiative, although significantly he cannot resist even here noting that the TVEI was launched by the Manpower Services Commission rather than by the Department of Education and Science, 'that repository of tradition and caution'.[60] The policy implications of this view of history were clear in Barnett's account: the 'educational Establishment' should be excluded from involvement in reform as far as possible because it was itself part of the problem.

Two specific failures of the reforms of the 1940s are singled out in this interpretation. First is the failure of the secondary technical schools to prosper as separate institutions in the post-war period. By the late 1950s, there were still fewer than 300 of these schools in England and Wales, and most of them were either closed or merged with other schools as comprehensive reorganisation developed in the 1960s.[61] Michael Sanderson mourns their demise, and argues, 'The failure to develop the junior technical and secondary technical schools is perhaps the greatest lost opportunity of twentieth century English education.'[62] He relates this to the continuing dominance of the grammar schools, 'with their academic and pure science values', and the 'chronic shortage of skilled labour which British labour has suffered since 1945'.[63] The lesson for contemporary reforms is stated explicitly. While acknowledging that 'we cannot turn the clock back to recreate this form as an alternative for non-academic teenagers', Sanderson supports the development of city technology colleges and the TVEI.[64]

Derek Aldcroft meanwhile links the problems encountered by the technical schools with a second failure of the 1944 Act, that of the county colleges. He suggests that 'The high hopes of the 1944 Act were not realised and subsequent attempts to reform the system have not, by and large, been met with any greater success.'[65] He concedes that, at least so far as formal schooling is concerned, 'the 1944 Education Act was not in principle the unmitigated disaster that some have alleged it to be', but blames the 'educational establishment' in general and the LEAs in particular for failing to implement its provisions to support technical schools.[66]

This right-wing revisionism had an important effect on the modernising reforms of the Conservative government in the 1980s and early 1990s. John MacGregor, Education Secretary from 1989 until 1991, explained that his own approach had been strongly influenced by the work of Wiener and Barnett in particular. He recalled:

> When I was asked by *The Times Educational Supplement* shortly after my appointment as Secretary of State to do a short piece for them, for a Christmas edition, on the three books I would pick out from my reading in the year just past, I think I caused some flutters in some circles by including Correlli Barnett's *The Audit of War*, which I re-read immediately on my appointment as Secretary of State.[67]

MacGregor admired what he saw as Barnett's 'devastating critique' which 'underlined the unjustified complacency that ran through so many strands of our national life and attributed much of it to the educational system of the previous many decades'. He acknowledged too that Wiener's book had a similar influence on him.[68] Indeed, he continued:

> Partly because of my view of the Martin Wiener problem and partly because of my anxiety to see the British economy developing in the way that I think it now is and certainly ought to in terms of enterprise and efficiency, recreating the enterprise spirit, I was very anxious to have a proper understanding taking place in schools of the processes of wealth creation. I have therefore welcomed all the youth enterprise initiatives and so on.[69]

More broadly, it was a perspective that strengthened the Conservatives' emphasis on accountability and 'parent power', and their suspicion of producer monopolies in education as elsewhere.

By the 1980s, therefore, the 1944 Act, despite its continuing statutory force, was widely regarded as a discredited and outdated document that urgently required overhaul and replacement. From different political stances the role and even the underlying purpose of the reforms of the 1940s were being challenged, and this helped to provide a strong incentive for a new cycle of reform. The education policies of the Conservative government from 1979, culminating first in the Education Reform Act of 1988 and then in the Education Act of 1993, strongly reflected the right-wing version of such 'lessons' of the past. At the same time, they were also encouraged and influenced by the liberal and socialist critiques that had undermined the 1944 settlement over the previous two decades.

The politics of nostalgia

Even as it was being condemned and uprooted, more ambivalent attitudes were beginning to reshape the familiar images of the 1944 Act. This process was again closely related to the changing political and social context. The Conservatives' education policies of the 1980s and early 1990s inspired fierce opposition even from many who had been critical of the shortcomings of the reforms of the 1940s. The need to respond to the changes of the present led some to adapt their views of the 1944 Act. Sympathisers of the Conservative reforms also found themselves revising their own notions of historical problems in order to justify the new developments.

Among critics of the Conservative education reforms, two distinct views of their historical significance are readily apparent. According to one view, the current changes were serving to intensify all of the worst aspects that had been identified in the reforms of the 1940s, especially the case in relation to educational and social inequalities. On the other hand, the second view stressed the failure of the Conservative reforms to repeat the achievement of the 1944 settlement, the lack of consensus involved in the reform process, and their disregard for the positive aspects of earlier reforms. This second view therefore tended to revive the image of the Act that had been dominant in the 1950s, in order to serve a new purpose towards the end of the century.

A common criticism of the 'choice' and 'diversity' envisaged in the Conservative reforms was that they recalled the tripartism of the 1940s, and presaged the emergence of an even more potent form of educational and social differentiation between different types of schools. The development of a middle tier of 'independent state schools' gave rise to particular concern. Between the independent schools and the remaining local authority schools, there would be a range of institutions such as grant-maintained schools, city technology colleges (CTCs), Technology Schools and Technology Colleges. Brian Simon, for example, warned against the consolidation of 'opted-out' schools and CTCs which would effectively create an intermediate tier of schools between 'the independent ("public" and private) schools for the better off, and the remnants of local authority schools for the masses left with the local authorities'.[70] Such analyses suggested the development of a 'new tripartism' in the 1990s that would reassert the divisions suggested in the Norwood Report. The White Paper *Choice and Diversity*, published in July 1992, gave further grounds for this general view. It was possible even for *The Times* to point out that 'The pattern most likely to emerge is roughly comparable to that obtaining under the 1944 Act, prior to the 1965 comprehensive reorganisation.'[71] According to *The Times*, the proposed changes ignored 'the clear danger of an educational underclass now emerging: of disappointed parents, rejected children and blighted schools'. Such a prospect would mean, it declared, that the education system would 'go back to 1944'.[72]

The curriculum reforms being developed in the 1980s and 1990s also invited jaundiced comparisons with the 1940s. In its early days, the Technical and Vocational Education Initiative (TVEI) gave rise to justifiable fears that it would create 'a divided curriculum perpetuating Victorian views of knowledge and social class'.[73] According to Maurice Holt, a prominent liberal critic of this initiative, it would rekindle old ideas in a new guise 'in a political context which seems itself to hark back to tripartism and old solutions to new problems'.[74] In the early 1990s, too, suggestions that academic and vocational streams should be developed from the age of 14 were met with protests that this would merely repeat the mistakes of the 1940s.[75]

Meanwhile, other critics of the new education policies being promoted by the Conservatives found much in the 1944 Act that they found preferable. This was especially the case as the Education Secretary John Patten was steering his Education Bill through Parliament towards the end of 1992. Michael Barber of the National Union of Teachers noted that the 1944 Act had been based on a broad consensus that was missing in the 1990s. The strength of the 1944 Act, he recalled, was 'based on the quality of Butler's consultations, his ability to respond to interests without being weak, and his shrewd combination of pragmatism and principle'.[76] Sir

Malcolm Thornton, the Conservative chairman of the House of Commons Select Committee on Education, Science and the Arts, pointed out that Butler's Act represented 'the fruits of balanced judgement of the developments and thinking which had been taking place over the years – particularly since the 1918 Act'. Moreover, he recalled, the 1944 Act had not given the Minister of Education such a wide range of powers as that of 1993 was to do: 'Significantly, it gave the Minister of Education a creative rather than just a controlling function – charging him or her with promoting education.'[77]

Again, there was in this vision of 1944 a clear contemporary message, that the new policies suffered by comparison with their predecessors both in general terms ('balanced judgement') and on specifics. Peter Watkins, former chief executive of the School Curriculum Development Committee, and another notable critic of many of the new policies, vigorously pursued a similar theme. The keynotes of the 1944 Act – expansion, consensus and partnership – had been destroyed, Watkins argued: 'The fiftieth anniversary of the Butler Education Act . . . is more likely to be a wake than a celebration.'[78] Replacing these sterling qualities, in his view, were contraction, conflict, and a lack of respect for the views and contributions of educators. This was also the stance adopted by the Labour Party's spokesperson on education in the House of Lords, Lord Judd, as he criticised the Education Bill towards the end of its passage in March 1993 for marking the last stage in the destruction of the '1944 consensus'.[79] Such perspectives underlined the importance of historical awareness in responding to contemporary policies. They used historical arguments to prove a contemporary point, to sharpen criticisms of present trends. No less interesting, in so doing they revived the positive vision of the 1944 Act that had been potent in the 1940s and 1950s – no longer as celebration of current changes and future potential, but now as nostalgic lament for the past.

Supporters of the education reforms of the 1990s tended meanwhile to distance themselves from the aims and outcomes of the 1944 Act. As has been seen, criticisms of the reforms of the 1940s from a range of perspectives had helped to give rise to this new cycle of policies, and their sponsors were anxious to avoid appearing to repeat the mistakes of the past. This is evident, for example, in the 1992 White Paper, *Choice and Diversity*. Part One of the White Paper suggests the general policy of the Government as being to build on the 'five great themes' of the 1980s: quality, diversity, increasing parental choice, greater autonomy for schools, and greater accountability.[80] These aims are contrasted with those of the 1940s:

> After wartime deliberations, and the Education Act 1944 which followed, those who argued so vigorously the pros and cons of selection and the 11 plus examination in the 1950s and 1960s lived in a different educational world, which had no National Curriculum taught in common throughout the tripartite system of secondary schools, ensuring equality of opportunity. Thus, the school system then offered no opportunity of an equal chance for all children.[81]

This is a very awkward and uncomfortable passage, but what it seems to convey is that the reforms of the 1940s were based on social inequality but that this would not now be the case because of the National Curriculum. Whatever their choice of school, pupils would have access to the same type of knowledge; indeed, it stressed, 'the whole emphasis of our changes in the education system – towards diversity, higher standards and choice – is designed to allow all children to realise their full potential'.[82]

Two especially significant implications of this stance seem to warrant close attention. First, it meant an acceptance of the kinds of criticisms of the 1944 settlement that left-wing critics had been making for the previous forty years. The Conservative government of the 1950s had strenuously denied such claims as it defended those reforms.[83] Sir David Eccles, Minister of Education in the 1950s, had gone so far as to argue in private that such differences in access to secondary schools were less important than the success of pupils after leaving school: 'In the long run, our maintained schools will not be judged by how fairly a child enters at 11 but by how successfully he leaves at 15-plus, i.e. how he makes his way into the big world.'[84] The Conservative government of the 1990s is acknowledging that this was insufficient. But at the same time, a further point would be that the 1992 White Paper presents this history as being remote and distant, as having nothing to do with contemporary problems. It was 'a different educational world', with different needs from those of the present, rather than an important source for understanding the continuing problems of educational reform.

On the other hand, despite such distancing from the reforms of the 1940s, there seems to be a certain nostalgia about the education settlement that was reached at that time among the sponsors and sympathisers of the Conservative reforms in the 1990s. This reflects in part a hankering for what are remembered as the golden days of the grammar school. Such an outlook has been described as 'a sad case of government by nostalgia', in which 'Many Conservative ministers, who are themselves beneficiaries of an excellent grammar school education, believe that the absence of that opportunity for today's children is the main reason for a slide in standards.'[85] This was especially apparent in the sympathies of the Prime Minister, John Major, who, it was mischievously observed, 'seems to hanker after a *Darling Buds of May* Britain, circa 1955, when every summer was warm, every village had its bakery, life revolved round the Rotary Club and the Women's Institute and every child sat attentively in front of a teacher in a cardigan reciting Shakespeare's sonnets'.[86] In this instance, the lessons drawn from personal experience seemed to be especially important in helping to motivate educational reform.

In contrast with this idealised view of the 'good old days', the reforms of the 1960s were regarded as being tainted with betrayal and failure – the decade of the Plowden Report and progressive child-centred education, of comprehensive schools and left-wing teachers. The egalitarian characteristics of these reforms were magnified and caricatured to portray them as the major source of Britain's educational and social problems. The failure of education to promote economic and industrial growth and the conspiracies of the 'educational Establishment' were again key themes in this view of the 1960s. Thus John Major argued that 'the problem of low standards stems in large part from the nature of the comprehensive system which the Labour Party ushered in in the 1960s, and the intellectual climate underpinning it that has tended to stress equality of outcome at the expense of equality of opportunity'.[87] He attacked the 'serious mistakes' of the 1960s, when 'tried and tested methods were cast aside and experimental techniques put in their place'.[88] Kenneth Clarke as Education Secretary also claimed that 'in the name of Plowden, grave damage has been done to parts of our education service'.[89] As a result of this, he insisted, 'anti-academic, anti-intellectual, eccentric views have permeated too many of our schools and must have contributed to the unacceptable variations in standards that our league tables are beginning to expose'.[90] This view was echoed by Clarke's successor, John Patten, who inveighed against the '"leave us alone and give us the money" secret garden of education theory of the 1960s'.[91] Patten's jibe invoked both the need for greater accountability in schools, and the importance of reducing the influence of dubious or 'eccentric' theories that had led the education system astray.

Sympathisers of the Conservative reforms reinforced these images of the 1960s which enhanced not only nostalgia for earlier lost 'standards', but also the need to promote aggressive new policies. A good example of this selective memory was Michael Jones, political editor of the *Sunday Times*. He remembered the primary school of his childhood, during the Second World War:

> Primary school was a happy time for me. About 40 of us sat at fixed wooden desks with ink wells and moved from them only with grudging permission. Teacher sat in a higher desk in front of us and moved only to the blackboard. She smelt of scent and inspired awe.[92]

This was then contrasted with an unfavourable image of the 1960s:

> The Plowden report changed all that in the 1960s, 20 years too late for me, thank God, but not, alas, for the generations that followed. My children spent their primary years in a showpiece school where they were allowed to wander around at will, develop their individuality and dodge the three Rs. It was all for the best, we were assured. But it was not. In that, as in much of their dogmatic orthodoxy, the disciples of the Plowden report served the nation ill.[93]

According to Jones, this 'dogmatic orthodoxy' led directly to educational decline: 'Throughout the 1970s and 1980s, hundreds of thousands of children were betrayed while the full extent of the damage was denied.'[94] He was therefore a fervent supporter of the reforms of the 1990s. Similarly, Anthony O'Hear, professor of philosophy at the University of Bradford and a member of the Council for the Accreditation of Teacher Education, derided the effects of the Plowden Report: 'The result of the educational establishment denigrating what it calls didactic teaching for two decades will be familiar to all parents: primary classrooms filled with noise, colour, movement and hubbub, and children emerging from them unstimulated, untaught and unable to concentrate.'[95] It was necessary, he argued, to reject this philosophy and thus 'transform our nation's primary classrooms from the playrooms they now so often resemble' to foster 'places where real learning might take place'.[96]

There was in this image of the 'educational Establishment' a significant shift from that which had been identified as having been responsible for the policies of the 1940s. The elite of the 1940s were castigated for their emphasis upon academic and liberal values, and caricatured as a group of unworldly mandarins who grew their fingernails long and preferred Greek to economics. The elite of the 1960s, on the other hand, were perceived as a clique of dangerously trendy radicals engaged in an untried social experiment akin to the Chinese Cultural Revolution. Despite the clear contradictions between these portrayals, they tended to be juxtaposed to create a composite image of an 'educational Establishment' whose influence any real reform would need to resist and destroy. The Plowden Report of 1967 may thus be seen as the equivalent of the Norwood Report of 1943, in the way that it symbolised for later generations the failures and flaws of the cycle of reforms that surrounded it.

The vivid contrast with the 1960s, then, served to encourage a nostalgia for the 1940s among sponsors and sympathisers of the Conservative reforms in the 1990s. Respect for the 1940s was heightened in such quarters out of a growing admiration for the durable nature of the settlement then reached. *Choice and Diversity* was intended to emulate this achievement: to provide the 'last piece of the jigsaw' of the Conservatives' reforms, and to set out the Government's vision of schooling for the next twenty to twenty-five years.[97] This aspiration had been clearly evident in Kenneth Baker's Education Reform Act of 1988.[98] As the 1993 Education Bill made its difficult way through Parliament, John Patten also expressed hopes that this would provide the basis for a major and lasting settlement, 'the third and most fundamental set of reforms of the way we educate our young people in this country'.[99] Like Baker before him, Patten emphasised the historic achievement of R.A. Butler in securing the passage of the 1944 Act, and styled himself in the same leading role:

Looking at Butler's photograph hanging in the waiting room outside my office at the Department for Education, I see in those then-youthful and relaxed features both conciliator *and* centraliser. Yes, he agreed that the churches and local authorities should run the schools – but according to a pattern that *he* laid down.[100]

This flattering interpretation of the 1944 Act also helped to legitimise Patten's own emphasis on central control of certain key features of education. Yet at the same time Patten continued to maintain a cautious distance between his own reforms and those of the 1940s. He made use of his own personal experience to criticise both the inequalities produced in the 1940s and the progressivism of the 1960s:

My own school days neatly straddled the two reforms. The Sixties had opened with schoolboys and schoolgirls patiently waiting to be tested at 11 and thereafter parcelled and graded like vegetables into grammar, technical or secondary [sic] children. They ended with the transmogrification of those uniformed and inky children into Biro-bearing 'kids', for whom difference was abhorred, diversity damned, choice condemned.[101]

This personal reminiscence again helped to justify Patten's contemporary purpose in pursuing radical education policies, as he concluded: 'We are now on another cusp between the second phase of post-war schooling and the third, just as in the Sixties as a schoolboy I saw that similar switch from the world of the 11-plus to the comprehensive experiment.'[102]

Just as the critics of the Conservative reforms began to develop a more ambivalent image of the 1944 Act, a similar process was evident among Conservative sympathisers. These signs of renewed sympathy seemed likely to increase as the controversies surrounding the Conservative reforms persisted. Even as the Education Bill was being introduced in November 1992, *The Times Educational Supplement* could suggest that 'There is now little support for the advance publicity claiming that a definitive Act to see out the century was in the making.'[103] Instead, it was evidently 'part of a continuing process, patching together the fabric of recent Acts where holes and weak seams were evident, and inevitably reformulating large sections of the 1944 Act in order to shift fundamental planning duties gradually away from local education authorities and into the hands of the Funding Agencies'.[104] By the time that the Act was passed in July 1993, there were already many predictions that another Education Bill would shortly be necessary, and complaints even from Conservative sympathisers that the reforms had failed.[105] The contrast with the 1940s was readily apparent. As the 1944 Education Act sank slowly in the west, it seemed to be bathed in a misty and roseate glow.

Back to the future

In November 1987, after the introduction of Kenneth Baker's Education Reform Bill, there appeared in *The Times Educational Supplement* a cartoon that symbolised the distance travelled since 1944. It is set at the graveside of R.A. Butler, where the lone mourner confides that 'I keep hearing these strange turning

"I keep hearing these strange turning noises . . ."

noises . . .' With him at the scene, as if looking out for suspicious circumstances, are a detective and a uniformed police officer.[106] The contrast with Partridge's optimistic 'New Boy' cartoon of 1945 could hardly be more complete, or more piquant. Yet this too served a contemporary point: the traditions and policies observed in the past were returning to reproach the present. Its sympathies for the 1944 Act undercut the Conservative reforms of the late 1980s, and deliberately so. Even after being laid to rest, the Butler Act remained an influential presence in education policy.

Visions of the 1944 Act had undergone many significant changes over the preceding half-century. Close at hand, its virtue and promise seemed its most important aspect. From a greater distance, its flaws and failures came more sharply into view. Finally, as though in reconciliation, all was forgiven – but not forgotten. Throughout these adaptations, the 1944 Act had represented both the merits and the faults of the 'English tradition'. On the positive side, it reflected aspirations for equality of opportunity, political consensus, and social partnership. Read negatively, it signified the power of elite groups to manipulate public provisions, leading either to entrenched social divisions and inequality, or to industrial decay and economic atrophy. Each of these visions of 1944 stretched further back towards the nineteenth century, reconstructing as they did so an overarching teleology. At the same time, they reached forward towards the future, to depict the consequences of this trend for English education and society in the twenty-first century. The alternative traditions and the projected outcomes of these are similarly integral to each of these visions of 1944. Over this fifty year period, the Education Act of 1944 constituted a vehicle by which observers from different social and political positions were able to go 'back to the future'.

The relationship between these historical perspectives and changing social, political and policy patterns was complex and contested. The directions of influence ran both ways, and yet were often ignored or only tacitly accepted. Contemporary problems demanded particular representations of the 1944 Act; historical accounts could challenge these ideas but could often reinforce them or become co-opted to them in simplified and usable forms. To view such processes at work must raise worrying questions about the detachment of even the most refined historical scholarship. But it underlines the importance of acknowledging and grappling with the importance of history in education policy; for if we do not, its influence, unremarked, will be insidious and unchallenged.

NOTES

1. Joan Simon, 'Promoting educational reform on the home front: *The TES* and *The Times* 1940–1944', *History of Education*, 18/3 (1989), pp.195–211, on the general background of Dent's work.
2. H.C. Dent, *The Education Act, 1944* (London: University of London Press, 1944), p.3.
3. H.C. Dent, *Education in Transition: A Sociological Study of the Impact of War on English Education, 1939–1943*(London: Routledge & Kegan Paul, 1944), p.78.
4. Ibid., p.vi.
5. Ibid., p 230.
6. *TES*, 3 March 1945, leading article, 'The great adventure'.
7. H.C. Dent, *Change in English Education: A Historical Survey* (London: University of London Press, 1952), p.19.
8. H.C. Dent, *Growth in English Education, 1946–1952* (London: Routledge & Kegan Paul, 1954), pp.44–5.
9. Ibid., p.viii.
10. Ibid.
11. H.C. Dent, 'To cover the country with good schools: a century's effort', *BJES*, 19/2 (1971), p.134.
12. Ibid.
13. Ibid., p.138.
14. G.A.N. Lowndes, *The Silent Social Revolution: An Account of the Expansion of Public Education in England and Wales 1895–1965* (Oxford: OUP, 1965), p.221.
15. Ibid., Ch.15.
16. S.J. Curtis, *History of Education in Great Britain* (London: University Tutorial Press, 7th edn, 1968), p.378.
17. Ibid., p.383.
18. Ministry of Education, *The New Secondary Education* (pamphlet no.9, London: HMSO, 1947), p.8.
19. Ibid., p.11.
20. Ibid., p.8.
21. Ministry of Education, *Secondary Education For All: A New Drive* (Cmnd. 604: London: HMSO, 1958), p.3.
22. Ibid.
23. See Roger Woods, 'Margaret Thatcher and secondary school reorganisation, 1970–74', *JEAH*, 13/2 (1981), pp.51–61;., Peter Gosden, *The Education System Since 1944* (Oxford: Martin Robertson, 1983), p.41; Brian Simon, *Education and the Social Order, 1940–1990* (London: Lawrence & Wishart, 1991), pp.413–20.
24. Nigel Middleton and Sophia Weitzman, *A Place for Everyone: A History of State Education from the End of the 18th Century to the 1970s* (London: Gollancz, 1976), pp.308–9. This was written by Middleton with the use of Weitzman's draft manuscript of the history of education.
25. Ibid., p.307.
26. Ibid., p.383.
27. Ibid., p.375.
28. R.A. Butler, *The Art of the Possible* (London: Penguin, 1973), p.125.
29. Sir William Alexander, *Towards a New Education Act* (London: Councils and Education Press, 1969), p.5.
30. Ibid.
31. Ibid., p.7.
32. Ibid., p.8.
33. Ibid., p.67.
34. *TES*, 3 August 1984, leading article, 'Forty years on . . .'
35. Richard Aldrich, Patricia Leighton, *Education: Time for a New Act?* (Bedford Way Papers 23, Institute of Education University of London, 1985), p.9.
36. Ibid., pp.73–4.
37. Ibid., p.74.
38. G.C.T. Giles, *The New School Tie* (London: Pilot Press, 1946).

39. Brian Simon, *The Common Secondary School* (London: Lawrence & Wishart, 1955), p.151.
40. Brian Simon, 'The 1944 Education Act: a Conservative measure?', *History of Education*, 15/1 (1986), p.38.
41. Ibid., pp.38–9.
42. Ibid., p.39.
43. Ibid., p.40. See also Brian Simon, *The Politics of Educational Reform, 1920–1940* (1974), pp.323–33; and Brian Simon, *Education and the Social Order, 1940–1990* (1991), Ch.1.
44. Simon, *Education and the Social Order*, p.74.
45. Simon, 'The 1944 Education Act', p.43.
46. Angus Calder, *The People's War: Britain 1939–1945* (London: Panther, 1971), pp.626–7.
47. Peter Gordon, *Selection for Secondary Education* (London: Woburn, 1980), p.192.
48. J. Lawson and H. Silver, *A Social History of Education in England* (London: Methuen, 1973), p.432.
49. Roy Lowe, *Education in the Post-War Years: A Social History* (London: Routledge, 1988), p.37.
50. Felicity Hunt, *Gender and Policy in English Education: Schooling for Girls 1902–1944* (New York: Harvester, 1991), pp.133–4.
51. Other works with similar implications include Gail Savage, 'Social class and social policy: the civil service and secondary education in England during the interwar period', *Journal of Contemporary History*, 18 (1983), pp.261–80; and Deborah Thom, 'The 1944 Education Act: the "art of the possible"?', in H. Smith (ed.), *War And Social Change* (Manchester: Manchester University Press, 1986), pp.101–28.
52. Tony Benn, diary, 25 October 1976, in Tony Benn, *Against the Tide: Diaries 1973–76* (London: Arrow Books, 1989), p.629.
53. Caroline Benn and Brian Simon, *Half Way There: Report on the British Comprehensive School Reform* (London: Penguin, 2nd edn 1972). A later statement of Caroline Benn's position, reflecting the strong influence of Simon, is Caroline Benn, 'Common education and the radical tradition', in A. Rattansi and D. Reeder (eds.), *Rethinking Radical Education* (London: Lawrence & Wishart, 1992), pp.143–65.
54. Martin Wiener, *English Culture and the Decline of the Industrial Spirit, 1850–1980* (Cambridge: CUP, 1981), p.17.
55. Ibid., p.22.
56. Correlli Barnett, *The Audit of War: The Illusion and Reality of Britain as a Great Nation* (London: Macmillan, 1986), p.8.
57. Ibid., p.276.
58. Ibid., p.299.
59. Ibid., p.302.
60. Ibid.
61. McCulloch, *The Secondary Technical School* (London: Falmer, 1989).
62. Michael Sanderson, *Educational Opportunity and Social Change In England* (London: Faber & Faber, 1987), p.60.
63. Ibid., pp.60–61.
64. Ibid., pp.6–7.
65. Derek Aldcroft, *Education, Training and Economic Performance 1944 to 1990* (Manchester: Manchester University Press, 1992), p.49.
66. Ibid., p.148.
67. John MacGregor, 'The education debate II', in M. Williams, R. Dougherty and F. Banks (eds.), *Continuing the Education Debate* (Swansea 1992), p.18.
68. Ibid.
69. Ibid., p.19.
70. Brian Simon, *What Future for Education?* (London: Lawrence & Wishart, 1992), p.56.
71. *The Times*, 29 July 1992, leading article, 'State knows best'.
72. Ibid.
73. Maurice Holt, 'The great education robbery', *TES*, 3 December 1992.
74. Maurice Holt, 'Vocationalism on the hoof', in M. Holt (ed.), *Skills And Vocationalism:*

The Easy Answer (Milton Keynes: Open University Press, 1987), p.82.

75. e.g. Sally Tomlinson, 'Yet another repeat', TES, 1 November 1991.
76. Michael Barber, 'An uncommon consensus', TES, 9 October 1992.
77. Sir Malcolm Thornton, 'The role of government in education', in C. Chitty and B. Simon (eds.), Education Answers Back: Critical Responses to Government Policy (London: Lawrence & Wishart, 1993), p.162.
78. Peter Watkins, 'Unhappy returns', TES, 26 March 1993.
79. The Independent, 24 March 1993, report, 'Lords attack Education Bill'.
80. Department for Education, Choice and Diversity (London: HMSO, 1992), para 1.9.
81. Ibid., para 1.49.
82. Ibid., para 1.50.
83. See D.W. Dean, 'Consensus or conflict? The Churchill government and educational policy, 1951–55', History of Education, 21/1 (1992), pp. 15–35.
84. D. Eccles, note, 'Secondary technical schools', 24 January 1955 (Ministry of Education papers, ED.147/207).
85. The Independent, 28 February 1992, leading article, 'Nostalgia is no solution'.
86. Sunday Times, 7 February 1993, leading article, 'Darling buds of Major'.
87. The Independent, 28 February 1992, report, 'Major puts blame for low standards on comprehensives'.
88. Sunday Times, 10 February 1991, report, 'Major puts schools at the top of his agenda'.
89. Kenneth Clarke, 'Education's insane bandwagon finally goes into the ditch', Sunday Times, 26 January 1992.
90. Ibid.
91. John Patten, 'Britain opts in to a better kind of school', Sunday Times, 31 January 1993.
92. Michael Jones, 'At last, trendy teachers' days are numbered', Sunday Times, 8 December 1991.
93. Ibid.
94. Ibid.
95. Anthony O'Hear, 'Putting work before play in primary school', Sunday Times, 8 December 1991.
96. Ibid. Also e.g. Sunday Times, 26 January 1992, report, 'The great betrayal'.
97. The Independent, 19 May 1992, report, 'Patten sees growth in school specialisation'.
98. See e.g. Michael Flude and Merril Hammer (eds.), The Education Reform Act 1988: Its Origins and Implications (London: Falmer, 1990).
99. John Patten, 'A learning-by-choice revolution', The Independent, 5 April 1993.
100. Ibid.
101. Ibid.
102. Ibid.
103. TES, 6 November 1992, leading article, 'The last word is yet to come'.
104. Ibid.
105. TES, 30 July 1993, report, 'The longest Act draws to a close'; TES, 14 August 1993, report, 'Councils demand new Bill'.
106. TES, 27 November 1987.

5

Three Types of Child

The Education Act of 1944 did not itself mention the idea of developing three different types of secondary school. Even so, as the last chapter showed, this 'tripartite' division became one of the dominant images of the reforms of the 1940s. In this chapter, the character of tripartism in the 1940s will be considered in greater depth, together with the notion of the 'three types of child' on which it was based. It is also helpful to understand the extent to which these reforms depended on the hope that the different types of school would achieve 'parity of esteem'. The relationship between these reforms and longer-term trends influencing current policies in the 1990s is a further key issue that needs investigation.

Tripartism and the Norwood Report

The categories of secondary schools related to three different types of mind that were presented in the Norwood Report of 1943 are a well known reference point for understanding tripartite divisions in education. Part I of the Report identified three 'rough groupings' of pupils which, 'whatever may be their ground, have in fact established themselves in general educational experience'.[1] It argued that these distinctions should be acknowledged and catered for in the future provision of secondary education.

The first type of pupil was 'the pupil who is interested in learning for its own sake, who can grasp an argument or follow a piece of connected reasoning'. Formerly, such pupils had been associated with the grammar schools, and they had generally gone into the learned professions or higher administrative or business posts. The curriculum best suited for these pupils was one that 'treats the various fields of knowledge as suitable for coherent and systematic study for their own sake apart from immediate considerations of occupation'.[2] According to the Report, grammar schools should continue to provide such a curriculum, in order to uphold an ideal of 'disciplined thought provided by an introduction to the main fields of systematic knowledge, which is valued first for its own sake and later invoked to meet the needs of life'.[3]

The second type of pupil was identified as showing 'interests and abilities' that lay 'markedly in the field of applied science or applied art'.[4] These pupils were especially well suited to a curriculum that was 'closely, though not wholly, directed to the special data and skills associated with a particular kind of occupation',[5] and this could be developed in secondary technical schools that would be designed for this purpose.

Lastly, the Norwood Report perceived a grouping of pupils who dealt 'more easily with concrete things than with ideas', and who demanded 'immediate returns' from any endeavour: 'His horizon is near and within a limited area his movement is generally slow, though it may be surprisingly rapid in seizing a particular point or in taking up a special line.'[6] For these pupils it suggested a curriculum with 'a balanced training of mind and body and a correlated approach to humanities, Natural Science and the arts', not to prepare for any specific job or occupation but to 'make a direct appeal to interests, which it would awaken by practical touch with affairs'.[7] Secondary modern schools should be developed to cater for these pupils, the Report concluded.

These recommendations suggested a framework for secondary education in which the needs of the 'three broad groups of pupils' could be met within 'three broad types of secondary education, each type containing the possibility of variation and each school offering alternative courses which would yet keep the school true to type'.[8] Such a reorganisation of secondary education would meet the needs both of the nation as a whole and of individual pupils, since in the view of the Report:

> The existing Secondary Schools would continue to perform their proper task without distraction; the secondary Technical Schools would provide an access of pupils well able to profit by the courses which they provide; the Modern Schools still in process of formulating their aim and methods would gain the scope necessary to them to fulfil the promise which they already show, and we do not regard it as impossible that eventually pupils of over 16+ may be found in them.[9]

It was therefore this arrangement of three types of school, rather than the multilateral schools which combined these functions, that the Norwood Report strongly supported.

The Norwood Report was far from alone in its general support for a tripartite structure of secondary education based on the notion of three different types of child. Such an ideal was widely advocated and was deeply rooted in the politics and society of the 1930s and 1940s. This immediate social and political context helps to explain the currency of such an approach. In its basic form, it had been conceived in the 1920s as a possible means of extending secondary education to all children while recognising their different backgrounds, aptitudes and interests. The Hadow Report of 1926, on *The Education of the Adolescent*, argued that post-primary education should begin at the age of 11-plus and should be 'envisaged so far as possible as a single whole' but embracing 'a variety in the types of education supplied'.[10] From this age, it suggested, children with different interests and abilities could be catered for 'by means of schools of varying types, but which have, nevertheless, a broad common foundation'.[11] Because there were 'diversities of gifts', the Hadow Report reasoned, 'there must be diversity of educational provision'.[12] It proposed that these should include the existing secondary grammar schools, together with central schools with a 'realistic or practical trend' which would be known as 'Modern Schools'. Senior classes and similar arrangements in elementary schools would also be included in these post-primary arrangements. It hoped that such a development would protect the existing secondary schools from the likely effects of growing numbers of pupils, while providing the curriculum that was 'most likely to be suitable for the pupils concerned'.[13] Each of these types of school would be 'concerned with an education which should logically be regarded as Secondary, and differ from each other merely as the different species of a single genus'.[14] At the same time, the Hadow Report envisaged that junior technical schools and trade schools would be retained along their existing lines, rather than being broadened and included in this framework of post-primary provision.

The Spens Report on secondary education, published at the end of 1938, pursued this theme further. This Report argued that the curriculum of the existing grammar schools should be broadened, but also recommended that junior technical schools should be upgraded to secondary school status to become 'technical high schools'. However, several problems arose from these recommendations which led the Report to be effectively shelved. It was not clear why the existing grammar school curriculum needed to be reformed to cater for a wider clientele, as the Report suggested, if at the same time there were to be three different types of schools for pupils of different types and capacities. A further issue was the extent to which the proposed technical high schools would achieve parity with the existing secondary schools, as the Spens Report envisaged.

The Spens proposals to broaden the curriculum of the existing secondary schools also attracted opposition from conservative officials at the Board of Education such as G.G. Williams (soon to become principal assistant secretary in the Secondary Branch), who argued that 'In an effort to correct the academic bias of the Secondary School let us not go to the other extreme . . . For many pupils this type of education may not be the most appropriate; but to say that we are justified in excluding it in favour of a more strongly vocational type of school for all pupils is to lose one of our most precious heritages.'[14] It was possible to argue, therefore, that the proposals of the Spens Report would neither improve the status of the new types of secondary schools, nor uphold the integrity of the existing ones. The financial implications of providing additional facilities for technical high schools constituted a further major barrier to implementing the Spens proposals, especially when preparation for a likely war was the main priority at the Treasury.[15] Part One of the Norwood Report may be read as an attempt to provide a coherent basis for a pattern of post-primary education that would satisfy both grammar school traditionalists, such as Williams, and those who sought broader and more diverse secondary school provision for a wider school population.

The general principle of trying to define three different types of secondary school was broadly accepted during the war. The idea presented no difficulty to R.H. Tawney, who had himself been a member of the Hadow Committee, and who continued to support the notion of different kinds of school for pupils of different abilities and aptitudes. In September 1940, Tawney perceived 'new and fruitful possibilities', especially as in his view 'The policy of a universal system of secondary education, embracing schools varying in educational type and methods, but equal in quality, has made much progress outside official and political circles.'[16] He was mainly concerned to see a general raising of the compulsory school leaving age to fifteen, and if possible to sixteen, and the abolition of fees in all secondary schools assisted by the State.

By the early months of 1943, Tawney was optimistic that Butler's reforms would indeed extend secondary education to all children more or less on the basis that he had envisaged: 'I wish to see all children going on to one or other of varying types of secondary education, and that view now seems to be fairly generally accepted.'[17] On the other hand, the struggle to ensure that 'schools should be free, in order that the choice between them may be made on educational grounds, and not biased by the fact that some schools charge fees, and others do not', remained to be won.[18] He therefore approved of the White Paper *Educational Reconstruction*, which referred to grammar schools, technical schools and modern schools being provided for all children,[19] and which argued that 'A system under which fees are charged in one type of post-primary school and prohibited in the other offends against the canon that the nature of a child's education should be determined by his capacity and promise and not by the financial circumstances of his parent.'[20] Tawney took advantage of this argument to claim that the Education Bill should 'act on the logic of the White Paper's premises, and abolish fees in Direct Grant, as well as other, Secondary Schools'.[21] He was less interested in the Norwood Report; Butler sent him a personal copy, and he confessed that he had 'not as yet done more than glance through it'.[22] To Tawney, it merely spelled out the terms of a political victory that had already been won, whereas he was more concerned with issues that remained contentious.

Another influential supporter of a tripartite system of secondary education, Harold Dent, the editor of *The Times Educational Supplement*, went further in his defence of the principles involved in it. He agreed with the Norwood Report that, as he put it, 'Tripartitism was a natural result of the historical evolution of post-primary education in England and Wales.'[23] It was not 'as many people appear to imagine, the result of a modern passion for administrative tidiness, nor as even more seem to believe, a sinister plot to deprive "working-class" children of the educational opportunities which are theirs by right'. It was, rather, 'a manifestation of the "tradition of the society", with long and deep historical roots, and should be treated as such'.[24] Thus Dent related tripartite distinctions, and the idea of three types of child, to an English tradition in education that he felt was broadly accepted.

The argument of the Norwood Report was thus widely shared, and reflected a prevalent general logic among the educational reformers of the 1940s. This is not to suggest that there was no opposition to such a view. The multilateral alternative had won support in Labour Party circles to the extent that its education advisory sub-committee recommended the introduction of a common secondary school from the age of eleven.[25] The London County Council, the largest in the country, was soon to choose a system of comprehensive high schools rather than one that involved different types of secondary school.[26] Nor can it be denied that there were many officials at the Board of Education who found a tripartite structure of education convenient to their social values or political interests. On the other hand, it seems important to recognise that there was also a substantial body of support for such thinking, grounded in the social and political aspirations of educational reform over the previous twenty years.

Types of tripartism

The tripartite divisions accepted in the 1940s must also be understood in relation to a longer-term historical tendency in English education towards social differentiation between different types of schools and curricula. These social distinctions echoed those of the Taunton Report of 1868 which, as Goodson points out, sanctioned 'a social and political order for schooling, based on a hierarchy of mentalities'.[27] In the educational reforms of the 1980s and 1990s, too, historians such as Simon and Lowe have discerned the potential contours of a new tripartite system consisting of independent schools in one category, grant maintained schools and city technology colleges in the second, and the schools left under local authority control in the third.[28] And yet the historical processes involved in this are less simple and straightforward than such accounts would tend to convey. Tripartism has not been a static or unchanging notion, but has been perceived to exist in several different forms. There are at least five different types of tripartism that have had an effect on English educational institutions in the twentieth century. It is in the contestation between them that their importance would seem to lie, both in relation to the 1940s and for the 1990s.

The first type of tripartism is a view based on a social hierarchy correlating in a straightforward manner with an educational hierarchy. As in Plato's scheme of education devised in classical Greece, the academic or 'liberal' approach was at the apex, the technical or vocational was assigned a poor second place, and the plebeian or banausic came in last. Indeed English education has often seemed to constitute a life-size working model of Plato's educational ideals.[29] As John Dancy pointed out in the 1960s, 'Plato was a social and intellectual snob rolled into one, a combination irresistible to the English. *His* intellectual theory matched and reinforced *our* traditional social practice.'[30] In the nineteenth century, the reinvigorated public schools provided the philosopher-kings; a range of technical institutions struggled to survive as an intermediate tier; the elementary schools that were grudgingly and belatedly created were clearly intended to create the workers of tomorrow. In the early decades of the twentieth century, the elite group was broadened, if often imperceptibly, to include the 'meritocracy' of the new state grammar schools (almost) alongside the 'aristocracy' of the public schools. The junior technical schools and the elementary schools continued in these circumstances to perform pre-ordained and familiar roles. Fred Clarke, professor of education in South Africa in the 1920s, could observe from a distance the maintenance of social distinctions in this period, reflected for example in upper-class opinion that could see 'something incongruous and almost indecent in the phenomenon of the coachman's or butler's son learning Latin'. On this view, Latin was 'like polo or pheasant-shooting – the prerogative of a gentleman, and should not be prostituted to base plebeian churls'.[31]

It is not difficult to detect a similar hierarchical pattern re-emerging in the tripartite system after the Second World War. Indeed, this was noted with increasing discomfort by the classics-trained administrators of the period. Sir Robert Wood, as Deputy Secretary at the Ministry, now emphasised that the education system was 'attaining Plato's rule that "children must be placed not according to their father's conditions, but the faculties of their minds"'. On the other hand, he conceded the possibility that it might thereby replace 'social class distinction by equally objectionable intellectual distinctions – creating an aristocracy of intellect in the grammar schools and putting the "runners-up" in the Secondary (Technical) Schools, and "the field" in the Modern Schools'.[32]

By the mid-1950s, another thoughtful senior official at the Ministry, Toby Weaver, feared entrenching 'for as long as we can foresee the three-tier system of Plato's Republic that is already hardening – the "fliers", whether humanists or technologists, in academic grammar schools, the technicians and managers in second creaming technical schools, and the "pedestrians" in banausic modern schools with little hope of challenge or standard in their courses'.[33] This latter prospect seems to have been reflected in practice in many secondary modern schools. For example, the headmaster of one secondary modern, in Middlesex, was happy to point out that the school took many children 'of under-average intelligence', who 'as adults will fill the more lowly positions in life'. This being so, his object was 'not to get his children through the examinations but to make their school life happy and, at the same time, provide them with a background of interests and a balanced view that will serve them after they leave school'.[34]

But this clear hierarchical pecking order has not been the only type or manifestation of the social distinctions represented in tripartism. The second type has been reflected in social emulation of the established, and more prestigious, institutions, curricula, and traditions. As Michael Young noted in his brilliant satire *The Rise of the Meritocracy*, first published in 1958: 'In a hierarchical system like ours, every institution has always modelled itself on the one immediately superior, which has usually meant the older – the new professions on the old, the modern universities on the ancient, and the comprehensive schools on the grammar.'[35] Such emulation also influenced the character of tripartism, as the less well established forms of provision – technical and modern – imitated the grammar schools. This type of tripartism has therefore tended to minimise the differences between types of institutions, but on the terms dictated by the already entrenched cultural forms. Such processes involved a tacit acknowledgement of status differences. In some cases, it meant avoiding an open declaration of type, approach, or background. Thus, for example, while the Ministry of Education was anxious to encourage the local development of three different kinds of educational provision, it announced that the titles of secondary schools should 'emphasise unity rather than diversity in the secondary system'. They should, therefore, avoid the use of such terms as 'grammar', 'technical' and 'modern' as well as street names.[36] This could be described, as the *TES* noted, as 'heavy-going tactfulness', but it also had the potential of concealing different purposes behind 'a list of names which are consistently euphonious, digified, and vague'.[37]

In other cases, such emulation involved the new and less prestigious institution emphasising what it had in common with the established institution, and where necessary taking steps to foster and publicise such similarities rather than their supposed differences. In the 1940s and 1950s, this meant that many technical and modern schools developed houses, sports, and other facets of a recognisable moral curriculum that derived from the grammar and public schools. They also imitated the academic curriculum of the grammar schools, especially through the use of examinations which the Hadow and Spens Reports had hoped they would avoid. In these ways, they sought to play down any association with the senior, central and trade schools from which most of them originated. A.G. Gooch, senior inspector for secondary technical schools, found in the mid-1950s that the 'least expected development' in such schools had been their 'trend towards the use of external examinations'.[38]

According to Gooch, these schools had also tried to develop sixth forms, 'often mainly for prestige reasons', although in reality some 'so-called sixth forms' consisted entirely of pupils aged 16 to 18 preparing for Ordinary, as opposed to Advanced, Level examinations.[39] Modern schools also made increasing use of external examinations in the 1950s. Such developments were often resisted as inappropriate by the Ministry of Education. Thus, for instance, it was hoped that 'secondary modern schools would not copy grammar schools in the pattern and scope of homework', although 'There was much to be said for semi-voluntary homework, or the gathering of information for some project.'[40]

Then again, a third type of tripartism emphasised the distinctive qualities of novel institutions as being superior to the old. With respect to secondary technical schools, Dr H. Frazer, Head of Gateway School in Leicester, declared that 'we are blazing the trail for the pattern of approach to education throughout the whole of the country in all types of schools'.[41] In relation to modern schools, D.R. Hardman, Parliamentary Secretary to the Minister of Education, told his Minister, Ellen Wilkinson, that their job was 'to educate many in our party [that is, the Labour Party] to a new and better conception of education for the adolescent, rather than an apish imitation of what in many respects in secondary education has been a failure in the past'.[42] With this in view, he insisted: 'What is wanted in the Modern secondary school is NOT a tame copy of a so-called superior education taken up to 16 at a Grammar School; nor is it to be a hotch-potch of manual jobs with a bit of art thrown in.'[43] On the other hand, what this 'new and better conception of education for the adolescent' should have been was never worked out in any detail or coherence.

The last two types of tripartism attempted in different ways to avoid the value judgements about the alternative forms of provision that each of the first three types involved. A fourth notion of tripartism, more agnostic in character, sought to allow individual schools and other educational institutions to find their own level. This was the position put forward by the Norwood Report in 1943, despite Cyril Norwood's own often stated preference for grammar schools. The idea here was that the emphasis should be placed on individual schools transcending or overcoming their limitations and official typologies in order to gain public acceptance. The three types of school, it argued, 'should have such parity as amenities and conditions can bestow', since acceptance 'can only be won by the school itself'.[44] This would allow secondary schools to offer 'equivalence of opportunity to all children in the only sense in which it has valid meaning, namely, the opportunity to receive the education for which each pupil is best suited for such time and to such a point as is fully profitable to him'.[45]

On the other hand, a fifth type of tripartism suggested a much stronger notion of parity of esteem between the different types of school. According to this view, each of the alternative kinds of secondary school were to be regarded as equal or equivalent to each other, and should therefore be accorded equal respect by pupils, parents, and the community at large. This notion often received official sanction, and yet rarely became established in practice. The Hadow Report of 1926 had envisaged different kinds of educational institution being accorded equal esteem, and the Spens Report on secondary education attempted to demonstrate in detail how this could be achieved. The White Paper *Educational Reconstruction* talked of secondary education 'of diversified types, but on equal standing'.[46] But the tripartism of the 1940s and 1950s failed to bring about 'parity of esteem'. This was partly because 'esteem' was not in the gift of the Ministry of Education to dispense or to withhold, and also because the competing interpretations of tripartism continually interfered with the ideal of 'parity'.

Other important social factors have also conditioned the character of tripartism, and these too need to be taken into account. Gender in particular has been a key source of social differentiation and inequality which has in some ways heightened tripartite divisions because of its effect on social and educational expectations. In 1960, for example, it was suggested that girls with examination passes in physics 'might prove more useful to industry as technicians before marriage and then returning to work after motherhood'.[47] In other words, because they were girls, grammar-type qualifications should lead to technical posts. Even this does not convey the full nature of the gender inequality. As was noted at the same time: 'There seems to be no reason why girls should not be recruited in larger numbers as technicians, except that industry does not wish to train them . . . A girl is obviously less attractive than a boy, because the chances are that she will marry and leave her job.'[48] This kind of factor provides a familiar and recurring influence over the nature and outcomes of educational provision during the past half century. More research is needed on the position of girls and women in relation to the separate tripartite domains, and indeed also in challenging and seeking to break down these kinds of distinctions.

At the same time, shifting ideological bases suggest change no less than continuity. The Spens Report of 1938, strongly influenced by Cyril Burt, Professor of Psychology at University College, London, justified its notion of tripartism in terms of child psychology and 'intelligence'.[49] The Norwood Report leaned more towards an argument based on a mythical 'national tradition'. If we have in some sense a revival of tripartism in the 1980s and 1990s it has been couched, by contrast, in the language of parental choice; that is, in the psychology of parents' views about what makes a good school and the needs of their own offspring.[50] This kind of emphasis brings its own ambiguities. On the face of it, for example, the city technology colleges constitute the contemporary equivalent of the secondary technical schools. Yet at one of the open evenings for parents at Kingshurst CTC, according to Walford and Miller, one parent called the CTCs 'the new grammar schools'. Although this parent was corrected by the college principal, 'other parents had appeared to agree with his description'.[51] Tensions surrounding such innovations can be read in terms of the confused echoes of the tripartite provisions of the 1940s, which continue to bear conflicting and unresolved messages for the present and the future.

Within a reconstituted tripartite pattern, to what extent do the CTCs represent the 'new grammar schools', and how far are they a swept-up version of the secondary technical schools? The nature of national policy edicts holds some of the answer, but much is likely to be found in the fears and ambitions of local parents. Contestation takes place in many different sites and arenas: in and around the educational State, and in the micropolitics and 'micro-markets' of schools and local districts.[52] It would in this situation be over-stating the case to suggest that the outcome of current policies in education will be determined by what happened in the past. It would be over-simplifying the case, too, to assume the survival of an 'ideal type' of tripartite provision. At the same time, it seems demonstrably true that our understanding of underlying trends, factors, relationships and tensions that will play a major role in the outcome of present policies is crucially enhanced by an awareness of their history.

Parity of esteem?

It is often assumed that parity of esteem constituted the underlying basis for the tripartism of the 1940s. Jack Demaine, for example, argues that '"Parity of esteem" is precisely what the architects of the tripartite system aimed for, and so hopelessly failed to achieve.'[53]

However, the idea of parity of esteem was highly problematic in its character and role. As has already been seen, it did not co-exist comfortably with the several different forms of tripartism that were current. There were also at least two different versions of parity of esteem itself, as the President of the Board of Education from 1924 until 1929, Lord Eustace Percy, later acknowledged in his memoirs. Percy preferred the idea of creating 'parity between two educational "ladders", one leading through the secondary school to the university, the other through the senior and technical schools to the college of technology, with ample facilities for changing from one to the other at almost any rung'.[54] This bipartite notion, reflecting a duality between the 'liberal' and the 'vocational', was taken further by Sir David Eccles as Minister of Education in the 1950s and was evident in the Crowther Report of 1959.[55] On the other hand, Percy was sceptical about the prospect of creating parity of esteem between different kinds of secondary education.[56]

There was, indeed, a keen debate from the 1920s onwards over whether it was really possible to foster parity of esteem between alternative forms of secondary school, and about the kinds of reforms and conditions that might help to bring this about. Following the Hadow Report of 1926, officials at the Board of Education were already pondering the likely effects of upgrading central and senior schools. It was noted that such a development might help to 'remove the stigma of social inferiority which appeared to attach in some areas to the central as opposed to the secondary school', while at the same time 'retaining the central (or modern) school as an alternative to the secondary school in areas where it seemed to be a type of school best suited to the needs of the particular area'.[57] On the other hand, it was already recognised that in order to remove the 'stigma' other steps would be necessary.

One official pointed out at this time that if these schools were to be included under 'Higher Education', they should continue to be 'subject to the existing conditions as regards fees, attendance, age limits, religious instruction and salaries'. The reasons for this, he added, were 'partly social, partly educational, partly financial and partly political'.[58] The potential contradictions were obvious. It would be very difficult to retain fees in existing secondary schools and not have fees in the new secondary schools, and still expect parity of esteem to develop between them. Since the payment of fees in modern schools was not 'practical politics', this meant that the development of free secondary education appeared to be 'an inevitable development, at least so far as the great mass of Secondary

Schools depending on public funds were concerned'.[59] It was also likely to mean bringing religious instruction in modern schools into line with existing secondary schools, which could be done by including them under Section 72(3) of the Education Act of 1921.[60]

At the same time, some of the practical and political difficulties that would be involved in developing parity of esteem between different kinds of school were also becoming clear by the end of the 1920s. In his capacity as chairman of the Secondary School Examinations Council, Cyril Norwood warned in 1928 of the likely consequences of the spread of secondary education to a 'veritable flood of new material', which would be 'not of the best intellectual quality'.[61] In order to avoid weakening the School Certificate examination, he suggested maintaining this in its present form while creating the award of a General Secondary Certificate for pupils who gained a pass in Group I and any four subjects.[62] The latter, which it was noted could involve a combination of subjects such as English, music, art, needlework and cookery,[63] would be for pupils in modern schools. Norwood's proposal was greeted with suspicion because of the damage that it would cause to the idea of parity. It was pointed out indignantly by one official at the Board that 'the establishment of a suitable examination for Modern Schools is a matter at once delicate and important and the Examination, if it is to appeal to teachers, and above all employers, must have all the prestige of a fresh and living attempt to focus the work of the new schools'.[64] In this situation, 'Dr Norwood presents us, rather contemptuously, with an Examination not good enough for the ordinary Secondary School pupil, but good enough for those who cannot take "the full Secondary School course" and "are not of the best intellectual quality", "not the right sort of material for the First School Examination"'.[65] The result would be to stamp the modern school as 'an inferior option to the Secondary School', and to 'play into the hands of those who regard the Central School with suspicion'.[66] Any such device, whether created deliberately or without due regard for its potential consequences, would impair the prospects of establishing parity of esteem between the older and the newer schools, and the pupils who went to them.

This issue came sharply into focus in the 1930s as the Spens Committee prepared its Report on secondary education. A sub-committee was created to consider the possibility of securing 'equality of conditions in post-primary schools of different types'.[67] It was apparent that this would prove very difficult to achieve. Tawney felt that the Board of Education would resist such a

development, partly on the grounds of cost, such as the implications
for teachers' salaries, but also because of 'the real issue which
won't be stated – principle'.[68] He insisted even so, as an interested
observer advising the radical educator Lady Simon who was a
member of the Spens Committee, that the introduction to the
Report should reflect the weight of evidence from LEAs and
others 'in favour of equality for all kinds of post-primary education'.[69] This idea was weakened as the work of the committee
continued, the term 'equality' being largely displaced by 'parity'.
Lady Simon herself was highly conscious of this development, as
she told Tawney: 'I wish I had fought "parity" earlier. I am afraid
that I let it go, and now it is so deeply embedded in the Report that
it would be impossible to get it changed.'[70] She explained that
Spens and W.A. Brockington, Director of Education for Leicester-
shire and also a member of the consultative committee, had
opposed the term 'equality' because it 'smacks too much of
Bolshevism'.[71]

Lady Simon was also highly critical of the chapter on administration which was drafted by Brockington, because it failed to show
how parity between all post-primary schools would be brought
about: 'With one exception there are no clear cut recommendations,
and I cannot help feeling that the impression on the general reader,
will be one of vagueness and bewilderment.'[72] She therefore helped
to redraft this chapter, Chapter Nine of the final Report, including
its key paragraph on the parity between different types of school.
This favoured what it called the 'multilateral idea' that 'so far as
possible there should be equality of status among all schools in the
secondary stage, and that the differences between them should be
dependent only upon the educational work which they were called
upon to do'.[73] Such a notion implied tackling the barriers that
already existed:

> Differences in the codes of regulations under which the schools are
> administered, in the conditions as regards both entrance tests and
> school fees under which the children are admitted, in the conditions of
> teaching service, in the amenities of school buildings, in the size of
> classes and in the minimum school leaving-age, have given to certain
> schools a prestige which secures their preference on other than
> educational grounds.[74]

The Report made several recommendations in order to avoid this
problem. Grammar schools, modern schools, and technical high
schools would all be administered under a new Code of Regulations

for Secondary Schools. Teachers' salaries would no longer depend directly on the type of school. The maximum size of classes should be the same in the modern school as in the grammar school. Building requirements, including playing fields, gymnasiums, dining rooms and common rooms were to be generally the same in the grammar school as in the modern school, 'apart from the fuller provision necessary in Grammar Schools for the teaching of certain subjects of the curriculum, and the provision of smaller classrooms for Sixth Form use'.[75] School fees should be abolished in all secondary schools, and the minimum leaving age should be raised to the same general level. The Report also supported the spread of schools with 'a strong technical bias', which would have 'equal prestige with grammar schools'.[76]

In these ways, the Spens Report was able to make specific recommendations as to the kinds of reforms and conditions that might encourage parity of esteem between different types of schools. Even before the publication of the Report, however, strong doubts were being expressed as to whether this was a realistic possibility. In particular, R.S. (later Sir Robert) Wood at the Board of Education, at this time Principal Assistant Secretary in the technical branch, was openly sceptical. He acknowledged that the proposals being developed would no doubt 'eliminate to some extent the inferiority complex about an education confined to a so-called Elementary School', but even so he anticipated that 'there might grow up again a feeling that special advantage attached to the Grammar or High School'. This might lead to further demands for an 'unreasonable expansion' of this kind of provision, with other forms being spurned as 'an elaborate attempt to spoof the public mind'. Merely to give schools 'a new wrapper and a new name' would not persuade the public to accept 'the old cheaper article as the higher class goods', Wood warned.[77] He concluded that the 'disparity of prestige' between grammar schools and technical schools was unlikely to be alleviated by the proposals put forward by the Spens Committee, especially as the technical high schools would lack a recognised public examination such as the School Certificate, which was 'well dug in as the hall-mark of a "proper education", and the passport to the black-coated jobs and professions'.[78] The basis of parity of esteem seemed very much open to question.

Such doubts and reservations were also expressed in the 1940s. The Norwood Committee was from the beginning highly sceptical about the likely outcome of Spens's plan. It asked pointedly: 'Can parity of esteem be secured? by equalization of buildings and amenities? of size of classes? of teachers' salaries and opportunities? by a single code for all schools? Can a school with a leaving age of 16 ever have parity of esteem with one with a leaving age of 18? Is it all a game of "Let's pretend"?'[79] One member of the committee, the secretary of the Association of Education Committees Sir Percival Sharp, 'protested that such parity could not be given by any fiat of administration, but must be won by the schools'.[80] The committee agreed that the phrase tended to create 'confusion of thought', and that 'the Report should not give any encouragement to the use of the phrase but should rather expose it as meaningless'.[81] It was with this aim in view that the Norwood Report proposed the alternative doctrine of individual schools winning esteem on their own merits.[82]

It seems clear, then, that although the idea of parity of esteem was indeed a powerful influence in the 1930s and 1940s, it was contested throughout this period by many supporters of tripartite policy. It was associated with the Spens Report rather than the Norwood Report, which is usually regarded as the classic statement of tripartism. Reservations about the likelihood of parity of esteem becoming established were expressed within the Board of Education, and this encouraged speculation about possible alternatives.

Rehabilitating parity

By the late 1940s, such doubts and reservations were vindicated as the ideal of parity of esteem became confounded by the realities of the 'new secondary education'. It was soon noted that a deep sense of disappointment followed the realisation that 'the number of secondary school places available – in the sense that the word "secondary" has hitherto been understood – is really no more than when the Act passed into law'.[83] In spite of the new official designations and titles attached to the schools, 'as parents well know, they are the same schools and many of them fall far short in personnel, premises and equipment of the old secondary school standard'.[84] In this situation, parity of esteem was exposed as a pious and unrealistic hope. Grammar schools, technical schools and modern schools were completely different from each other in their histories and respective roles:

> How then, it is asked, can entities so different in their social and cultural origins come to be regarded as having 'parity of esteem'?

Administrative action of itself could hardly achieve the result. Can it ever be achieved in English society apart from profound changes in prevailing social attitude and habits? Until it is achieved the hope of free and unobstructed transfer from one type of school to another is, to say the least, over-sanguine.[85]

In the short term, the failure to achieve parity of esteem between different forms of secondary school in the 1940s and 1950s led to wider support for the alternative policy of establishing multilateral or comprehensive schools.[86] Over the longer term, the notion of 'parity of esteem' itself appeared to be thoroughly discredited, together with the idea of identifying three different types of child or school with which it was associated. Yet despite its failure and apparent demise, parity of esteem re-established itself with particular strength in the educational policies of the 1980s and 1990s. First, the bipartite ideal of the liberal and the vocational acquiring equal esteem surfaced again, for example in the 1991 White Paper *Education and Training in the 21st Century*. The Foreword to this White Paper, by the Prime Minister John Major, expressed confidence that 'With the introduction of a new Advanced Diploma, we will end the artificial divide between academic and vocational qualifications, so that young people can pursue the kind of education that best suits their needs.'[87] According to Chapter Four of this White Paper, entitled 'Equal Status for Academic and Vocational Education', it was the intention of the government to 'remove the remaining barriers to equal status between the so-called academic and vocational routes' because 'We want academic and vocational qualifications to be held in equal esteem.'[88]

The idea of parity of esteem between different types of secondary school also made a spectacular comeback at this time. According to the 1992 White Paper *Choice and Diversity*, 'There will be a rich array of schools and colleges, all teaching the National Curriculum and playing to their strengths, allowing parents to choose the schools best suited to their children's needs, and all enjoying parity of esteem.'[89] It pursued this point to explain that

> The Government is committed to parity of esteem between academic, technological and creative skills, with all children – whatever their aptitude and in whatever type of school – being taught the National Curriculum to the same high standards. The Government wants to ensure that there are no tiers of schools within the maintained system, but rather parity of esteem between different schools, in order to offer parents a wealth of choice.[90]

Even though it distanced itself from the connotations of the 1940s and tried to emphasise the potential significance of the National Curriculum, the White Paper of 1992 revived the same language of parity of esteem.

The publication of the final Dearing Report on the National Curriculum and its assessment at the beginning of 1994 also served to highlight this development. The Dearing Report recommended that the National Curriculum should be 'slimmed down', and that 'alternative pathways' should be developed from the age of 14. These pathways would be academic, vocational, and occupational respectively, and they should be 'of equal quality, leading to parity of esteem'.[91] There is an especially resonant echo here of the ideals that were widely voiced in the 1940s, and which were rapidly frustrated at that time.

The rehabilitation of parity as a policy goal in the 1990s clearly owes much to a political imperative to encourage high expectations of each of the different types of school while at the same time developing an emphasis upon differentiation and specialisation. In the 1992 White Paper, the National Curriculum becomes a device to secure equality of opportunity whatever the type of school attended. It was always open to doubt whether the National Curriculum was capable of satisfying such an expectation. It experienced major difficulties in becoming established so far as the character of the different subjects was concerned, and also in relation to the time allocated to subjects, the kinds of assessment used, and other issues. In practice, too, it was likely to be interpreted in different ways according to the type of school and the role of the teachers involved.[92] But even if the National Curriculum were not so problematic in its character and role, it was still unlikely that it could overcome the historical and cultural differences between different forms of education that have been so pervasive in the past. The further reforms recommended by Dearing, to enhance curriculum differentiation within no less than between schools, must heighten such doubts.

The view that the National Curriculum can perform such a task depends largely on the idea that education policy can provide a 'technical fix', drawing a line as it were beneath the problems of past generations. It might equally be described as a triumph of hope over experience. In reality, the issues involved are likely to remain important for the foreseeable future. The resilience of tripartism, the unresolved tensions between different ideals and images, and attempts to encourage parity among them are all endemic and familiar features of English education. It seems especially important in attempting to address them first to recognise their historical and cultural characteristics. Although the context, methods, and immediate problems will change, the twenty-first century is likely still to witness further attempts to provide in different ways for three types of child.

NOTES

1. Norwood Report, p.2.
2. Ibid., p.4.
3. Ibid., p.7.
4. Ibid., p.3.
5. Ibid., p.4.
6. Ibid., p.3.
7. Ibid., p.4.
8. Ibid., p.14.
9. Ibid., p.15.
10. Board of Education, *Report of the Consultative Committee on the Education of the Adolescent* (Hadow Report, 1926), p.71.
11. Ibid., p.74.
12. Ibid., p.78.
13. Ibid., p.83.
14. G.G. Williams, 'Notes on the Spens Report: Scarborough, 16/6/39' (Board of Education papers, ED.134.131).
15. Sir John Simon (Chancellor of Exchequer) to Earl de la Warr (Minster of Education), 4 May 1939 (Board of Education papers, ED.136/132). Note also Bill Bailey, 'The development of technical education, 1934–1939', *History of Education*, 16/1 (1987), pp.49–63.
16. R.H. Tawney to F. Clarke, 30 September 1940 (Tawney papers, Institute of Education, London).
17. R.H. Tawney to D. Miller, 30 January 1943 (Tawney papers, Institute of Education).
18. Ibid.
19. *Educational Reconstruction*, paragraph 31.
20. Ibid., paragraph 20.
21. R.H. Tawney to R.A. Butler, 1 August 1943 (Tawney papers, Institute of Education).
22. Ibid.
23. H.C. Dent, *Growth in English Education: 1946–1952* (London: Routledge & Kegan Paul, 1954), p.76.
24. H.C. Dent, *Change in English Education: A Historical Survey* (London: University of London Press, 1952), p.93.
25. Labour Party education advisory sub-committee, R.D.R. 167/December 1942, 'The new secondary school' (Tawney papers, BLPES, 23/5).
26. London County Council, *London School Plan* (London, 1947).
27. Ivor Goodson, 'On curriculum form: notes towards a theory of curriculum', *Sociology of Education*, 65/1 (1992), p.71.
28. See especially Roy Lowe (ed.), *The Changing Secondary School* (London: Falmer, 1889) and Brian Simon, *What Future for Education?* (London: Lawrence & Wishart, 1992).
29. See McCulloch, *Philosophers and Kings*.
30. John Dancy, 'Technology in a liberal education', *Advancement of Science*, October 1965, p.385.
31. Fred Clarke, *Essays in the Politics of Education* (Oxford: OUP, 1923), p.51.
32. Sir Robert Wood, minute, 15 April 1946 (Ministry of Education papers, ED.147/207).

33. T.R. Weaver, 'Secondary technical schools', 14 January 1955 (Ministry of Education papers, ED.147/207).
34. *Manchester Guardian*, 22 June 1946, article, '"Modern" schools of the future: problem dependent upon the attitude of teachers'.
35. Michael Young, *The Rise of the Meritocracy, 1870–2033* (London: Penguin, 1958; 1963 edn.), p.51.
36. *TES*, 17 July 1948, 'Comment in brief'.
37. Ibid.
38. A.G. Gooch, 'Secondary technical education', 28 December 1954 (Ministry of Education papers, ED.147/207).
39. Ibid. For further details on such schools see McCulloch, *The Secondary Technical School* (1989).
40. Inspectorate secondary education panel, 24 April 1959, minute 4(c) (Ministry of Education papers, ED.158/20).
41. Dr H. Frazer, report of AHSTS 6th annual conference, 9–10 March 1956 (AHSTS papers).
42. D.R. Hardman, memo to Minister of Education, 19 March 1946 (Ministry of Education papers, ES,136/788).
43. D.R. Hardman, memo to Minister, n.d. (1946) (Ministry of Education papers, ED.136/788).
44. Norwood Report, p.14.
45. Ibid., p.24.
46. Board of Education, *Educational Reconstruction* (1943), paragraph 2.
47. Ministerial meeting, 12 January 1960, on 'Scientific and technical education' (Ministry of Education papers, ED.147/794).
48. A. Thompson, note, 'Output of craftsmen and technicians', 20 January 1960 (Ministry of Education papers, ED.147/794).
49. Spens Report (1938), esp. Ch.3.
50. See e.g. M. Adler, A. Petch and J. Tweedie, *Parental Choice and Educational Policy* (Edinburgh: Edinburgh University Press, 1989), and Miriam David, *Parents, Gender and Education Reform* (Oxford: Polity Press, 1993).
51. G. Walford and H. Miller, *City Technology College* (Milton Keynes: Open University Press, 1991), p.119.
52. See also R. Bowe and S. Ball with A. Gold, *Reforming Education and Changing Schools: Case Studies in Policy Sociology* (London: Routledge, 1992), esp. Chs.1, 2.
53. J. Demaine, in review symposium on 'Freedom, inequality and the market in further and higher education', *British Journal of Sociology of Education*, 13/1 (1992), p.120.
54. Eustace Percy, *Some Memories* (London: Eyre & Spottiswoode, 1958), p.101.
55. See Gary McCulloch, 'Views of the Alternative Road: the Crowther concept', in D. Layton (ed.), *The Alternative Road: The Rehabilitation of the Practical* (Leeds: University of Leeds Press, 1984), pp.57–73.
56. Percy, *Some Memories*, p.101.
57. 'Modern schools' – discussion on Wednesday 25 May [1927?] (Board of Education papers, ED.24/1264).
58. Note to Sir E. Phipps (by Mr Watkins?), 1 June 1927 (Board of Education papers, ED.24/1264).
59. Note of discussion by the PASs Committee on amendments to the Education Act of 1921, 4 October 1928 (Board of Education papers, ED.24/1264).
60. Ibid. Section 72(3) of the 1921 Education Act, referring to the higher education powers of LEAs, stated that 'No catechism or formulary distinctive of any particular religious denomination shall be taught in any school, college, or hostel provided by the council, except in cases where the council at the request of parents of scholars, at such times and under such conditions as the council think desirable, allow any religious instruction to be given in the school, college, or hostel, otherwise than at the cost of the council; but in the exercise of this power no unfair preference shall be shown to any religious denomination.'
61. C. Norwood, memo, 'The School Certificate' (n.d; January 1928?) (Board of Education papers, ED.12/255).

62. Ibid.
63. F.B. Stead, note to M.G. Holmes (Board of Education), 20 February 1928 (Board of Education papers, ED.12/255).
64. W.R. Richardson, note, 26 March 1928 (Board of Education papers, ED.12/255).
65. Ibid.
66. Ibid.
67. M.F. Young (secretary of Spens Committee) to Lady Simon, 26 February 1936 (Lady Simon papers, Manchester Central Library, M14/2/2/3).
68. R.H. Tawney to Lady Simon, 26 February 1936 (Lady Simon papers, M14/2/2/4).
69. R.H. Tawney to Lady Simon, 2 January 1937 (Lady Simon papers, M14/2/2/4).
70. Lady Simon to R.H. Tawney, 12 September 1938 (Lady Simon papers, M14/2/2/4).
71. Ibid.
72. Lady Simon to Sir Will Spens, 21 May 1938 (Lady Simon papers, M14/2/2/3).
73. Spens Report, p.293.
74. Ibid.
75. Ibid., p.378.
76. Ibid., p.339.
77. R.S. Wood, memo, 30 July 1937 (Board of Education papers, ED.10/273).
78. R.S. Wood, further note (n.d; 30 July 1937) (Board of Education papers, ED.10/273).
79. Norwood Committee, 'Detailed agenda for meetings', January 1942, IIv (IAAM papers, E1/1 file 3).
80. 3rd meeting of Norwood Committee, 5–7 January 1942, minute 4 (IAAM papers, E1/1 file 3).
81. Ibid.
82. Norwood Report, p.78.
83. Central Advisory Council draft report, *School and Life*, Ch.1, 'The contrast between theory and practice', 10 May 1946 (Ministry of Education papers, ED.146/13).
84. Ibid.
85. C.A.C. memo (n.d; 1947) 'Current criticisms of the proposed triad of secondary school types' (Ministry of Education papers, ED.146/13).
86. See e.g. Olive Banks, *Parity and Prestige in English Secondary Education* (London: Routledge & Kegan Paul, 1955), esp. Introduction.
87. Department of Education and Science, *Education and Training in the 21st Century*, Vol.1 (1991), Foreword.
88. Ibid., paragraph 4.2.
89. Department for Education, *Choice and Diversity* (1992), paragraph 15.3.
90. Ibid., paragraph 1.49.
91. Ron Dearing, *Final Report: The National Curriculum and its Assessment* (London: School Curriculum and Assessment Authority, 1994), paragraph 3.19.
92. See e.g. Bowe and Ball, *Reforming Education and Changing Schools*, esp. Ch.4.

6

Education as a Civic Project

The civic dimensions of the reforms of the 1940s had one thing in common with their tripartite facets: they were virtually concealed from view in the 1944 Act. However, while the idea of identifying three types of child has become one of the most familiar images of these reforms, their aspiration to promote education as a civic project is often forgotten. This chapter focuses on the social vision that underlay the Act, the ways in which it was effectively contested, and the character of its enduring influence and importance.

The 1944 Education Act included only one reference to the idea of 'education for citizenship'. Section 43 provided for all LEAs to establish and maintain county colleges in order to give 'for young persons who are not in full-time attendance at any school or other educational institution such training, as will enable them to develop their various aptitudes and capacities and will prepare them for the responsibilities of citizenship'.[1] The inclusion of this reference, brief and fleeting though it may have been, was significant in itself; according to Dent, this was 'the first time in our educational history' that education for citizenship had been 'specifically mentioned in an Act of Parliament'.[2] Behind this, all but hidden in the actual legislation, was the strong emphasis that was placed in the reform cycle of the 1940s upon the idea of education as a civic project.

A framework for deconstruction?

It is the disintegration of or retreat from this project that surely represents one of the key shifts since the 1940s, against which the reforms both of the 1940s and of the 1990s need to be understood. The civic dimensions of education, and the decline and fragmentation of the 'liberal framework', have been clearly understood by American historians.[3] It is possible to draw up a similar case to match the British context. On such a reading, 1944 could be read as the high-water mark of education as a civic project in this country. Educational reform was seen not only as a means of achieving equality of opportunity, but also as a way to enhance citizenship. This project involved a strong sense of the power of education to foster social solidarity and cohesion, a notion of commitment to a wider goal, and even of sacrifice in the interests of the group. It drew on the major intellectual influences of eighteenth- and nineteenth-century Europe out of which schooling itself had emerged in its recognisably modern form. It embraced the idea of 'social engineering' which would involve an important role for the State. In the 1930s and especially during the Second World War, it based itself on the protection of democratic rights against the threat of the fascist dictators. Education was envisaged as a key means of this defence, just as much as air raid shelters or the Home Guard.

One of the most widely noted criticisms of the reform cycle of the 1980s and 1990s is that it has failed to provide a similar vision of social integration or cohesion. Although many critics have attacked the current reforms as having little philosophical basis or social mission, it is clearly the case that they have been informed by a strong, though not always consistent, ideological thrust – 'neo-conservative', for example, as well as 'neo-liberal'.[4] Other labels have also been applied – 'New Right', conservative modernisers, free marketeers, preservationists. The real question is whether this provides an adequate substitute or successor to the ideology and social objectives of the 1940s.

Underpinning many of the reforms involved, especially in the 1980s, has been a free-market, 'neo-liberal' approach that effectively eschewed State intervention on behalf of civic values and rights. Stewart Ranson observed that the Education Reform Act of 1988 encompassed 'the vision of a consumer democracy that is intended to replace the purported weary assumptions of the liberal democratic state which have lasted for a generation and more.'[5] This new vision constituted, according to Ranson, 'a moral order of individual self-interest in a market society'.[6] Even so, Ranson insists, consumerism is not citizenship, and cannot achieve 'public choice'. Reliance on the market was such a poor substitute for a civic mission that it failed to provide an effective rationale, or integrative code, for a public education system.

The reforms of the early 1990s were vulnerable to similar criticisms. The 1992 White Paper, *Choice and Diversity*, stated baldly that 'Parents know best the needs of their children – certainly better than educational theorists or administrators, better even than our mostly excellent teachers.'[7] This seemed to ring hollow as an educational philosophy that was supposed to underlie a national education policy, tending towards an abdication of the State's responsibility to encourage a collective ethic through the education of the young. There were several echoes of earlier projects, for example in the quote from John Ruskin with which the White Paper begins. The first paragraph of the White Paper insists that '130 years after Ruskin wrote, the message is the same, the duty on government and parents is identical. For without good schools there can be little development – personal, moral or economic – for our children. What schools offer to the individual they offer to the community equally.'[8] The White Paper also places much emphasis on 'spiritual and moral development', and declares that 'At the heart of every school's educational and pastoral policy and practice should lie a set of shared values which is promoted through the curriculum, through expectations governing the behaviour of pupils and staff and through day to day contact between them.'[9] Even so, such strictures sat uncomfortably with free market consumerism, with a suspicion of theory, with a celebration of competition as against co-operation.

Such tensions made it difficult for *Choice and Diversity* to set out clearly the government's social vision of schooling and its purposes for the next generation. Although citizenship was designated as a 'cross-curricular theme' in the National Curriculum, and although copies of the 'Citizens' Charter' were widely distributed, it was the lack of a coherent civic mission that appeared most striking to critical observers. Eric Bolton, former Chief Inspector of schools, complained that without an overarching vision or 'underpinning philosophy', the education system 'risks becoming a stifling bureaucratic monster intent upon its own day-to-day survival in which people are treated like so much lost-property'. There was, he continued, 'no clarity at present about the Government's vision for the public education service of this country'. Implicitly, 'The notion of a free-market economy, allied with a narrow concentration on basic skills, that characterised some of the thinking of advisors to the early Thatcher Governments is still around and is reflected in some of what is now being enacted.' But there was little in the way of an explicit statement of long-term aims, and indeed, Bolton concluded: 'I suspect that if we were able to lift the veil hiding the Government's intentions for education we would find, not a coherent vision, worrying or otherwise, but uncertainty, confusion and incoherence.'[10] Similar concerns were voiced by *The Times Educational Supplement*, which described the 1992 White Paper as a 'framework for deconstruction' rather than one for reconstruction.[11] The Bishop of Guildford, Chairman of the Church of England Board of Education, attacked the government's

education policies for their lack of a 'common vision'.[12] The
Education Act of 1993 was castigated even as it became law for
creating an 'unholy mess'.[13] A civic charter for the twenty-first
century, which *Choice and Diversity* had promised to provide,
seemed a distant prospect in these unpromising circumstances.

The Association for Education in Citizenship

It is therefore especially important for us to try to understand the
character of education as a civic project, as it was envisaged in the
1940s; that is, its limitations and contradictions no less than its
strengths. The Association for Education in Citizenship (AEC),
formed in 1934, was one important focus for activity in this area
whose significance has tended hitherto to be neglected. Founded
by the industrialist and former Liberal MP Sir Ernest Simon, this
Association tried to cultivate greater civic awareness in the schools
and also in official committees such as that of Spens. While not
altogether successful in its efforts, its ideas and general approach
make it a suitable starting point for a more detailed examination of
such aspirations in relation to the reform cycle of the 1940s.

Probably the most important factor in the creation and development of the AEC was the perceived need to respond to the threat
to democracy posed by the fascist dictators of the 1930s. The AEC
attempted to direct attention towards the idea of democratic values
in the schools and in wider educational circles, in the hope that this
would help to foster greater awareness of the importance of
democracy and citizenship in society as a whole. Simon was concerned to use educational channels to develop a more 'critical and
discriminating' public opinion that would be in a better position
to defend democracy against contemporary threats.[14] He was
conscious that this would be a long-term process, and indeed con-
fided to the National Labour peer Lord Allen of Hurtwood that
'your job is to save democracy here and now; mine to lay the basis
for saving it in future by better education if it can survive the next
five or ten years'.[15] His crusade was therefore based on a conviction
rooted in the Enlightenment and familiar in the nineteenth century:
that education of the young could channel their characters and
energies into new and potentially more positive directions.

The nature of the AEC's efforts was determined by its approach
to three major issues: its political stance, its notion of the place of
'citizenship' in the school curriculum, and its view of the role of
teachers in fostering such an ideal. In terms of its politics, Simon

sought to ensure that it represented a broad range of 'mainstream' and conservative opinion, to such an extent that he preferred to avoid active association with causes that were identified as left-wing. Among the leading members of the education policy community whom he was hoping to influence was Will Spens, Master of Corpus Christi College, Cambridge, who had just been appointed to chair the Board of Education's consultative committee to prepare a report on secondary education. Spens declared himself sympathetic to Simon's aims: 'I entirely agree as to the importance of education for citizenship; if it is not education for citizenship education has no meaning.'[16] On the other hand, he was concerned that the AEC's published list of prominent supporters 'leaned pretty heavily to the Left', and that it should be made 'less one-sided politically'. He added: 'I realise only too well that it is difficult to get people who are Conservatives to come in to this sort of thing, but I have no doubt that it is important, both so as to secure an adequate representation of that element in our own discussions and so as to give greater weight to your conclusions.'[17]

Simon heeded Spens's advice, and approached the Conservative historian Arthur Bryant to join the AEC's executive committee. Bryant was especially important in this regard, as he had close links with the Conservative Party leader Stanley Baldwin, and Simon hoped that Bryant would persuade Baldwin to associate himself with the AEC. Simon hoped that Bryant would be 'successful in keeping our Bolshevik tendencies in order!' At the same time, he assured him that 'my one desire is to get education which will turn out exactly the kind of responsible citizen of whom Mr Baldwin spoke so eloquently over the wireless some weeks ago'. It was important, he emphasised, for the Association to be admired by 'somebody who is interested in education and has the Conservative point of view in the front of his mind'.[18] Baldwin's reassuring, rustic brand of citizenship seemed likely to broaden the appeal of the Association beyond a core group of activists. Bryant accepted Simon's invitation to join the Executive Committee, and carried out his promise to talk to Baldwin. He reported on the outcome: 'His point of view is much as I thought it would be. But once he felt assured that the Association was providing sound and impartial knowledge "for the extirpation of ignorancy" among the future electorate, I am sure that he and every other reasonable Conservative would give it their sympathy and support.'[19] Bryant also spelled out for Simon's benefit the practical implications of such support: 'What I want to ensure, and what I think you want me to ensure, is that in our working committees and in our lists of text books etc the traditionalist and evolutionary as opposed to the purely revolutionary view (in politics, religion and philosophy) shall have due representation. Once this is clear, the rest I am sure will follow.'[20]

These negotiations bore fruit by 1938, as Baldwin agreed to become President of the Association after he left high office. They also helped to harden Simon against involving the AEC in activities that would be regarded as left-wing in character. Thus, for example, towards the end of 1937 he declined an invitation by the publisher Victor Gollancz to speak at a rally in the Albert Hall under the auspices of the Left Book Club. The LBC had also been created to provide 'education for citizenship' as a response to the threat of fascism, but was at this time closely associated with the Communist Party.[21] This association had brought it into conflict with the leaders of the Labour Party, despite Gollancz's protestations that 'the Left Book Club is a purely educational body: that it has no policy whatever, with the vital exception that it is opposed to War and Fascism, and in favour of a higher standard of life: that it is in no sense whatsoever, nor can it become, a political party or a wing or organ of a political party'.[22] Simon was certainly suspicious of its political stance, and insisted to Gollancz that he must avoid 'anything that could be regarded as party politics'.[23]

Gollancz professed himself to be 'rather surprised' at Simon's view, since, as he put it, '"education for citizenship" is precisely the object of the Left Book Club'; moreover, he added, 'our platform at the Albert Hall (apart from the club selectors) consists of a Communist, a Liberal Party Whip, and two Ex-Cabinet Ministers of the Labour Party'.[24] But Simon was clear and determined on the kind of political distinction that he wanted to draw: 'The Left Book Club is, of course, very effective education for citizenship, but it is left-wing citizenship and its publications are partly democratic and partly anti-democratic; I am afraid the balance is considerably on the "anti" side.'[25] Thus, the political tensions of the 1930s helped to discourage broad alliances in favour of 'education for citizenship'.[26] The AEC attempted to define itself so as to attract 'democratic' and Conservative support, which would help it to influence key individuals and committees. However, this meant that it effectively eschewed active involvement in some of the most vigorous and prominent campaigns of the time.

The second key problem that faced the AEC was how to formulate 'education for citizenship' within the restrictions imposed by the school curriculum. This involved deciding whether it should be taught directly, as a separate subject in the curriculum, or indirectly, as a dimension of the curriculum as a whole. The Association as a whole seems to have been ambivalent on this issue, and certainly more research is needed in relation to the attitudes of teachers and local activists. Early pamphlets produced by the AEC referred to its role as a 'Subject Association', but on the other hand some of its widely circulated published works in the mid-1930s such as *Education for Citizenship in Secondary Schools* emphasised the possibility of exploiting existing disciplines and subject bases.[27] Simon himself was strongly inclined towards more direct methods of teaching citizenship. He was emphatic that in view of the new complexities and difficulties of the political world, 'it is essential to train men just as consciously and deliberately for their duties as citizens as for their vocation or profession.'[28] This would include teaching them to 'reason correctly in the social sciences where their own prejudices and passions are often involved,' and also to acquire knowledge of the 'broad facts of the political and economic world'. It would involve at the same time imparting a 'sense of social responsibility' and a 'love of truth and freedom'.[29] Simon argued that these qualities could not be taught through indirect methods.

Indeed, Simon often expressed hostility to indirect approaches to education for citizenship. One of its 'greatest enemies', he declared, was 'the belief that clear thinking is taught just as well by Latin prose or by physics or by whatever subject the particular teacher happens to be interested in, as by a proper course of training'.[30] Even more to the point, the 'enemy' was actually 'the teacher who half-heartedly believes in education for citizenship and alleges that he teaches it indirectly with incidental direct references'. Such indirect teaching, he insisted, 'really means nothing except education of some sort', whereas 'the whole emphasis of our Association must be laid on more direct teaching'.[31] What this meant was that the AEC had to argue for room to be found in an already crowded curriculum for a new subject such as Civics, that the character and syllabus of such a new subject would need to be defined and promoted, and that eventually suitable teachers would have to be found to give it meaning. Simon and his associates had very little notion of what these developments would involve.

The third major difficulty that confronted the AEC was how to prescribe particular approaches to education for citizenship without dictatorial control of the school curriculum. Fascist and authoritarian regimes on the Continent were extending their powers in this direction to enhance allegiance to their rule. As has recently been noted, the Soviet Union, National Socialist Germany, and Fascist Italy 'undertook the education of a new generation of citizens with unprecedented thoroughness', as they 'strengthened their control over school curricula, textbooks, and teachers through strict censorship and compulsory youth organisations'.[32] In Austria, too, according to Esden-Tempska, the clerico-fascists of the mid-1930s 'attempted to foster a deep emotional attachment to the state as the embodiment of a national myth, and they reorganised the curriculum to present all subjects from this viewpoint'.[33] The aims of the AEC were to foster democratic notions of citizenship in order to combat the doctrines of fascism, and so it could not be seen to be adopting the same techniques in relation to the school curriculum. Indeed, no doubt in part as a reaction against fascist and totalitarian tendencies, during the 1930s and 1940s the idea of the State actively intervening to control the school curriculum towards particular social ends became highly suspect in Britain. Simon himself was uncomfortable on the issue, and had to emphasise that he was hoping to 'persuade' rather than force teachers to bring 'definite views on citizenship' clearly and constantly before their pupils: 'our Association never dreamt of suggesting that it should be made *compulsory* on teachers to teach any special kind of citizenship.'[34] This remained a difficult problem during the war, as the educational reforms were being planned. For the AEC, as for any other agency that hoped to influence the character of the school curriculum at this time, it tended to inhibit calls for stronger curriculum control.

Simon, Norwood, and the Spens Committee

In his search for an appropriate model for integrating education for citizenship into the school curriculum, Simon became a strong supporter of ideas that Cyril Norwood was putting forward in the 1930s. Although his educational philosophy emphasised 'tripartite' divisions, Norwood also sought to foster ideals of citizenship through education.[35] Both of these strands in his thought stemmed from Plato, but his ideas on citizenship were also influenced by T.H. Green and the Idealist school of the late nineteenth century.[36] Jose Harris notes that Plato's ideal of the ethical nature of citizenship was one in which 'individual citizens found happiness and

fulfilment not in transient sensory satisfactions, but in the development of "mind" and "character" and in service to a larger whole'.[37]
Norwood had already attempted to relate this ideal to the public
schools, and to his own interpretation of the 'English tradition' in
education.[38] During the 1930s, he attempted to spell out what this
would mean in more practical terms for the grammar school
curriculum.

Norwood's ideas were well reflected in his evidence to the Spens
Committee on secondary education. He argued that the secondary
school curriculum tended to be dominated by the requirements of
the School Certificate examination, and that there was a need to
aim for a definite purpose in the curriculum. He defined this
purpose as 'training for citizenship', and 'so far as the whole school
life is concerned, as the development of personality'.[39] The foundation for this process, Norwood proposed, should be 'English
culture'. English studies would involve the training of pupils in
speech, writing and reading, and would include History and
Geography for all. Physical education and hygiene would be more
important than hitherto, and all pupils would have some training in
handicraft, art, and musical appreciation. These areas of the
curriculum would be given greater priority than the one foreign
language that would be taught, or Mathematics, or Science.[40] He
explained that in his view the primary object of the secondary
school curriculum should be to 'inculcate a measure of English
culture', whereas 'At present pupils tend to leave school with a
very slight knowledge of the history and manners of the country in
which they live.' Moreover, the aim of producing good citizens
should be emphasised throughout: 'the pupil must one day become
a citizen, and his education should be designed and organised with
this end in view.'[41]

Norwood's ideas came to Simon's attention during 1936, and he
was so struck by their potential that he decided to publish two of
Norwood's recent speeches on the topic in a single pamphlet under
the auspices of the AEC.[42] Simon was especially hopeful that this
would help to influence the ideas of the Spens Committee towards
an emphasis upon education for citizenship. Indeed, he was highly
encouraged when Spens told him that he was already 'thinking very
much along Norwood's lines'.[43] Others, such as Spencer Leeson,
headmaster of Winchester College, were more cautious over
whether the AEC should commit itself to supporting Norwood's
ideas.[44] But Simon insisted on the grounds that Norwood's approach
was at least worth considering by the Spens Committee and by

secondary school heads, and was worthy of wider circulation.[45] The pamphlet, *The Curriculum In Secondary Schools*, was produced in March 1937, with mixed results. R.F. Young, secretary to the Spens Committee, assured Simon that 'This document is of first-rate importance to the Committee for their present Inquiry, though of course most of them have a general notion of Dr Norwood's views on the topic in question.'[46] Headteachers had also in many cases already formed an opinion on Norwood's ideas, not always a favourable one. According to Hugh Lyon at Rugby, 'Much that Norwood says about the importance of the main English subjects is becoming a matter of general agreement and will, I hope, find a reflection in the decisions of the Consultative Committee in due course. I do not go all the way with him for various reasons, but I certainly subscribe to his main principles.'[47] On the other hand, an 'eminent headmaster in Liverpool and a real friend' (Arnold Gibson of Liverpool Collegiate School) told Simon that 'Norwood is an object of hatred and contempt among most secondary school masters for preaching exaggerated stuff now which he never made the remotest attempt to put into force himself.'[48]

It is not altogether clear why Simon supported Norwood's ideas so strongly when they failed to make room for 'citizenship' as a separate subject. Norwood's own calculations, included in the AEC pamphlet, provided for six hours for English, six hours for History and Geography, eight hours for Mathematics and Science, six hours for Physical Training, and six hours for Art, Music and Handicraft. This made up 32 hours, which still did not allow a foreign language to be taught.[49] In Simon's terms, this meant that citizenship would have to be taught 'indirectly' rather than directly. Presumably, Simon must have been strongly impressed by the general spirit and ideals in which Norwood's proposals were couched. It seems likely that he hoped to develop ideas for a separate subject once the 'main principles' had been more widely accepted. Subsequent events were to show that he had not given up his ambitions in this area.

So far as the Spens Committee was concerned, Simon's persistent lobbying had some effect, but not as much as he had hoped. His wife, Shena, as a member of the consultative committee, was able to keep him informed on its discussions.[50] By the start of 1938, he had become pessimistic about the outcome of the final Report of the Spens Committee, and began to argue for the Board of Education to set up a further committee to focus on the issue of education for citizenship.[51] This idea was strongly resisted both by Spens himself and by Maurice Holmes, the Permanent Secretary of the Board, leading Simon to make a strategic retreat.[52] In fact, however, the Spens Report, published at the end of 1938, did make a number of effective points emphasising the importance of the issue. In particular, the last two pages of the Introduction declared that 'all teaching should contribute to this end'. Indeed, it continued, 'On the extent to which the youth of this country can be fitted to fulfil later their duties, and to take advantage of their opportunities, as citizens of a democratic State may well turn the whole future of democracy, and that not only in this island.'[53] It accepted that pupils should be given information about local government and about national and international affairs, and recognised that some teachers had made 'excellent use' of courses of 'civics'. Despite this, however, it argued that in general existing subjects such as History, Mathematics and Science should be developed so as to bring out wider issues, and to encourage a 'transfer' of logical arguments to the social and political domain.[54]

These arguments were clearly informed by Simon's books, pamphlets and personal influence, even where they did not agree with his views. Simon himself accepted that useful progress had been made, as he told Spens: 'No previous public document in this country has put the case for education for citizenship with anything like the same knowledge and vigour; your report therefore marks, I think, a real advance in public appreciation of the importance of this aspect of education.'[55] Even so, he remained dissatisfied, and added that he would still like to see 'a great deal *more* emphasis laid on the necessity of educating for democracy than is done in your report!'[56] The Spens Report reflected a measure of success in the AEC's chosen strategy of influencing established and authoritative agencies about the importance of promoting 'education for citizenship'. On the other hand, Simon and his associates had clearly failed to do more than gain a general acceptance of the principle involved before the threat of a world war turned into a reality.

Education for social reconstruction

This civic aspiration tended to traverse the conventional political boundaries. As has been seen, the Left Book Club was also committed to the promotion of education for citizenship, although in the 1930s at least it was difficult for groups such as this to collaborate with more conservative organisations like the AEC. The onset of

war both renewed the incentive to emphasise the civic project, and
made earlier political differences appear less important. Prominent
left-wing publicists who shared many of the enthusiasms of Simon
and Norwood in this regard also included R.H. Tawney and Fred
Clarke. The educational 'settlement' of the 1940s owed much to
the general cross-party agreement of such influential figures on the
need to foster a stronger community ethos.

Tawney, a dominant influence in left-wing circles since the
1920s, stressed the close relationship of this ideal to the aim of
social equality. Unhappy that young people were being brought
up in a world with 'no fixed standards, moral or intellectual, by
which to judge political conduct',[57] he saw educational reform as
potentially mobilising 'unity of spirit'. Tawney's socialism was
fundamentally ethical in character, stressing the immorality of the
structures and assumptions of the 'English tradition' which he
associated with capitalism.[58] He urged that to develop a stronger
civic ideal would also involve a frontal assault on social and
economic inequality. It was for this reason that he was dissatisfied
with Simon's approach to the problem, sympathetic though he was
to the general project of the AEC. Tawney argued, however, that
Simon failed to appreciate the importance 'of whole environment,
the class system, public schools, the short education, and that compared to all that the curriculum is of relatively no importance'.[59]
Thus, Tawney located the issue within profound socio-political
antagonisms which Simon failed to address.

Despite the cataclysmic threat of 'barbarians at the gate' that it
represented, the onset of war also suggested to Tawney as for many
other radicals and left-wing thinkers important new possibilities
for social reconstruction. While Hitler was promising a 'New
Order' for Europe, it seemed insufficient for Britain to fight for the
status quo ante bellum. The war could instead be conceived as
revolutionary in nature, offering the promise of a new civilisation
to follow its successful conclusion. The alternative notions of
fascist and democratic citizenship that had already been current in
the 1930s could now be drawn even more starkly. Tawney insisted
that 'If Great Britain is to rally other peoples and inspire her own,
she must prove by her actions, not merely by words, that she is no
insular egoist or imperial profiteer, but the champion of causes
which touch the hearts of all mankind.'[60] The idea of citizenship,
like other notions such as federalism and human rights, became
very fashionable for its potential to provide a solution to the world
crisis.

Such aspirations were also voiced by Fred Clarke, now Director of the Institute of Education in London. He was influenced by the new situation to seek to adapt the existing educational institutions to fresh social challenges. In particular, he argued, education needed to be able to provide a basis for social cohesion.[61] Clarke strongly supported a more self-conscious and assertive approach to educational planning, but hoped that this would also involve the 'application of a social philosophy in harmony with that which inspires a generous education'.[62] He was to develop this idea further after the war in his work on several major committees, undertaken in the hope that improved education would create a 'strong increase of genuine *community* cutting across the divisions both of traditional class and of occupation'.[63] Such ambitions made the particular details of educational plans seem less important than the spirit or ideals on which they were founded.

They also came into conflict with other views and assumptions that had become entrenched. A significant example of this was the idea of individual rights and freedoms as against civic duties and obligations; emphasising the latter represented a challenge to the former. It was in this context that the public schools appeared to be in danger during this period, while support for common schools grew. The potential contradictions between the two ideals were clearly identified by Maurice Holmes at the Board of Education at the beginning of 1942. He noted that there was no educational objection to retaining preparatory schools, nor any educational advantage in requiring all children to go through a common school. The argument between the two approaches was in his view political rather than educational in nature. On the one hand, he suggested: 'There will be those who will argue that if parents choose to send their children at their own expense to schools outside the public system which are admittedly as efficient as those within the system, why on earth shouldn't they?' On the other hand, however, 'it will be argued that national unity depends on a national system of education for all and that the smaller classes of the preparatory schools give an unfair advantage to the child who attends them.' Which of these two views would prevail depended in Holmes's view 'in some measure on the duration of the war'.[64] Since it was the war itself that had helped to stimulate civic and national ideals, it was the same factor that would largely determine their fate; an early return to peace might encourage the resumption of earlier social patterns and relationships.

This tension between individual and community rights also

influenced Tawney's suspicions of direct grant schools that were financed and controlled by the Board of Education, rather than by the local education authority. He observed privately that he was 'not much impressed by general talk about educational freedom'. Indeed, he declared, 'Some of those who are most eloquent on the subject seem to me to talk in the spirit of a mediaeval seigneur defending his "liberties" against the Crown. We all of us want to be free to do exactly what we like without being accountable to anyone else, and few, if any of us, ought to be allowed to gratify that natural desire.'[65]

It is important to note also that the principal architects of the Act, Butler and Chuter Ede, were equally resolute in their support for this expansive civic and integrationist ideal during this decisive phase. Chuter Ede argued in favour of a broader educational high-way on the grounds that secondary education was now a necessity rather than a luxury, and he therefore opposed the payment of school fees at this level. Moreover, he detected the prospect that 'The post-war Britain may well find itself subjected to social strains far more severe than those which were felt in the twelve years prior to 1939.' In such circumstances, he claimed, 'a broader based secondary education, with its various institutions genuinely open to a wide range of aptitudes and to which admission can be obtained by individual ability to profit will be a greater cohesive force than any other'. By contrast, however, 'A suspicion that the ability of the parent to pay a fee reserves for the child a particular place, and places that child outside the craftsman's class, will be socially disastrous.'[66] Butler had similar ambitions as he aspired towards 'introducing in this country a real sense of national purpose – both moral, spiritual and political – and of inculcating a philosophy of public life in those who cross over from the threshold of youth to active participation in national affairs'.[67] He did recognise other weaknesses, especially what he called 'an unnecessarily wide gulf twixt Parent and School',[68] but was committed to this broader social and educational aim.

It was in relation to this broad aspiration of social reconstruction, embracing as it did a strong civic ideal, that the White Paper *Educational Reconstruction*, published in July 1943, received warm approval. In its very first paragraph it struck what had become the dominant note: 'It is just as important to achieve diversity as it is to ensure equality of educational opportunity. But such diversity must not impair the social unity within the educational system which will open the way to a more closely knit society and give us strength to face the tasks ahead.'[69] It aimed, therefore, to 'fit the schemes for educational reform into the general picture of social reconstruction'.[70] It declared its opposition to the social inequalities of the existing education system – large classes, competitive examinations at the age of eleven, the payment of fees in secondary schools. It added also that fresh approaches would be necessary in the teaching of history, geography, and modern languages 'to arouse and quicken in the pupils a livelier interest in the meaning and responsibilities of citizenship of this country, the Empire and of the world abroad'. Indeed, according to the White Paper, somewhat grandly, 'Education in the future must be a process of gradually widening horizons, from the family to the local community, from the community to the nation, and from the nation to the world.'[71] These precepts commanded wide support, even if there appeared to be few guidelines on exactly how they were to be achieved. Tawney was far from alone in admiring the White Paper's 'comprehensiveness and vision', nor in his hope that it would help to mobilise a 'unity of spirit' in the years ahead.[72]

Citizenship and the Norwood Report

No less notable than the civic aspirations of the 1943 White Paper was the strong strain of citizenship evident in the Norwood Report that followed it. This theme, and the ways in which it was articulated, derived in large part from the ideals that the chairman of the Norwood Committee, Cyril Norwood (since 1938, Sir Cyril), had developed in the inter-war years. It also represented an attempt to transcend the tripartite divisions into 'three kinds of child' that were such an important dimension of the reforms of the 1940s.

Norwood was deeply conscious of the opportunity that the war provided for general social reconstruction, and aligned himself with this aim. Within a few months of the beginning of the war, even before the crisis and change of government that took place in the summer of 1940, he was expressing the hope that there would be 'a good scheme for national education to be embarked on when the war is over – a common education leading up to common national service for all at 18–19'.[73] This represented, he was convinced, 'a big cause which would have the bulk of the nation behind it', and which would also require 'a statesman of real vision at the Board to lead it, when the time comes'.[74]

Despite the differences between particular forms of education that he felt were appropriate to different 'types of mind', Norwood felt that education could still provide the basis for a common citizenship, and that this should form the basis for reform. He was attracted to the idea of keeping national service after the war as 'a transition from adolescence to manhood [sic] in equality of service, for some between their earlier and their final training, for others after the completion of their education, and before they enter upon the work which will occupy their mature life'.[75] His ideas for the curriculum were equally 'inspired by the ideal of public service' and intended to build on 'the supremacy of those spiritual values which are cast into deadly hazard by the present war'.[76] Thus, he noted, 'Though there must be greater variety of type, a more conscious and consistent effort must be made to impart a common stock of ideas and a common knowledge as the basis of citizenship.'[77] It was this general aim that lay behind his efforts associated with the Norwood Committee from 1941 onwards: in order to 'make the young men dream dreams . . . this old man will try to see a vision.'[78] At the same time, the particular characteristics of the kind of school curriculum that Norwood had supported in the 1930s remained central to his plans for reform during the war. An important aspect of this was his preference for retaining established subjects such as History and Geography to emphasise 'education for citizenship', rather than creating new subjects such as Civics for the purpose. This was evident in the dealings of the Norwood Committee with Sir Ernest Simon and the Association for Education in Citizenship (AEC).

On the outbreak of the war, Simon and his associates had at first decided 'more or less automatically' to close down the AEC.[79] It was significant that they then decided to maintain its existence on the grounds that, as Simon argued, 'education for democracy is more important now than it ever has been before.' According to Simon, it had become essential to 'make people think not only what we are fighting against, but also positively what we are fighting for, especially from the point of view of the post-war world.'[80] Simon himself was appointed to a position in the Ministry of Information, but this lasted for only a short period. Although his energies were increasingly diverted elsewhere, the major part of his efforts towards educational reform during the war was therefore through the agency of the AEC, which continued the strategy adopted in the 1930s of attempting to influence the ideas of key members and committees of the education policy community. The Norwood Committee was a natural focus for its activities, especially as it was chaired by a clearly identified ally of the AEC's cause.

The AEC's hopes for the future were clearly expressed in a lengthy memorandum forwarded to the Norwood Committee. It continued to base its views on the priorities that it had announced in the 1930s, but stressed the new opportunities and threats posed by the war. It insisted therefore that education for citizenship should be a 'fundamental aim' of every secondary school.[81] This would involve the cultivation of both moral and intellectual qualities. 'Social Studies', or 'the study of man in his environment – of family, district, country or world', was recommended to assume 'a highly important place in the curriculum of the Secondary School in every age group'.[82] A further submission to the Norwood Committee by the newly constituted Council for Curriculum Reform, closely associated with the AEC, pursued similar themes and also proposed a consolidated 'Social Studies': 'Integration is vital in this area; the social studies should provide a common matrix from which the specialized studies of history, geography, economics, etc may emerge at a later stage.'[83]

However, there was strong opposition to the idea of a distinct 'Social Studies', even among those who were sympathetic to the general ideal of education for citizenship. Even the AEC's own president, Sir Richard Livingstone, was suspicious of 'Social Studies', and distanced himself from Simon on this question. This in turn helped to undermine the effect of Simon's approach to the Norwood Committee. Livingstone, who had taken over as President of the AEC from the former Prime Minister Earl Baldwin, gave oral evidence to the Norwood Committee in June 1942, and according to the transcript of the discussion emphasised that 'the subjects of the curriculum should remain much as at present'. He described Languages, Mathematics, Science, History and Literature as the core subjects of the curriculum, and argued that some of the subjects that were being recommended for inclusion in the school curriculum 'were more suitable for adult education'.[84]

Livingstone's stance became an embarrassment when Simon and two of his close colleagues met the committee the following month. They were confronted with this contradictory advice, and were forced to disagree. They argued instead that the subjects currently in the curriculum were 'inert' and held places 'assigned by tradition'. In order to redress this situation, 'it would be better to start from the idea of a core of subjects consisting of Social Studies, English, Geography and Science and to determine from this starting point what time could be allowed to other subjects'.[85] In spite of their efforts, however, an important division of opinion had been clearly exposed; a division clarified further in Living-stone's own explanation to Simon: 'The point where I fancy I differ from you is scepticism as to the value of what are called civics . . . at the secondary school – unless of course you have a teacher with real keenness in it and a great power of putting it across.'[86]

There was little doubt about which of these two approaches the Norwood Committee would adopt. The final Report was generally opposed to the introduction of new subjects into the curriculum, especially as they would tend to limit the time available to existing subjects.[87] In relation to education for citizenship, it echoed Livingstone's point by noting the potential harm of 'attempts to interest pupils prematurely in matters which imply the experience of an adult'.[88] This indeed also reflected the opinion of Butler as President of the Board, who insisted that 'children are too young to learn Civics', and preferred to seek further development of adult education for such tasks.[89] The Report also emphasised the view that Norwood himself had previously espoused: 'Teaching of the kind desired can best be given incidentally, by appropriate illustra-tion and comment and digression, through the ordinary school subjects, particularly History, Geography, English and foreign Languages and Literatures.'[90] On the other hand, lessons on 'Public Affairs' might be developed at the Sixth Form stage – as Norwood had once done at Harrow.

And yet in spite of this important difference of opinion on how to approach the teaching of citizenship, it is clear that the Norwood Report was a strong advocate of the general proposition that was involved. While emphasising the special character of the grammar school curriculum for a limited number of pupils, it also addressed the social and spiritual values with which all secondary school pupils should be imbued. Thus, it suggested that although 'in the Grammar School the pupil is offered, because he is capable of reaching towards it, a conception of knowledge which is different from that which can be and should be encouraged in other types of school', in other respects 'the ideals of all types of school are generally similar'.[91] This was an especially notable feature of Part III of the Report, which focused on the curriculum. The three essential elements of education, more important than any particular subjects, were declared to be first, training of the body, second, training of character, and third, training in habits of clear thought and clear expression of thought in the English language.[92] In its treatment of History and Geography, it also stressed the need to establish 'a good foundation for enlightened citizenship'.[93]

It was perhaps this general civic aspiration, shared as it was despite differences of emphasis across social and political lines, that was most important in establishing the broad coherence and authority of the reforms of the 1940s. It provided a strong rationale for educational reform around which all parties could unite. It also implied a unifying and optimistic vision of the future that was consistent with prevailing national 'traditions'. In ideological terms, it was a comfortable and reassuring vision with which all groups could identify, rather than a confrontational or threatening one that would polarise opinion and foster alienation. The civic ideology contains vital clues to why the settlement of 1944 attracted such broad and durable support, no less than to why it was to be mistily remembered with affection and nostalgia after half a century had passed.

Flaws and contradictions

It is important to note that these aspirations carried with them inconsistencies that were ultimately to lead to frustration and failure. Civic ideals seemed increasingly to contradict the tripartite divisions that also lay at the heart of the 1944 settlement. Citizenship still seemed to give most advantages to boys in grammar and public schools. It was the Norwood Report that symbolised this fatal contradiction most vividly, and which as has already been seen was increasingly blamed for the disappointments that followed.

It is true also that these general ideals, even those articulated in specific policy recommendations, were not necessarily reflected in the educational practices of the late 1940s and 1950s. The Norwood Report well exemplified the distance between curriculum policy and curriculum practice. Norwood himself was acutely conscious of this distance and the problems that it implied for reform, and even told Butler that 'we ought to try to "debunk" much of the stuff that is circulating now, particularly the notion that by a stroke of the pen you can create a New Order in Education'.[94] The proposals for county colleges, which inspired the only explicit reference to citizenship in the 1944 Act, are symbolic also of the problematic character of the imposition of policy. Just as the 1918 Act had failed to secure the development of day continuation schools, so the 1944 Act was unsuccessful in its provision for county colleges.[95]

Indeed, in retrospect it is in the lack of practical means to ensure the realisation of civic ideals in the school curriculum that the most striking omission or flaw in this dimension of the 1944 settlement might be seen. The suspicion of direct state intervention in the content of the curriculum, strengthened by its contemporary association with totalitarian education policies, obviated any attempt to pursue such an approach. Thus, for example, when the Foreign Office suggested a scheme for explaining to schoolchildren the proposals of the Potsdam Conference on international relations, Maurice Holmes at the Ministry of Education was immediately on his guard against the likely implications. Holmes noted that 'This Department is under constant pressure to secure that this or that subject is included in the curriculum of schools. The duty of the citizen to fight for his country and the desirability of seeing that the younger generation is air-minded are recent instances that occur to me.'[96] He preferred what he called the 'traditional and, I think, wholesome practice' in which 'We have always resisted such proposals on the ground that in this country the details of the curriculum are not controlled or directed by the Ministry but are left to the determination of the LEAs and the teachers.'[97] The new Minister, Ellen Wilkinson, was no less suspicious of such departures: 'I couldn't agree more,' she minuted to the dependable Holmes.[98]

As Chitty (among others) has pointed out, over the following half-century this view gave way to increasingly strong direct central control over the school curriculum, culminating by the late 1980s in the introduction of a National Curriculum.[99] Some measure of the transformation that was involved in this has been documented by Duncan Graham, the first chairperson and chief executive of the National Curriculum Council from 1988 until 1991. According to Graham, Kenneth Baker intervened directly as Secretary of State for Education to require that primary school children should learn poetry by heart; 'Harmless as it was, Baker's intervention was the first indication that ministerial whim could be enshrined in law.'[100] Moreover, when Kenneth Clarke became Secretary of State, he sought successfully to restrict the scope of 'history' to prevent the inclusion of 'current affairs'.[101]

It might be argued that this latter incident also symbolised the change in emphasis relating to civic ideals in the school curriculum. Norwood, Butler, and the reformers of the 1940s generally supported the development of 'education for citizenship' through the established subjects of the curriculum, although they were unwilling to legislate for this. The National Curriculum of the 1990s provides for entrenched academic subjects, with the cross-curricular theme of 'education for citizenship' which has been described as 'safe' and 'irredeemably Anglocentric'.[102] Whereas the reforms of the 1940s pursued a strongly civic goal but lacked adequate means to achieve it, those of the 1990s seem to have acquired the means but forgotten the ends.

NOTES

1. 1944 Education Act, Section 43 (1).
2. Dent, *The Education Act, 1944*, p.49.
3. e.g. B.M. Franklin, *Building the American Community: The School Curriculum and the Search for Social Control* (London: Falmer, 1986); P.S. Fass, *Outside In: Minorities and the Transformation of American Education* (Oxford: OUP, 1989); J.R. Rosario, W.S. Barnett and B. Franklin, 'On "Politics, Markets, and American Schools"', *Journal of Education Policy*, 7/2 (1992), pp.223–35.
4. See e.g. R. Johnson, 'Radical education and the New Right', in A. Rattansi and D. Reeder (eds.), *Rethinking Radical Education* (London: Lawrence & Wishart, 1992); and C. Chitty, 'The changing role of the state in education provision', *History of Education*, 21/1 (1992), pp.1–14.
5. Stewart Ranson, 'From 1944 to 1988: education, citizenship and democracy', *Local Government Studies*, 14/1 (1988), p.1.
6. Ibid., p.14.
7. *Choice And Diversity* (1992), paragraph 1.6.
8. Ibid., paragraph 1.1.
9. Ibid., paragraph 8.3.
10. Eric Bolton, 'Imaginary gardens with real toads', in C. Chitty and B. Simon (eds.), *Education Answers Back: Critical Responses to Government Policy* (London: Lawrence & Wishart, 1993), pp.9–10.
11. *TES*, Comment, 'A framework for deconstruction', 31 July 1992.
12. *The Independent*, 8 February 1993, report, 'Bishop condemns changes to education'.
13. *TES*, 13 August 1993, report, 'Councils demand new Bill'.
14. Sir Ernest Simon to Professor W. Biddle, 1 February 1937 (Simon papers, Manchester Central Library, M11/14/15. I am most grateful to Mr Roger Simon for permission to consult and quote from these papers.)
15. Sir Ernest Simon to Lord Allen of Hurtwood, 30 November 1934 (Simon papers, M11/14/14).
16. Will Spens to Sir Ernest Simon, 30 June 1934 (Simon papers, M11/14/14).
17. Ibid.
18. Sir Ernest Simon to Arthur Bryant, 27 November 1934 (Simon papers, M11/14/14).
19. Arthur Bryant to Sir Ernest Simon, 6 December 1934 (Simon papers, M11/14/14).
20. Ibid.
21. See e.g. Gary McCulloch, '"Teachers and missionaries": the Left Book Club as an educational agency', *History of Education*, 14/2 (1985), pp.137–53.
22. V. Gollancz to C. Attlee, 10 November 1937 (John Strachey papers, private).
23. Sir Ernest Simon to Victor Gollancz, 23 October 1937 (Simon papers, M11/14/16).
24. V. Gollancz to Sir Ernest Simon, 25 October 1937 (Simon papers, M11/14/16).
25. Sir Ernest Simon to V. Gollancz, 27 October 1937 (Simon papers, M11/14/16).
26. See also e.g. Ben Pimlott, *Labour and the Left in the 1930s* (Cambridge: CUP, 1977), esp. Part 4.
27. e.g. Eva Hubback, E.D. Simon, *Education For Citizenship* (London, AEC, n.d; 1934?), p.28.
28. Ibid., p.11.
29. Ibid.
30. Sir Ernest Simon to Professor G.C. Field, 26 October 1934 (Simon papers, M11/14/14).
31. Sir Ernest Simon to Eva Hubback, 5 July 1937 (Simon papers, M11/14/14).
32. Carla Esden-Tempska, 'Civic education in authoritarian Austria, 1934–38', *History*

of Education Quarterly, 30/2 (1990), p.187.
33. Ibid., p.189.
34. Sir Ernest Simon to Professor Joseph Jones, 27 July 1935 (Simon papers, M11/14/14).
35. See McCulloch, *Philosophers and Kings*, Ch.4.
36. See Melvin Richter, *The Politics of Conscience: T.H. Green and his Age* (London: Weidenfeld & Nicholson, 1964), Andrew Vincent and Raymond Plant, *Philosophy, Politics and Citizenship: The Life and Thought of the British Idealists* (London: Basil Blackwell, 1984), and I.M. Greengarten, *Thomas Hill Green and the Development of Liberal and Democratic Thought* (Toronto: University of Toronto Press, 1981), on T.H. Green's philosophy; on its influence in relation to education, Peter Gordon and John White, *Philosophers as Educational Reformers: The Influence of Idealism on British Educational Thought and Practice* (London: Woburn Press, 1979).
37. Jose Harris, 'Political thought and the Welfare State 1870–1940: an intellectual framework for British social policy', *Past and Present* 135 (1992), p.127.
38. Cyril Norwood, *The English Tradition of Education* (London: John Murray, 1929).
39. Dr Cyril Norwood, memo to consultative committee (n.d; 1933) (Board of Education papers, ED.10/151).
40. Ibid.
41. Dr Cyril Norwood, oral evidence to Spens committee, 24 November 1933 (Board of Education papers, ED.10/151).
42. Sir Ernest Simon to Eva Hubback, 24 December 1936 (Simon papers, M11/14/15).
43. Sir Ernest Simon to Spencer Leeson, 30 December 1936 (Simon papers, M11/14/15).
44. Spencer Leeson to Sir Ernest Simon, n.d. [January 1937] (Simon papers, M11/14/15).
45. Sir Ernest Simon to Spencer Leeson, 14 January 1937 (Simon papers, M11/14/15).
46. R.F. Young to Sir Ernest Simon, 31 March 1937 (Simon papers, M11/14/15).
47. Hugh Lyon to Sir Ernest Simon, 1 January 1937 (Simon papers, M11/14/16).
48. Sir Ernest Simon to Eva Hubback, 9 June 1937 (Simon papers, M11/14/15); Sir Ernest Simon to Sir Percy Jackson, 2 May 1938 (Simon papers, M11/14/16).
49. Meeting of Principal Assistant and Assistant Secretaries with Chief Inspectors, 14 October 1937 (Board of Education papers, ED.10/273).
50. Sir Ernest Simon to Eva Hubback, 9 October 1937 (Simon papers, M11/14/16).
51. Sir Ernest Simon to Will Spens, 17 February 1938 (Simon papers, M11/14/16).
52. Sir Ernest Simon to Maurice Holmes, 8 March 1938; Simon to Spens, 9 March 1938; Spens to Simon, 11 March 1938 (Simon papers, M11/14/16).
53. Spens Report, p.xxxvii.
54. Ibid., p.xxxviii.
55. Sir Ernest Simon to Sir Will Spens, 10 January 1939 (Simon papers, M11/14/17).
56. Ibid.
57. R.H. Tawney to Sir Ernest Simon, 22 December 1939 (Simon papers, M11/14/17).
58. See e.g. Ross Terrill, *R.H. Tawney and his Times: Socialism as Fellowship* (Harvard: Harvard UP, 1973).
59. Sir Ernest Simon to Eva Hubback, 26 April 1937 (Simon papers, M11/14/15).
60. R.H. Tawney, *Why Britain Fights* (Macmillan war pamphlet no.13, 1941), p.46.
61. F. Clarke, *Education and Social Change: An English Interpretation* (London: Sheldon Press, 1940).
62. Fred Clarke to R.H. Tawney, 5 October 1940 (Tawney papers, Institute of Education, London).
63. Sir Fred Clarke, 'Notes on the Enquiry into the Education of the Young Worker' (n.d; 1947?) (Ministry of Education papers, ED.147/15).
64. M. Holmes, note to R.A. Butler, 26 January 1942 (Board of Education papers, ED.136/294).
65. R.H. Tawney to D. Miller, 30 January 1943 (Tawney papers, Institute of Education).
66. J. Chuter Ede to R.A. Butler, 27 April 1943 (Board of Education papers, ED.136/642).
67. R.A. Butler to Captain C. Allport, 21 August 1942 (Butler papers, Trinity College Cambridge, G14).
68. R.A. Butler, note, 4 May 1942 (Board of Education papers, ED.11/254).
69. *Educational Reconstruction*, paragraph 1.

70. Ibid., paragraph 5.
71. Ibid., paragraph 35.
72. R.H. Tawney to R.A. Butler, 1 August 1943 (Tawney papers, Institute of Education).
73. Sir Cyril Norwood to G.G. Williams, 3 December 1939 (Board of Education papers, ED.12/518).
74. Ibid.
75. Sir Cyril Norwood, 'The crisis in education – II', *The Spectator*, 16 February 1940.
76. Ibid.
77. Sir Cyril Norwood, 'Some aspects of educational reconstruction', *The Fortnightly*, February 1941.
78. C. Norwood to G.G. Williams, 13 August 1941 (Board of Education papers, ED.12/478).
79. E. Simon to E.G. Savage (Board of Education), 15 September 1939 (Simon papers, M11/14/17).
80. Ibid.
81. AEC, memo to Norwood Committee, n.d. [1942] (IAAM papers, E1/4 file 4).
82. Ibid.
83. Council for Curriculum Reform, evidence for the Committee on Curriculum and Examinations (June 1942) (IAAM papers, E1/3 file 2).
84. Sir Richard Livingstone, oral evidence to Norwood Committee, 12–13 June 1942 (IAAM papers, E1/1 file 3).
85. AEC, oral evidence to Norwood Committee, 10–11 July 1942 (IAAM papers, E1/1 file 3).
86. Sir Richard Livingstone to Sir Ernest Simon, 15 July 1942 (Simon papers, M11/14/18).
87. Norwood Report, p.58.
88. Ibid., p.57.
89. R.A. Butler to Captain C. Allport, 21 August 1942 (Butler papers, G14).
90. Norwood Report, p.88.
91. Ibid., p.7.
92. Ibid., p.66.
93. Ibid., p.104. See also McCulloch, *Philosophers and Kings*, esp. pp.55–62.
94. Sir Cyril Norwood to R.A. Butler, 6 June 1942 (Board of Education papers, ED.136/681).
95. See also W. Silto, 'Compulsory day continuation schools: their origins, objectives and development, with special reference to H.A.L. Fisher's 1918 experiment' (Ph.D. thesis, London, 1993), for more detailed discussion of the links between the day continuation schools and the county colleges. Further research with particular reference to the 1944 Act would be useful.
96. Sir M. Holmes to A.A. Part, 13 August 1945 (Ministry of Education papers, ED.147/21).
97. Ibid.
98. E. Wilkinson, note to Sir M. Holmes, 13 August 1945 (Ministry of Education papers, ED.147/21).
99. Clyde Chitty, 'Central control of the school curriculum, 1944-87', *History of Education*, 17/4 (1988), pp.321–34.
100. D. Graham with D. Tytler, *A Lesson for us All* (London: Routledge, 1992), p.51.
101. Ibid., p.70.
102. W.E. Marsden, 'Recycling religious instruction? Historical perspectives on contemporary cross-curricular issues', *History of Education*, 22/4 (1993), p.330.

7

Contesting the Curriculum

Competition between opposing ideologies and interests inside and around the educational State was clearly thriving in the 1940s, and reached an often uneasy equipoise in the Education Act of 1944. Earlier chapters have shown how the Act itself was interpreted in different ways, and how its silences and its shades of meaning, always richly ambiguous, established new tensions in subsequent decades. Notions such as tripartism and citizenship could be negotiated in many different ways. Alternative approaches, themselves with long and chequered histories, were examined often in minute detail during this crucial phase of reform. The outcome was in some cases to ensure the dominance of particular kinds of assumption, structure or relationship for the next generation or more. Other approaches were effectively consigned through this process to the outer margins of the educational settlement reached in 1944.

Debates around the curriculum, pedagogy and assessment were also fiercely fought. The present chapter will focus on the ways in which the grammar school curriculum was contested between different outlooks represented on the one hand by the Spens Report of 1938, and on the other by the Norwood Report of 1943. Such differences help to illuminate the contestation that underlay the settlement of 1944, the alternative possibilities that were articulated during this period, and the nature of the modern 'educational State'. More specifically, they also highlight the unresolved debates that surround the secondary school curriculum.

From Spens to Norwood

At first sight, the processes through which the Spens Report gave way to the Norwood Report would not appear to be promising as an example of this kind of contestation. Indeed, according to F.R.G. Duckworth, the senior Chief Inspector of Secondary Schools, in 1943, the two Reports were broadly in line with each other. Commenting on the proposals put forward by the Norwood Report shortly before its publication, Duckworth concluded that 'there does not seem to be any serious divergence of views between the two Reports.' What had happened, he suggested, was that 'the

Norwood Committee has expanded at great length what the Spens Committee had to say about curriculum and examinations, and in doing so has put forward recommendations which, although not included in the Spens Report, cannot be said to be out of line with it.'[1] Thus, for example, both Reports called for grammar schools to have freedom to frame their own courses of instruction and to draw up syllabuses. Likewise, both insisted on the importance of English, although Norwood was 'less emphatic about Mathematics and Science'. Both regarded multilateral schools with 'guarded disapproval', but supported 'a combination of Grammar and Modern Schools in thinly populated areas'; that is, they both favoured the allocation of pupils to different types of secondary schools on the basis of their aptitudes and abilities.[2]

Duckworth did note a few differences between the two Reports. For instance, he pointed out, 'Spens insists on bringing studies "into closer contact than at present with the practical affairs of life". Norwood touches on the same point but with slightly less emphasis.'[3] Thus whereas Spens appeared to emphasise the 'vocational element' in grammar school education, Norwood stressed 'the importance of sound learning for its own sake'. However, in Duckworth's view, 'The only essential difference in the general lay-out of secondary education which the Spens Report proposed was the creation of the Technical High School.'[4] Since Norwood also endorsed the creation of 'secondary technical schools' as one of the three major types of secondary school envisaged for the new age of secondary education for all, even this one 'essential difference' must have appeared relatively minor.

However, closer scrutiny reveals much greater incoherence and disagreement than is conveyed in Duckworth's bland commentary. The disagreements involved can be seen first in the unresolved tensions between the Spens Committee and the Norwood Committee. Moreover, major differences in the educational values and priorities represented in the two Reports are evident from a close comparison of their recommendations. This is especially true in relation to their approaches to the secondary school curriculum. They reflected competing and contradictory positions on the curriculum that had been in opposition to each other throughout the twentieth century, and which maintained a basic tension after the war.

Writing in the early 1950s, Harold Dent perceived this tension in terms of Spens's preference to provide a *general* education for ils who would leave school at fifteen to go into employment, and Norwood's aspiration to provide a *preliminary* education for pupils aiming at the professions. Within the 1944 Act, he suggested, there were 'two distinct and different functions' for the grammar school that were 'actively contending for supremacy'.[5] Moreover, he added, it was 'impossible to prophesy which will prevail'.[6] But the Spens and Norwood Reports also reflected other continuing struggles over the nature of the secondary school curriculum that were no less significant for the future. These included debates about the role of school subjects, the importance of individuals and the role of the community, and differences between material and spiritual ideals.

First indications of tension between Spens and Norwood involve expressions of rivalry over the respective territory, scope and role of the Reports. To some extent, this rivalry might be interpreted in personal terms as a dispute between the chairmen of the two committees, Sir Will Spens and Sir Cyril Norwood, both distinguished and senior educators who had become key members of the education policy community. At the same time, it represented a contest over rights and powers between two major policy agencies attached to the Board of Education. The Spens Report was a product of the Board's consultative committee, which had been the principal agency responsible for major inquiries into specific areas of policy since the beginning of the century. The Norwood Report, on the other hand, was put together by a specially appointed subcommittee of the Secondary School Examinations Council (SSEC). The SSEC had been created in 1917 to oversee the new School Certificate and Higher School Certificate examinations, and included representatives of the eight university examining boards, the local education authorities, and secondary school teachers. Friction involving the bodies headed by Spens and Norwood demonstrates the existence of competing interests between what Ball describes as 'sites and agencies' within the educational State, with direct implications for policy formation.

The Norwood Committee was initially set up at the start of 1941 to recommend suitable changes to the School Certificate examination.[7] However, the following summer, the new President of the Board of Education, R.A. Butler, decided to widen the terms of reference of Norwood's Committee to include curriculum issues.[8] The issue in pursuing this aim was how to define the purposes and scope of Norwood's Committee in such a way as to avoid a clear invasion of the territory covered by the Spens Committee. In developing the role of Norwood's Committee in this way, there w

obvious strategic problems that needed initially to be faced. First, since the committee was chosen only from the members of the SSEC, it had a limited claim to be representative of different kinds of opinion and indeed was technically entitled to discuss only matters directly relevant to secondary school examinations. Norwood and Butler agreed therefore that they should be cautious in framing the committee's new terms of reference. If they were framed too broadly, Norwood noted, 'then the criticism may be made that the Committee is not rightly constituted', that is, that the SSEC was going beyond its legitimate sphere of interest.[9] Norwood proposed that this could be avoided through making the terms of reference 'To consider suggested changes in the secondary school curriculum and the question of School Examinations in relation thereto'.[10] In this way, he hoped, 'we can start from the Spens report, and get our minds on the whole problem, while considering primarily the examinations which are the natural outcome of the work done in schools'.[11] This was a formula that suggested a particular focus but allowed considerable freedom for discussion. Indeed at the first meeting of the committee in October 1941, Norwood felt able to declare that it 'had an opportunity of reviewing the whole field of secondary education after the War'.[12] In effect, the new terms of reference of the committee enabled it to extend the range of the SSEC's interests in education policy matters, at a critical stage in the development of post-war reforms.

The issue of the committee's proper sphere of interest was especially important since it was now in a position to revisit the proposals of the Spens Report and, potentially, to contradict the findings of the Board's own consultative committee. The need to prevent a clear clash with Spens led to further careful negotiations over the scope and aims of Norwood's committee. As late as November 1941, Butler remained uncertain about 'the extent to which the Committee is to go in considering the future of secondary education in the wide sense, i.e. including technical and modern schools'.[13] G.G. Williams warned Norwood that although Butler was 'already satisfied that there is no reason to think that we are acting improperly vis-à-vis the Spens Report', he might 'wonder whether we are properly constituted to go beyond the range of Grammar Schools'.[14] In this situation, the safest course appeared to be to restrict Norwood to issues relating to the curriculum and examinations in grammar schools, thus limiting the scope for his committee to interfere in the wider areas dealt with by Spens. Norwood himself hoped to include a discussion of public schools in his Report, 'to show that a boarding-school system is essential to the country, and that therefore it is our business to make it accessible'.[15] The Spens Report had not in fact discussed the problems of the public schools, and Norwood was of course an experienced and sympathetic observer of the issues involved with them. However, in the interests of restricting the scope of the committee it was agreed to avoid dealing in detail either with the public schools, or with technical and modern schools. By the end of the year, Norwood accepted that the committee should focus on 'the scope of Grammar Schools in the wider field of Secondary Education', and that it was 'not the job of the Committee to examine in detail problems of Modern or Technical or Public Schools', even though, as he argued, 'something must be said of our approach to them'.[16] It was these negotiations surrounding the genesis of the Norwood Committee that determined both the general scope and the bounds or limitations of its eventual Report. They ensured that discussion would continue to be framed generally in terms of grammar, technical and modern schools: that is, in a tripartite pattern of provision. They also reflected the existence of outstanding issues for debate, and the potential for conflict between two major agencies associated with the Board in framing education policy.

Despite the care that was taken to restrict Norwood's territorial ambitions, rivalry between Spens and Norwood persisted and was well known inside the Board of Education. Maurice Holmes, Permanent Secretary to the Board, outlined the background to this 'rivalry' in a memorandum to Butler, headed 'Spens v. Norwood', as the Norwood Committee was beginning its work. Holmes felt that 'any animus that there may be is on Sir Will's side', and that this resulted from the fact that

> As Chairman of the Board's Consultative Committee he feels that on any question of importance the Board should consult him rather than anyone else, and he is probably annoyed because the terms of reference of Sir Cyril Norwood's Committee have been enlarged by the inclusion of the curriculum of Secondary Schools, a subject which he regards as peculiarly his own.

Holmes, however, recommended that Norwood be supported in his new role, especially as 'I feel pretty clear that the educational world would be more ready to put their money on Sir Cyril Norwood than on Sir Will Spens.'[17] The following spring, Spens took his grievances direct to Butler, registering his 'great alarm' at the activities of the Norwood Committee, and expressing 'great distrust' of Norwood himself.[18] But by this time it was too late to prevent Norwood from carrying out his work. When the Committee finally completed its Report in June 1943, Butler considered his support for Norwood well justified: 'This well-written report will serve our book very well – particularly its layout of the Secondary world.' He could not refrain from adding at the same time: 'Spens will be furious.'[19]

Contesting the curriculum

The tensions between Spens and Norwood are not only to be explained in terms of personal and institutional competition for influence over educational policy change. They also involved substantial policy differences. These were reflected in the approach adopted towards particular issues by the Norwood Committee, often explicitly against the thrust of what Spens had proposed. Several important shifts in policy and outlook are evident in the Norwood Report. It took up its own distinctive positions on the school curriculum, and in so doing it radically opposed Spens's notion of the aims and aspirations of secondary education.

The two Reports represented widely contrasting views of the grammar school curriculum. Spens emphasised criticisms of the existing curriculum, and argued that owing to rapid social and economic changes it was important to make a 'thorough reconsideration' of its framework and content.[20] This was especially necessary, according to Spens, as the large increase in the number of pupils attending grammar schools over the past twenty-five years raised questions as to whether the traditional academic curriculum was suited to this new clientele. Spens suggested, therefore, that 'the studies of the ordinary secondary school should be brought into closer contact than at present with the practical affairs of life'.[21] It proposed that what it called the 'utility phase' in the development of pupils' interests should be more strongly reflected in the secondary school curriculum, for example in Mathematics, Physical Science, Art and Handicraft, and that in particular 'the interests of the less able pupils will always be best met by a greater stress on the utility of a subject than on the phase of generalisation'.[22] If such a reform could be achieved, it argued, 'Pupils would leave school with a better equipment for practical affairs of many kinds and with some understanding of the way in which those affairs depend upon exact knowledge, and would be better prepared to pursue such knowledge with intelligence upon the technical plane.'[23] The Norwood Committee, on the other hand, was more anxious to retain the most distinctive characteristics of the grammar school curriculum. Norwood argued at the first meeting of the committee that 'the tradition of secondary education, the best in the world, must be preserved'.[24] The logic of a generally tripartite structure of secondary education seemed to Norwood to confirm the role of the existing grammar schools, with their traditional curriculum, for those pupils best able to benefit from them. The purpose of a grammar school was defined as suiting 'the boy or girl who shows promise of ability to deal with abstract notions – who is quick at seizing the relatedness of related things'.[25] According to Norwood, this 'grammatical' treatment was 'concerned with knowledge for its own sake more than any other treatment is likely to be'.[26] Spens's criticisms of the curriculum were therefore directly challenged by the Norwood Committee, and the Norwood Report itself developed a strong rebuttal of such charges. It concluded, indeed, that 'we strongly suspect that part of the criticism directed against the curriculum is really directed not against the curriculum itself but against its suitability for many of the pupils now in the extended Secondary Schools of the country'.[27] Thus the Norwood Committee addressed what was regarded as the inconsistency of the Spens Committee on the character of a grammar school curriculum within a tripartite structure of provision, by drawing more heavily and much less critically upon existing traditions.

A further major difference between the two Reports relates to the importance attached to school subjects in the grammar school curriculum. Spens argued that the core of the grammar school curriculum should be arranged through the 'English subjects', by which it meant 'careful training in comprehension of what is read and in the expression of ideas both orally and in writing', together with History, Geography, English Literature, and Scripture.[28] It regarded school subjects as useful categories in forming the basis of school studies, although it conceded that wider activities and projects could also be helpful. It insisted therefore that 'the school "subjects" stand for traditions of practical, aesthetic and intellectual activity, each having its own distinctive individuality'. According to Spens, they needed to be pursued as such, actively, 'and not merely be assimilated by memory and understanding'.[29] It resisted notions of unifying established separate subjects such as History and Geography. It also talked of 'balancing the curriculum' and of a 'parity of subjects'.[30]

By contrast, the Norwood Committee was critical of the notion of separate subjects, which Spens had treated as the building blocks of the curriculum, and argued that their development had been harmful for the school curriculum as a whole. A memorandum circulated to the committee and 'on the whole accepted'[31] noted that 'barriers' had been set up between subjects, 'partly because differences of content of subject have been emphasised at the expense of their common purposes'.[32] As a result of this, it contended, 'Each subject has now built round itself a vested interest; each stresses what it claims to be its own subject value and to minimise what is common to all. This has resulted in extreme specialism and neglect of common ground.'[33] On the basis of this argument, the Norwood Report was hostile to subjects conceived as 'preserves, belonging to specialist teachers', and complained that 'The school course has come to resemble the "hundred yards" course, each subject following a track marked off from the others by a tape.'[34] It opposed the idea of 'weighting' subjects in relation to each other because this seemed to assume that they each had 'claims of their own, independent of the needs of the pupil'.[35] There had developed, it remarked in conclusion, an 'uneasy equilibrium' in the school curriculum in which the 'demands of specialists and subjects and examinations' were 'nicely adjusted and compensated'.[36] It was anxious to break through this specialising tendency and to emphasise instead the 'common ground', and thus in this area conveyed a more radical response to the existing situation than that which Spens had adopted. It looked more towards a 'grammar of sound learning' running through related subjects and expressed partly in related content, 'but much more in common methods and ideals'. It defined the 'common ground' in terms of three 'essential elements': training of the body, training of character, and training in 'habits of clear thought and clear expression of thought in the English language'.[37] It declared, moreover, that these 'elements' were of much greater importance than were any 'subjects', so that 'no matter what may be the subject or subjects to which a teacher may give most of his time, the subject or subjects should be of minor importance to him compared with the general welfare of the "whole" pupil'.[38]

Spens and Norwood differed also in the emphasis given to the importance of individuals and the role of the community. Spens sought to foster the 'free growth of individuality' by encouraging schools to help 'every boy and girl to achieve the highest degree of individual development of which he or she is capable'.[39] The prime duty of secondary schools, it argued, was 'to provide for the needs of children who are entering and passing through the phase of adolescence'.[40] It was highly conscious of differences between individuals going through this 'phase', and devoted a chapter to the physical, mental, and emotional development of adolescents. Spens was also concerned to measure differences in individual development, especially through intelligence tests in the case of mental development. Its priority for individuality and the notion of equality of educational opportunity to which this gave rise were strongly influenced by the findings of modern psychology, especially those endorsed by Professor Cyril Burt. The Report dealt also with the duties of individuals in society, especially as citizens. As has been seen above, it was willing to assert the central role of education in developing this, especially in the context of the need to promote alternative social values from those of the European dictators.[41] The Norwood Committee, however, went much further in emphasising the importance of community and citizenship, and was less concerned to define and measure individual differences.

Closely related to this difference of emphasis between individuality and communal values was a further contrast between Spens's espousal of 'material' ideals and Norwood's preference for the 'spiritual'. Norwood argued vigorously that 'the spiritual values of truth, goodness and beauty' should be regarded as 'absolute values', and as indispensable to the task of education.[42] He adhered to this in opposition to what he described as 'the alternative modern theory' which, he suggested, 'holds that there are no absolute values; that truth, goodness and beauty, are all relative; that education has hitherto been backward-looking, designed to confirm and entrench established names; that the new world requires a forward-looking education, based on science, using scientific method to adapt conduct to changing needs, and knowledge to changing circumstances . . . that biology and psychology should replace Christian teaching'.[43]

The Spens Report was seen as characteristic of this latter tradition in its general treatment of modern social, intellectual and scientific movements. In pursuing its discussion of criticisms of the grammar school curriculum, for example, Spens pointed out that 'the existing framework was completed in the second half of the nineteenth century during a phase of civilisation which was largely static, and is accordingly more suited to a static than to a dynamic phase in which we live to-day'.[44] However, owing to the 'many and great changes' of the past forty years, 'the world in which the modern child is born and in which he grows up is a very different world from that of the Victorian child'.[45] Advances in technological knowledge and practice, the breakdown of 'old lines of social cleavage',[46] and improved means of intercommunication and transport needed on this view to be reflected in the school curriculum. The 'great advance in the science of psychology' also suggested a need to adjust the curriculum in line with a new awareness of 'the natures of boys and girls'.[47]

Such an argument was anathema to Norwood in his stern defence of lasting moral and spiritual values that transcended social change. It was this that led the Norwood Report to insist that 'education cannot stop short of recognising the ideals of truth and beauty and goodness as final and binding for all times and in all places, as ultimate values'.[48] Such ideals, it averred, were not of 'temporary convenience only, as devices for holding together society till they can be dispensed with as knowledge grows and organisation becomes more scientific'.[49] It found no sympathy for 'a theory of education which presupposes that its aim can be dictated by the provisional findings of special Sciences, whether biological, psychological or sociological, that the function of education is to fit pupils to determine their outlook and conduct according to the changing needs and the changing standards of the day'.[50] In all of this, its view that 'education from its own nature must be ultimately concerned with values which are independent of time or particular environment, though realisable under changing forms in both',[51] was a barely disguised rebuttal of the social-scientific evolutionism of the Spens Report. This aim is especially clear in the background memoranda that were prepared for the Norwood Committee, in which Norwood himself declared: 'It is important that the report should make it clear that in all educational reconstruction a firm stand should be taken on the question of spiritual as opposed to material ideals.'[52]

In the same vein, Norwood was particularly forceful in his criticisms of Spens's approach to religious education and the scriptures. Chapter Five of the Spens Report argued in favour of a 'historical and objective' outlook in the study of scripture, intended to promote an understanding of its original meaning. This approach would involve specialist training for teachers of scripture in order to acquire 'increased professional knowledge', although Spens conceded at the same time that 'the best teacher is one whose interest in the subject and desire to teach it proceed from religious faith'.[53] Norwood was clearly suspicious about the implications of

Spens's notion of religious education, and was anxious to, as he put it, 'develop further Chapter V of the Spens Report'.[54] He agreed that 'literary criticism and historical background' were necessary in order to bring out the meaning of the Bible, although he felt that Spens seemed to 'over-simplify' this aim. At the same time, he argued that this on its own was insufficient: 'the value of the book still remains religious value and that value cannot be well represented, no matter how objective the method, unless a religious interpretation of life means something to the teacher'.[55] This conviction led him to suggest that a 'religious outlook on life' was 'indispensable to any successful teacher of religious instruction'. Thus to 'intellectual equipment', such as that stressed by Spens, Norwood added 'a belief in the study's own specific value, i.e. a religious interpretation of life'. Moreover, he held that this needed to be developed in the wider context of a school in which 'spiritual values are the standards embodied in its life and activities', and that it should not be confined to particular classrooms or specialist studies.[56] These notions were again vividly reflected in the Norwood Report itself, which elevated 'religious consciousness' above the restrictions of subjects in the syllabus.[57]

A grammar school curriculum?

The Spens and Norwood Reports represented overall very different stances in relation to the character and role of the grammar school curriculum. These differences have tended to go unnoticed because of their common endorsement of a tripartite structure, but they are significant none the less. Spens favoured a curriculum that would promote individual opportunities and differences, and emphasised the need to adapt in accord with a changing society. Norwood leaned more towards late nineteenth-century notions of social hierarchy, conscience, morality and community. These were approaches that were directly opposed to each other and, attached as they were to distinct interests, formed the basis for contestation in and around the educational State in this important phase in the negotiation of reform. The parameters for debate within the policy community and inside the educational State therefore continued to be broad, allowing scope for fundamental disagreements on the proper direction for reform that are not explained adequately in an unproblematic, monolithic model of the 'educational Establishment' type.

This contestation took place at a time when the agencies and sites involved were themselves being transformed. The Board of Education was reconstituted to become the Ministry of Education, stronger and potentially more active in its policy role.[58] The consultative committee was converted into two Central Advisory Councils, for England and for Wales. Meanwhile, the SSEC's position was radically changed after the war through the exclusion of the university examining bodies. Both Spens and Norwood, pivotal figures in the policy community during the previous decade, lost their organisational base and much of their influence partly as a result of these developments, and also due to the challenge of the rising generation.

The configurations and therefore the power relationships within the educational State had undergone important changes in this process. These brought new individuals and groups to the fore and diminished the role of others in the post-war era. It is in developing the links between these changes that important research challenges remain; also in understanding the ways in which contestation developed around the educational State in each of the subsequent decades. In many ways the scale and complexity of the educational State appear to increase greatly in the fifty years following the Education Act of 1944, while the landscape and the terrain itself are transformed on several occasions. And yet underlying the shifts and the convulsions, it is no less important to identify the inherited battles and ideological fault-lines that relate the debates of the 1960s, 1970s, 1980s and 1990s to those that took place before and during the Second World War.

Dent's view of a contested grammar school curriculum suggests just such a theme. It has become common to acknowledge specific continuities in the school curriculum. Goodson, for example, notes the incorporation of the 'grammar school curriculum' into the comprehensive schools in the decades after the war, to argue that a hierarchy of academic subjects was substantially maintained. According to Goodson, 'The dominance of academic subjects with high-status examination credentials would need to be in close harmony with the vested interests of subject groups to explain the strength of this structure over so long a period.'[59] In relation to the National Curriculum, also, some historians have discerned lines of descent from progenitors such as the Revised Code of 1862 and the Secondary School Regulations of 1904.[60] It remains important to combine an awareness of the historical dimensions of the contemporary curriculum, with an understanding of the ways in which it has been contested between rival values and interests.

Such an understanding should foster new insights into the contested nature of the 'grammar school curriculum'. That is to say, it is not enough to imagine it as a simple, static and timeless entity. For example, in coming to terms with the extent to which the 'grammar school curriculum' maintained its dominance in comprehensive schools, it is important to recognise the many dimensions and the changing and keenly debated character of the curriculum in grammar schools, even in the first half of the twentieth century.

The importance of changes in wider social and cultural values also seems paramount in explaining curriculum change over a number of years. Butler remarked in his diary in 1943 that political interest had shifted during the twentieth century 'from the soul of man to his economic position', and that this had affected the debate over his Bill compared with the Education Act of 1902.[61] Even so, both sets of values were involved in the contest between Spens and Norwood that prefigured and shaped the Bill of 1943: the more materialistic, individualist, scientific concerns of the Spens Report, and the moral, community-oriented curriculum of the Norwood Report. The differences between these ideals, and their respective influence, deserve more detailed attention in future analysis of the secondary school curriculum.

The basic tension between Spens's emphasis on general education and the mass of secondary school pupils, and Norwood's focus on the preliminary education of pupils intending to go into higher education and the professions, again signals a profound and long-term curriculum issue. This debate echoed nineteenth- and early twentieth-century arguments about whether secondary education should cater especially for a small elite, or whether it should broaden its appeal to a wider clientele. These alternatives had always carried clear implications for the curriculum. Catering for an elite would tend to mean a more specialised, academic curriculum, whereas larger numbers of pupils would suggest greater breadth in the curriculum and scope for practical and vocational approaches.

In terms of this debate, the Spens Report was consciously in the same tradition as the Bryce Report on secondary education of 1895, while the Norwood Report seemed to critics and admirers alike to hark back to the ideals of Sir Robert Morant and the Education Act of 1902. Indeed, in this respect it is particularly apt to draw a direct comparison between the phase of educational reform that began with Bryce and culminated in the 1902 Act, and the reform cycle of the 1940s. During both periods, the nature of the secondary school curriculum was subjected to vigorous and open debate within the educational policy community. During the 1940s, no less than in the 1890s, there remained ample scope for this kind of highly charged argument to occur within and around the educational State. In spite of the increasingly glacial and impervious impression conveyed in the official accounts, such as that of F.R.G. Duckworth in 1943, the curriculum continued to be contested between powerful, directly opposed and deeply rooted interests.

Such debates also find potent and ironic resonance in the educational reforms of the late twentieth century. The conflict between materialism, individualism, and science, on the one hand, and spirituality, community and religion, on the other, has been in marked evidence during the 1980s and 1990s. Unlike Kenneth Baker and Kenneth Clarke, John Patten has adopted a strong moral stance, reflected partly in the White Paper *Choice and Diversity*, and also in his later emphasis on religious education.[62] The moral dimension of 'back to basics' in the early 1990s could be regarded as a remnant of earlier crusades, reminiscent of such battles also in the way that it manoeuvred uneasily for its position in relation to rival interests.

There were also continuing debates over the relative value of school subjects and cross-curricular themes, which have again emerged as a key issue in the development of the National Curriculum in the early 1990s. Despite the efforts of Duncan Graham, the founding chairman of the National Curriculum Council, officials apparently resisted discussion of broad cross-curricular themes in preference for an exclusive emphasis on the ten National Curriculum subjects. According to Graham, 'The council was told that its job was to deliver the ten national curriculum subjects: everything else could be dealt with once the original brief was achieved.'[63] Graham finally resorted to meeting Kenneth Baker, the then Secretary of State, secretly in a field behind a hotel in North Wales to discuss his concerns.[64] What the Norwood Report had described as barriers in a hundred yards racecourse, in which each subject followed a track marked off from the others by a tape, retained a powerful influence.

Similarly, the tensions around preparing a small elite for further studies, and providing a general education for all, were a major topic for discussion in the decades that followed the Education Act of 1944. C.P. Snow referred to the problem in the late 1950s in terms of his notion of the 'two cultures', in which, as he argued, 'Somehow we have set ourselves the task of producing a tiny *elite* – far smaller proportionately than in any comparable country – educated in one academic skill.'[65] In the 1990s, the Paul Hamlyn Foundation's National Commission on Education was no less aware that the education system had 'concentrated for too long on the needs of the academically able at the expense of the rest.'[66] In order to redress this problem, the Commission recommended a wider range of participation in education from the age of sixteen, but there remained acute difficulties over the kinds of pathways and signposts that would be provided for students. The contradictions highlighted in the curriculum debates between Spens and Norwood in the early 1940s still posed uncomfortable dilemmas for the future of education at the end of the twentieth century. The same was true of issues relating to the autonomy of school teachers and their responsibilities for assessment and examinations, and it is to these that we now turn.

NOTES

1. F.R.G. Duckworth, note on Norwood Report, 28 June 1943 (Board of Education papers, ED/136/681).
2. Ibid.
3. Ibid.
4. Ibid.
5. H.C. Dent, *Change in English Education: A Historical Survey* (London: University of London Press, 1952), p.71.
6. Ibid.
7. H. Ramsbotham to C. Norwood, 3 January 1941 (Board of Education papers, ED.12/478).
8. R.A. Butler, note, 31 July 1941 (Board of Education papers, ED.12/478).
9. Cyril Norwood to R.A. Butler, 20 September 1941 (Board of Education papers, ED/12/478).
10. Ibid.
11. Ibid.
12. 1st meeting of Norwood Committee, 18 October 1941, minute 2 (Board of Education papers, ED/136/681).
13. G.G. Williams to Cyril Norwood, 26 November 1941 (Board of Education papers, ED/136/681).
14. Ibid.
15. Cyril Norwood to G.G. Williams, 28 November 1941 (Board of Education papers, ED/12/478).
16. G.G. Williams, note to M. Holmes and R.A. Butler, 23 December 1941 (Board of Education papers, ED/12/478).
17. M.G. Holmes, memo to R.A. Butler, 20 October 1941 (Board of Education papers, ED/12/478).
18. R.A. Butler, note, 20 March 1942 (Board of Education papers, ED/136/131).
19. R.A. Butler, note to Secretary and G.G. Williams, 6 June 1943 (Board of Education papers, ED/136/681).
20. Board of Education, *Secondary Education with Special Reference to Grammar Schools*

    and Technical High Schools (Spens Report) (London, 1938), p.142.
21. Ibid., p.162.
22. Ibid., p.183.
23. Ibid., p.163.
24. Norwood Committee, minutes of 1st meeting, 18 October 1941, minute 2 (Board of Education papers, ED/136/681).
25. 'A note on the grammar school', memo to Norwood committee, n.d. (January 1942) (Board of Education papers, ED/136/681).
26. Ibid.
27. Board of Education, *Curriculum and Examinations in Secondary Schools* (Norwood Report) (London, 1943), p.12.
28. Spens Report, p.xxiv.
29. Ibid., p.159.
30. Ibid., pp.170, 205.
31. Norwood Committee, meeting 1–4 September 1942, minute 3 (Incorporated Association of Assistant Masters (IAAM) papers, E1/1 file 3).
32. Com. 28, 'Notes on the curriculum', n.d. (1942) (IAAM papers, E1/2 file 2).
33. Ibid.
34. Norwood Report, p.61.
35. Ibid., p.60.
36. Ibid., p.61.
37. Ibid., p.66.
38. Ibid.
39. Spens Report, pp.151–2.
40. Ibid., p.168.
41. See Chapter Six, above.
42. 'Detailed agenda for meetings', January 1942 (IAAM papers, E1/1 file 3).
43. Ibid.
44. Spens Report, p.142.
45. Ibid.
46. Ibid.
47. Ibid., pp.142–3.
48. Norwood Report, p.viii.
49. Ibid.
50. Ibid.
51. Ibid.
52. Memo to Norwood Committee, Com. 30, 'Religious education', n.d. (1942) (IAAM papers, E1/2 file 2).
53. Spens Report, pp. 209–10.
54. 'Detailed agenda for meetings', January 1942 (IAAM papers, E1/1 file 3).
55. Com. 30, 'Religious education' (IAAM papers).
56. Ibid.
57. Norwood Report, p.86.
58. See Peter Gosden, 'From Board to Ministry: the impact of the war on the education department', *History of Education*, 18/3 (1989), pp.183–93.
59. Ivor Goodson, *School Subjects and Curriculum Change* (London: Falmer, 1987 edn), p.31.
60. E.g. Richard Aldrich, 'The National Curriculum: An historical perspective', in D. Lawton and C. Chitty (eds.), *The National Curriculum* (Bedford Way Papers 33, London, 1988), pp.22–3.
61. R.A. Butler, diary, 9 September 1943 (Butler papers, Trinity College. Cambridge, G15).
62. Department for Education, *Choice and Diversity* (London: HMSO, 1992), Ch.9, 'Spiritual and moral development'; also e.g. *The Independent* 1 February 1994, report, 'Patten warns schools not to shun act of worship'.
63. Graham, *A Lesson for us All*, p.20.
64. Ibid., pp.20–21.
65. C.P. Snow, *The Two Cultures and a Second Look* (Cambridge: CUP, 1963), p.19.
66. National Commission on Education, *Learning to Succeed* (1993), p.239.

8

Teachers and Testing

The reforms of the last decade have often appeared likely to threaten what has been taken to be the professional role of school teachers, particularly in relation to their influence in the sphere of the school curriculum. The National Curriculum restricts the freedom of teachers to control the curriculum, although it does allow some scope for interpretation.[1] The interim Dearing report of August 1993 acknowledged the concerns expressed by teachers about the possible effects of the National Curriculum: 'the attempt to spell out the requirements of the National Curriculum subjects in a clear, unambiguous manner has led to a level of prescription that many teachers find unacceptably constricting.'[2] It therefore noted a need to review the balance between 'what is defined nationally' and 'what is left to the exercise of professional judgement'.[3] The Secretary of State for Education, John Patten, confirmed that issues such as the pattern of curriculum organisation were 'matters properly left to the professional judgment of teachers'.[4]

The role of teachers in testing and assessment, however, remained unclear and contested. Was this inextricably linked with the professional duties and authority of teachers in the sphere of the curriculum, or was it more properly a task in which effective control should be allocated elsewhere? Examination boards based on the universities enjoyed a great deal of influence in this area, but their role also came under close and critical scrutiny on the part of the government in the early 1990s. In 1992, for example, they were publicly criticised for allegedly allowing an erosion of standards in the GCSE examination. The Secretary of State pointed out on this occasion that although he did not control the boards, he had 'quite serious powers' that could be employed if he was not satisfied.[5] This incident brought the position of the examining boards into focus, and raised the question of whether they should be involved to a greater extent in the more general reforms of the education system. *The Independent* argued that 'There is no particular reason why we should have the boards we do. Like so many British institutions, they just grew. They might be better for pruning. Or they might benefit from competition. There is nothing to stop any suitable body from setting up in business as a provider of examination services.'[6] Alternatively, it was suggested that a single unified examining body might be set up for the whole country. As John Patten himself noted, in his speech to the Conservative Party annual conference in October 1992, 'I have a message for those exam boards. Listen very carefully. I will say this only once. "Get your act together."'[7]

The final Dearing Review, published at the beginning of 1994, confirmed that teachers should be allowed 'scope for professional judgement',[8] although this seemed to relate in particular to non-compulsory areas of the curriculum as it suggested 'a division of the content of the present National Curriculum Orders into the essential matters, skills and processes which any school must by law teach and the optional material which can be taught according to the professional judgement of teachers.'[9] The Report also argued that what it described as 'on-going teacher assessment' should be regarded as 'central to the assessment of the performance of the individual child'.[10] At the same time, it averred, such teacher assessment should be 'complemented with information from short, well-conceived national tests in the core subjects at the end of each key stage'.[11] The Dearing Review aspired towards an 'increased trust for teachers', but insisted that this should be matched by 'accountability to parents and society, including that from simple tests in the core subjects'.[12] It remained to be seen how these recommendations would affect the balance between teachers, examining bodies, and the State.

The reforms of the 1940s had also highlighted tensions involved in the control of assessment and examinations. These too focused on the different roles to be assumed by school teachers and by examination boards, and brought out conflicting arguments over the supposed professional responsibilities of teachers. Indeed, criticism of the role of examinations, especially in relation to the secondary school curriculum, reached a peak during the Second World War. Again the Norwood Committee was central to the dispute. Its Report of 1943 suggested an alternative approach emphasising the potential role of internal examinations to be controlled mainly by teachers, as opposed to external examinations administered by examination boards. It thus provides a historical episode that may suggest a framework by which we may be able to interpret more recent developments, and our own contemporary situation.

Assessing examinations

Sociologists of education have long recognised the importance of assessment as a social and ideological construct. The work of Patricia Broadfoot has been influential in highlighting the relationship between educational assessment and society.[13] Whitty and Eggleston, among others, have discussed the tensions involved in this relationship.[14] Issues of accountability and control are raised in Lingard's paper on secondary school assessment in Queensland.[15] Another recent contribution from New Zealand develops three distinct models of educational accountability – the 'professional' model, the 'market' model, and the 'management' model – and applies these to an investigation of recent assessment reforms.[16]

At the same time, a socio-historical literature on examinations and assessment has also appeared over the past decade. John Roach's earlier work located the emergence of public examinations in England within a wider social and political framework, as a means of understanding for example the strong role asserted by university-based examination boards.[17] MacLeod's research on science examinations in the late nineteenth century, and Sutherland's discussion of intelligence testing in the early twentieth century, are further examples of important socio-historical work in this area.[18] Musgrave's more recent study of the Victorian Universities Schools Examinations Board is a significant attempt to bring together the distinct interests developed in the 'sociological' and the 'historical' literature.[19] Latterly, too, there has been the emergence of socio-historical research on teachers and teaching, which also has important implications for the study of issues relating to assessment.[20]

Despite these developments there seems to be little sense of a socio-historical framework of debate between so-called 'internal' and 'external' examinations in the twentieth century, and scant recognition of the character and role of different types of *opposition* to public examinations over that time. There has been a continued tendency for assessment issues to be discussed in a technical language, detached from wider sociological, political, policy, and ideological considerations; that is, for such issues to be couched in terms of 'policy science' rather than of 'critical scholarship'.[21] Examples of this tendency might include Fisher's historical work on external examinations, and recent discussions of assessment reform by such as Desforges, and Riding and Butterfield.[22] And yet there seems to be much potential in this theme for exploration as a socio-political arena involving competing interests and ideologies.

Attention to this theme should give due recognition to the importance of assessment systems as historical and political in their characteristics, in the same way that such aspects of the school curriculum have been highlighted in research conducted over the past decade.[23] It would raise issues bound up with the work and status of schoolteachers – their involvement in the process of constructing and assessing examinable knowledge, and the extent of their alienation from this process. It should also provide a means of focusing on the use of 'assessment' as a method of encouraging competition between schools, and thus its relationship to market ideologies in education.[24] Further to this, it should inform a greater understanding of how schools and teachers have been rendered 'accountable' to different constituencies.

Over the longer term, three principal contestants for control and influence over secondary school examinations may readily be identified: the State, university examining boards, and teachers. Each of these have themselves represented arenas for debate on the best means of exercising and sharing authority in this area. In the late nineteenth century, the State tended to distance itself from secondary school examinations in favour of 'independent' examining bodies dominated by the universities. These examining bodies were responsible for administering 'external' public examinations, and continued in this role into the twentieth century.[25] In 1917, the Secondary School Examinations Council (SSEC) was set up by the Board of Education to co-ordinate secondary school examinations, and to consult the Board on issues of principle and policy. The eight examining bodies were each represented on the SSEC, and maintained a dominant influence. However, the SSEC provided an important forum for debate among rival interests over secondary school examinations.

Secondary school teachers and local education authorities were also represented on the SSEC. It was when Sir Cyril Norwood, as chairman of the SSEC, chose to support the rights of teachers in this sphere that the contestation between the three parties involved became explicit and acute. Norwood argued in favour of teachers asserting greater control over secondary school examinations by setting and marking them within the schools, that is, converting them from being externally-based to becoming 'internal'. This represented a direct challenge to the authority of the examining bodies, from a highly influential quarter within the 'educational state'. The Norwood Report and the debate that surrounded it therefore involved not only controversies over the 'tripartite system' of secondary education, the character of the school curriculum, and the civic goals of education, but also gave rise to a key struggle for control over secondary school examinations that was no less concerned with important educational and social issues.

The Norwood Report's championing of internal examinations, against determined opposition, raises several important issues. The first involves the ideologies and interests that were at stake in this contest: to what extent did the outcome influence power relationships and patterns of authority? The continuing tensions between the State, examining boards, and teachers are central to this first issue. The second is about perceptions of the proper role of school teachers in assessment and examinations, including the perceptions of the school teachers themselves: how far do these relate to the 'legitimated professionalism' that Grace has ascribed to school teachers in the post war years?[26] The Norwood Report seems to suggest a stronger notion of teacher professionalism in which assessment is brought more fully into the domain and control of the teacher. The third issue that needs to be addressed has to do with the notion of 'accountability' reflected in the debate and in its outcome: to what extent did the ultimate failure of the Norwood report in this area represent the defeat of an alternative set of priorities and values?

Norwood and teacher professionalism

The Spens Report of 1938 noted growing criticisms of the School Certificate examination, and of its effects on the curriculum and on the 'healthy growth of mind and body' of many children.[27] Sir Cyril Norwood, as chairman of the SSEC, was determined to go further than this, and to undermine external examinations in favour of internal ones – not only in the new technical and modern schools, but in grammar schools as well. Norwood had developed his views in this area during the 1920s and 1930s as the implications of the strong role of external examinations had become increasingly apparent.[28] In 1932, he had submitted a successful motion at the Headmasters' Conference 'that the school certificate in future cease to be accepted by itself as a sufficient qualification for entrance to a university'. On this occasion, he emphasised the need to give schools 'freedom to experiment', and claimed that 'At present the school certificate with its matriculation requirement was clamped on secondary education like a band of iron, stopping experiment whether in the curriculum or in method, and turning out masses of boys and girls who, through the unsuitability of the machine, had had their intellectual interests deadened.'[29] He was influenced by his public school background in his desire to give schools as much freedom from outside restrictions as possible, and also felt that only a small elite of pupils would be suitable to go on to further studies at the university. But his thinking also placed an emphasis on the needs of learners, which he argued that examinations tended to stifle, and on the potential role of teachers which he felt was being ignored.

Once the Norwood Committee had been established, Norwood lost little opportunity to expound on these views to his colleagues on the committee. He pointed out that 'in all consideration of educational problems the child must be the starting point'. The child, however, could not receive the education which was its due 'unless there were a teaching profession free of controls and inhibitions which hampered the work'. This improvement, he insisted, 'could not take place if secondary school teachers were tied to an external examination'. Thus, according to Norwood, 'A critical moment had occurred for the teaching profession; were teachers to stay where they were at the moment or to advance to real control in education?'[30] It was for this reason that he emphasised to the President of the Board of Education, R.A. Butler, that there was a need to 'reform the teaching profession' in order to ensure the success of the wider reforms.[31] Norwood elaborated on this view later in 1942, while giving evidence to the McNair Committee on teachers and youth leaders. Here, he argued that the status of the teaching profession would not be raised 'until the teachers were given more responsibility and made to face up to it'. Examinations were a key to this development: 'At present teachers taught to an Examination standard which was set by an outside Examining Body. Teachers should themselves be able to work out a scheme of education and to assess it.' If teachers could be trained to take responsibility in this area, he concluded, 'they might in time become a self-governing profession and be esteemed as such'.[32] In other words, by asserting their own control in this sphere of their work, they would be able to acquire a greater degree of professional status.

An especially clear and extended statement of this view was conveyed by Norwood to his committee in a memorandum on the 'internal exam'. He again pressed on them the urgency of radical reform: 'We can as a Committee either stultify ourselves by patching up the fabric, or lead boldly, and attempt to shape the broad outlines of a development which it will take the next two generations to carry out. Now is the time.'[33] Norwood also counselled his committee not to 'repeat the mistake of the Spens Report', which had seen the flaws of the system but had then 'proceeded to patch it up, although for their own child, the Technical High Schools, they planned the more excellent way of an internal examination'. Hence, he concluded: 'Let us be braver and more logical.' In arguing for internal rather than external exams, he stressed two central issues: the guidance of the child, and the freedom of the teacher. If teachers were to assume the 'harder and more skilled' task of guiding their children, 'they must have freedom, and they must have responsibility'. Indeed, he averred, 'Only so can they rise to the status of doctors and lawyers.' On the other hand, 'So long as they accept external control as to what they shall teach and external assessment of the way in which they have taught, they can never rise above the rank of journeymen.' Overall, Norwood concluded, 'Just as the Universities must be free to conduct their own teaching and research within their own domain, so must the school teachers be free in theirs.'[34] All of this suggested a strong notion of teacher responsibility, directly related to the professionalism of the teacher.

Under this kind of pressure, Norwood's Committee moved quickly towards a position of general support for the principle of internal examinations despite continued resistance on the part of some members. By September 1942, it could be noted that, 'at the invitation of the Chairman, each member of the Committee spoke provisionally on the proposal to replace the external examination by an internal examination with external assessment; all expressed opinions in favour of such a change provided that the safeguards which they considered necessary could be satisfactorily devised and operated'.[35] It was envisaged that the 'external assessment' would be carried out 'chiefly by teachers in other areas', and that it would be 'an assessment not of individuals but of the work of the schools and it would not aim at securing "equivalence" among schools'. Such an assessment would be 'a report on the degree of success which a school had achieved (1) in setting before itself a suitable objective, as expressed in syllabuses, (2) in realising that objective'. It was also made clear that 'The assessment would be of value to the teachers concerned and not to the public except indirectly as an assurance to the public that the school was obtaining the benefit of an external opinion on its own examinaions.'[36] This model asserted in the strongest terms teachers' own professional responsibility in the domain of examinations and assessment, against what was later to emerge as the 'market' view of the accountability of teachers and schools to 'the public' for the outcomes of public examinations.

Part Two of the Norwood Report expressed the rationale behind these proposals in cogent and optimistic fashion. It presented alternative views on external examinations, those in favour and those against, and then set out its own proposed scheme. The avowed intention was to transform the School Certificate examination after a transitional period of seven years, by making it 'entirely internal, that is to say, conducted by the teachers at the school on syllabuses and papers framed by themselves'.[37] Ultimately, it hoped, examinations would have only a 'subordinate part' in the school.[38] A new form of School Certificate would involve 'a record of the share which the pupil had taken in the general life of the school, games and societies and the like', together with a record of the pupil's achievement in an examination taken at the end of the school course.[39] The secondary technical school and the secondary modern school would also be free of external examinations, and the 'judgement of the teacher' would play a more important role both on the pupils' entry into secondary school and during their course. It concluded, in terms highly characteristic of Norwood's own earlier claims, that such developments would be in the interests both of the 'individual child' and of the 'increased freedom and responsibility of the teaching profession'.[40] Indeed, it asserted, 'On the basis of wider freedom and greater responsibility rests the increased status which in our opinion the teaching profession should in the future enjoy.'[41]

Such views help to explain the later comments of Sir John Wolfenden, chairman of the SSEC in the 1950s, that the Norwood Report had '"stuck its neck out" quite a long way' on this issue. According to Wolfenden, the Norwood Report had been regarded in its time as an 'advanced and progressive' document that tried to 'introduce more flexibility into the education system, and thereby to give more freedom to the schools'.[42] It was certainly a controversial document that posed a radical challenge, especially to the dominance of the university-based examination boards, and it aroused strong opposition and contestation.

The tyranny of examinations?

Opposition to the proposals put forward by the Norwood Committee was led, predictably enough, by the examination boards. It is noticeable also, however, that teachers' groups were at best lukewarm and often actually hostile in their reactions, and this raises issues about their own perceptions as to the proper role of the teacher.

It is important to note that the Norwood Committee was itself divided over the scope and extent of the reform that was envisaged. Nalder Williams, secretary of the Cambridge Local Examinations Syndicate, was a member of the committee, and he was especially prominent in responding to the views expressed by its chairman. The issue of internal examinations divided the committee from its inception until the autumn of 1942. At its meeting in January 1942, 'no decision was taken' despite a lengthy discussion.[43] At the end of May, Norwood was uncertain of success but clearly determined to press ahead with his ideas, as Butler noted following a private meeting: 'He said that he was not clear what results his Committee would reach about the examination, but that he would attempt to alter the present system. I said that I must leave the matter to him.'[44]

The matter had still not been resolved by July, when Williams circulated his own views to the committee in spirited defence of external examinations in general and the School Certificate in particular. He conceded that it might be necessary for the examination boards to make some concessions, and that a more 'elastic' scheme with more 'reasonable freedom of experiment' could be appropriate. But he also stressed that the structures and relationships surrounding examinations were already well entrenched. Thus, he argued, 'Since 1918 the first school examination has taken firm hold of the mind of teachers, pupils, parents and employers.' Employers attached value to external examinations; parents wanted them; pupils preferred them; and at the same time 'there is a large volume of opinion among teachers in favour of an external examination.'[45] Overall, he claimed, the work of the university examining boards had produced an 'increasingly fruitful partnership' which had become 'a factor of real value in the development of Secondary Education, and reacts in its turn on the University'.[46] Ending this 'disinterested' service might therefore involve 'serious loss to the community'.[47]

While Williams was courteous but firm, critics of the scheme outside the committee were uninhibited in their opposition. According to J.L. Brereton, Assistant Secretary of the Cambridge Local Examinations Syndicate, such examinations were 'an essential part of the machinery of education', rather than a 'necessary evil'.[48] He attacked the Norwood Report in the strongest terms for its proposal to replace external with internal examinations, 'a step which I believe will allow arbitrariness, favouritism, and patronage to raise their ugly heads again, and would cause a much greater disintegration of the secondary system than is yet fully realised'.[49] It came as no surprise that the Oxford and Cambridge examination boards led public opposition to the Norwood proposals. Norwood noted that these boards were in his view 'doing their best to undermine and belittle the Report from pure motives of self-interest',[50] and warned Butler of an attempt to 'sabotage the report, and to throw the older universities into strong opposition'.[51] At the meeting of the SSEC held mainly to receive the Norwood Report, according to Norwood, 'The Secretary of the Cambridge side of the O and C Joint Board had the effrontery to vote that our Report be *not* received – this after refusing to give evidence, or to answer our questions.'[52] It was agreed 'with one dissentient' to receive the Report.[53] This marked the beginning of a war of attrition between the interested parties as the new Ministry of Education redeveloped the examination system. The examining bodies succeeded in their propaganda war to the extent that they helped to undermine the reputation of the Report, and of Norwood himself, in the years following the war.[54] In this contest, the examining boards represented a 'managerial' view of examinations, but were competing with the new Ministry of Education for effective control. They tended to stress public accountability much more than the potential role of teachers. Although they lost some control, temporarily, to the Ministry, they were able to ward off the ideals championed by Norwood.

The views expressed by other educators and teachers as witnesses to the Norwood Committee suggested some important sources of support for the proposed scheme, but also reflected clear reservations. The evidence of industrial and professional bodies encouraged the Norwood Committee to believe that they 'may not be so attached to a general school examination as is supposed'.[55] It was noted, for example, that the firm of Tootal Broadhurst 'would prefer a well-thought-out system of reporting on pupils by schools rather than School Certificate.' Opinion among the Chambers of Commerce was apparently evenly divided for and against the external examination.[56] Observers such as Dr Ernest Barker, Dr Pickard Cambridge, Mr M.L. Jacks, Miss Linda Grier, the Trades Union Congress, the National Association of Inspectors of Schools and Educational Organisers, the Association of Headmistresses of Girls' Boarding Schools, the New Education

Fellowship, and several headteachers and teachers were recorded as favouring an internal examination with external assessors.[57] The Association of Municipal Corporations emphasised a need to 'work towards a solution aimed to achieve a greater freedom in the schools and more responsibility by the staffs of the schools in framing the syllabuses and schemes of work'.[58]

At the same time, most teachers, headteachers and subject associations showed themselves to be somewhat conservative and resistant to such a major reform. Just before the publication of the Norwood Report, Dr Terry Thomas, head of Leeds Grammar School and a member of the committee, expressed his dissent from the internal examination proposal. Norwood attributed this decision to 'pressure' from the Association of Headmasters, although he was comforted by the fact that the other 'active teachers' on the committee accepted the principle of the internal examination.[59] There were other clear indications of unwillingness on the part of teachers and headteachers to support this proposal. For example, Miss W.M. Casswell, Headmistress of Edgbaston High School in Birmingham, pronounced herself to be strongly against the abolition of external examinations: 'An outside examining body is a yardstick of achievement giving a certain standardisation which I think desirable.'[60] Professor Frank Smith, in his oral evidence to the Norwood Committee, was acutely aware of this kind of reluctance on the part of schools and teachers, as he commented that the abolition of the School Certificate was unlikely because '(a) examinations had established themselves in the public mind [and] (b) he was conscious of some unwillingness on the part of teachers to shoulder the responsibility which would fall on them'. Smith emphasised the role of examinations as 'a key, a bad key but real enough, to Opportunity', and added that 'Any substitute for the School Certificate would mean considerable training of teachers and of assessors.'[61]

It is noticeable that subject associations, even those representing subject areas that suffered under the established School Certificate, responded warily and in some cases negatively to Norwood's overtures. The Society for Education in Art, for example, voiced a fear that 'Although theoretically Art would no doubt flourish better and gain new vitality through the removal of the set syllabus of an examination, the subject would not hold its own against the academic subjects unless it were put on a parity with them in an external examination.' It did acknowledge that 'if there were not an external examination in any subjects, the freedom so given would be of benefit to the teachers who would gain much by being able to think for themselves'.[62] Even so, it was more inclined towards caution than to this kind of untried development. The Modern Languages Association, meanwhile, was expressly hostile to the idea as it suggested, with some scorn, that 'such catch-words as "the tyranny of examinations" have been uttered chiefly to bring comfort to the souls of those who are unable to pass them'. In the case of Modern Languages, the Association insisted, teachers were not hampered in their methods by the need to conform to an examination syllabus. In the end, it concluded, 'An examination can be regarded as an educational audit; if the auditor is an external body, the result of its findings commands more respect than an internal audit is likely to do.'[63] Such accountability to a wider public, in the view of the Modern Languages Association, outweighed any advantages that an internal examination might have in its favour.

Reconstructing past and present

Norwood responded to such setbacks by pointing to the views of women teachers, younger teachers, and those 'of weight and distinction' who, he claimed, were 'strongly in favour of internal examination as the way of progress'.[64] It is much more likely, however, that teacher conservatism was overall too strong to sanction such a change. It seems clear that teacher groups by and large favoured the relatively weak notion of 'legitimated professionalism' for school teachers that came through into the post-war period. This preference appears to support the claim put forward by J.C. Matthews that 'teachers seem to rely heavily on the externally prescribed goals of examination results as a prime motivator.'[65] It is in this context that Grace's emphasis on 'the considerable freedom which teachers in the state system experienced in school and classroom autonomy' in this period[66] may need to be modified. The notion of 'legitimated professionalism' conveyed by Grace suggests a willingness on the part of teachers to assert a strong contribution within their own sphere of authority. However, the failure of Norwood's attempt to enlist their support for internal examinations, on precisely these grounds, seems to imply that teachers defined this sphere of authority in a somewhat restricted way that reflected only limited ambitions. It is true that the hopes and ambitions of individual teachers, and of those in different subject areas, may well have differed from those of the groups and associations that were supposed to represent them. Further research would be helpful in developing this theme, in the spirit of Eisenmann's recent demand in the United States for deeper historical inquiry into 'how and what teachers taught in the classroom and how they exercised their professionalism'.[67] It also holds major implications for understanding the professionalism exercised by teachers in the rapidly changing educational and political context of the 1980s and 1990s, especially in relation to the demands of the National Curriculum and the kinds of testing of pupils that have recently been introduced.

Norwood had argued strenuously for a framework within which assessment would be part of the natural domain of teachers' control, together with the school curriculum. He linked this proposal explicitly to an enhancement in the professional authority of school teachers. But his approach failed to win enough support. Politically, more pragmatic opponents and established interests were too powerful to dislodge, and they were able to overcome Norwood's spirited but ephemeral challenge. Ideologically, stronger notions of accountability and the market prevailed over Norwood's emphasis upon the 'judgement of the teacher'. The latter approach was effectively consigned to the outer margins of the educational 'settlement' of the 1940s. As Stewart Mason remarked in Leicester, there were two powerful forces that favoured the more general development of external examinations in the post-war period: 'the parents, who will want a piece of paper of more than local currency to show employers and to some extent the pupils themselves will share their parents' desires in this respect; and those head teachers and their assistants who welcome an external exam as giving their pupils "something to work for", and also as providing a readymade standard of efficiency'.[68] Although the School Certificate examination was replaced in 1951, the use of external examinations to give this 'readymade standard of efficiency' was a central feature of educational developments after the Second World War.

The educational reforms of the 1980s and 1990s have generally tended, at least in their avowed aims, increasingly to strengthen notions of accountability and 'market forces'.[69] Examination boards and the State have maintained the uneasy tension over the management of public examinations that emerged from the 1940s settlement, although with increasing signs of instability in this arrangement. In the contest for control and authority over secondary school examinations in the early 1990s, the State was again in the process of asserting itself. Whereas in the 1940s it had done so on behalf of a notion of 'teacher responsibility', however, in the 1990s it was on behalf of the very different notion of 'public accountability'.

Over the long term, then, the aspirations and ideals represented by Norwood and his committee in the 1940s failed to overcome the ascendancy of the examination boards and the State. In recent times, heated debates over the position of more 'practical' and 'creative' subjects such as music in relation to examinations were a symptom of the decline of alternative notions of curriculum freedom. The idea of teachers' professional responsibility in the domain of assessment, as championed by Norwood, seemed increasingly remote in this context. Norwood's model or ideal can therefore be interpreted as an alternative vision of schooling which was socially and culturally based, and which found some support, but which was crowded out by competing interests and ideologies in and around the educational State, in the wider public discourse and expectations, and among teachers themselves. It represented a notion of responsibility, as distinct from accountability, that indicates something of the contrast between the timbre of the debates of the 1940s and those of the 1990s. The debate over internal examinations in the 1940s, and its eventual outcome, offer both a point of comparison with the developments of the present day, and an alternative vision of the role of the 'judgement of the teacher' whose practical implications remain to be realised. When discussing future power relationships in this area, or when developing particular aspects of the assessment debate, it seems highly important to recall the longer-term framework within which choices have been made and alternatives discarded. Only thus will it be possible to understand fully the assumptions underlying contemporary debates, and in particular their transience, which results in turn from their essentially ideological and contested characteristics.

NOTES

1. See e.g. Richard Bowe and Stephen Ball, *Reforming Education and Changing Schools* (London: Routledge, 1992), esp. Ch.4.
2. R. Dearing, *The National Curriculum and its Assessment: An Interim Report* (NCC/SEAC, 1993), p.5.
3. Ibid., pp.5–6.
4. *TES*, 22 October 1993, report, 'Patten "does trust teachers"'.
5. *The Independent*, 7 September 1992, report, 'Patten accused of scaremongering over GCSE'.

6. *The Independent*, 2 September 1992, editorial, 'Full marks for effort'.
7. *TES*, 9 October 1992, report, 'Another Tarzan sweeps in'.
8. R. Dearing, *The National Curriculum and its Assessment: Final Report* (NCC/SEAC, 1994), p.20.
9. Ibid., pp.20–21.
10. Ibid., p.24.
11. Ibid., p.25.
12. Ibid.
13. E.g. Patricia Broadfoot, *Assessment, Schools and Society* (London: Routledge & Kegan Paul, 1979); and Patricia Broadfoot (ed.), *Selection, Certification and Control: Social Issues in Educational Assessment* (London: Falmer, 1984).
14. E.g. G. Whitty, 'School examinations and the politics of school knowledge', in L. Barton and R. Meighan (eds.), *Sociological Interpretations of Schooling and Classrooms* (Driffield: Nafferton, 1978), pp.129–44.
15. B. Lingard, 'Accountability and control: a sociological account of secondary school assessment in Queensland', in *British Journal of Sociology of Education*, 11 (1990), pp.171–88.
16. D. Willis, 'Educational assessment and accountability: a New Zealand case study', *Journal of Education Policy*, 7 (1992), pp.205–221.
17. J. Roach, *Public Examinations in England, 1850–1900* (Cambridge: Cambridge University Press, 1971).
18. R. MacLeod (ed.), *Days of Judgement: Science, Examinations and the Organisation of Knowledge in Victorian England* (Driffield: Nafferton, 1982); and G. Sutherland, *Ability, Merit and Measurement: Mental Testing and English Education, 1880–1940* (Oxford: Clarendon Press, 1984).
19. P.W. Musgrave, *Whose Knowledge? A Case Study of the Victorian Universities Schools Examinations Board, 1964–79* (London: Falmer, 1988).
20. E.g. M. Lawn and G. Grace (eds.), *Teachers: The Culture and Politics of Work* (London: Falmer, 1987).
21. G. Grace, 'Urban education: policy science or critical scholarship?', in G. Grace (ed.), *Education and the City: Theory, History and Contemporary Practice* (London: Routledge & Kegan Paul, 1984).
22. P. Fisher, *External Examinations in Secondary Schools in England and Wales, 1944–1964* (Leeds: University of Leeds Press, 1982); C. Desforges, *Testing and Assessment* (London: Cassell, 1989); R. Riding and S. Butterfield (eds.), *Assessment and Examinations in the Secondary School* (London: Routledge, 1990).
23. E.g. Ivor Goodson, *The Making of Curriculum* (London: Falmer, 1988).
24. Bowe and Ball, *Reforming Education and Changing Schools* (1992).
25. Roach, *Public Examinations in England*, p.256.
26. G. Grace, 'Teachers and the state in Britain: a changing relation', in Lawn and Grace (eds.), *Teachers*.
27. Spens Report (1938), p.256.
28. See e.g. John Roach, 'Examinations and the secondary schools, 1900–1945', *History of Education*, 8 (1979), pp.45–58; Felicity Hunt, *Gender and Policy in English Education: Schooling for Girls, 1902–1944* (Hemel Hempstead: Harvester, 1991).
29. *The Times*, 23 December 1932, report, 'Matriculation system: headmasters' views'.
30. Norwood Committee, meeting, 26–27 June 1942, minute 6 (IAAM papers, E1/1/file 3).
31. R.A. Butler, note, 28 May 1942 (Board of Education papers, ED.136/681).
32. C. Norwood, memorandum of oral evidence to McNair committee, 29 September 1942 (McNair Committee papers).
33. C. Norwood, memo to Norwood Committee, 'The internal examination' (IAAM papers, E1/2 file 1).
34. Ibid.
35. Norwood Committee, meeting, 1–4 September 1942, minute 4 (IAAM papers), E1/1/file 3).
36. Norwood Committee, meeting, 26–27 June 1942, minute 6 (IAAM papers, E1/1/file 3).
37. Norwood Report (1943), p.140.
38. Ibid., p.45.

39. Ibid., p.48.
40. Ibid., p.140.
41. Ibid., p.45.
42. J. Wolfenden, 'The Secondary School Examinations Council and the evolution of policy on external examinations', in G.B. Jeffery (ed.), *External Examinations in Secondary Schools: Their Place and Function* (London: Harrap, 1958).
43. Norwood Committee, meeting, 5–7 January 1942 (IAAM papers, E1/1/file 3).
44. R.A. Butler, note, 28 May 1942 (Board of Education papers, ED.136/681).
45. W. Nalder Williams, memo, 'Note on proposed changes in the School Certificate examination' (1942) (IAAM papers, E1/2/file 1).
46. W. Nalder Williams, memo, 'University boards and the School Certificate examination' (1942) (IAAM papers, E1/2 file 1).
47. Ibid.
48. J.L. Brereton, *The Case for Examinations: An Account of their Place in Education with some Proposals for their Reform* (Cambridge: Cambridge University Press, 1944).
49. Ibid., p.187.
50. C. Norwood to G.G. Williams, 10 December 1943 (Board of Education papers, ED/12/480).
51. C. Norwood to R.A. Butler, 19 November 1943 (Board of Education papers, ED/12/480).
52. Ibid.
53. SSEC, 103rd meeting, 19 November 1943, minute 12 (Board of Education papers, ED/12/480).
54. See e.g. J.A. Petch, *Fifty Years of Examining: The Joint Matriculation Board, 1903–1953* (London: Harrap, 1953).
55. Norwood Committee, memo, 'Brief summary of views on the School Certificate examination' (IAAM papers, E1/2 file 2).
56. Ibid.
57. Ibid.
58. Association of Municipal Corporations, memo to Norwood Committee (1942) (IAAM papers, E1/3 file 1).
59. C. Norwood to R.A. Butler, 23 June 1943 (Board of Education papers, ED/136/681).
60. W.H. Casswell, memo to Norwood Committee (1942) (IAAM papers, E1/4 file 3).
61. F. Smith, oral evidence to Norwood Committee, 26–27 June 1942 (IAAM papers, E1/1 file 3).
62. Society for Education in Art, memo to Norwood Committee (1942) (IAAM papers, E1/1 file 3).
63. Modern Languages Association, memo to Norwood Committee (1942) (IAAM papers, E1/3 file 1).
64. C. Norwood, memo to Norwood Committee, 'The internal examination' (1942) (IAAM papers, E1/2 file 1).
65. J.C. Matthews, *Examinations: A Commentary* (London: George Allen and Unwin, 1985), p.23.
66. G. Grace, 'Teachers and the state in Britain: a changing relation', in Lawn and Grace (eds.), *Teachers* p.212.
67. L. Eisenmann, 'Teacher professionalism: a new analytical tool for the history of teachers', *Harvard Educational Review*, 61 (1991), p.224.
68. S. Mason to R.H. Charles, 5 March 1946 (Ministry of Education papers, ED/147/133).
69. E.g. Department for Education, *Choice and Diversity* (1992).

9

Antipodean Echoes

'Educational reconstruction' contains resonances that are comparative and international no less than national in character. The long-term frameworks of interpretation within which the 1944 Education Act may be located are also potentially to be found much further afield than within Britain itself. Change, continuity, and contestation in the influence of the Act are evident not only over time, but also over spatial distance. In this chapter, the similarities and differences of education in New Zealand are explored in order to begin to assess the extent to which the Antipodes provide echoes and reverberations of 'Home'.

Although located on the other side of the world, some 12,000 miles away, New Zealand has been strongly influenced by English attitudes, customs and traditions since being created a British colony under the Treaty of Waitangi in 1840. New Zealand society has been dominated by European settlers and their descendants (known as *pakehas*), often at the expense of the indigenous Maori population. In adopting British values and practices, educational institutions and processes in general and schools in particular were central to the colonisation of New Zealand. It might be expected, therefore, that the overall historical framework of changes in English education would have found especially strong echoes and reverberations in the case of New Zealand. There are certainly clear similarities that may be discerned in the reforms that took place, in New Zealand as in England, in the 1940s, and also in subsequent developments in the 1960s and the 1980s/1990s. On the other hand, educational reform in New Zealand has also involved important local and specific factors that modify, and to some extent challenge, straightforward assumptions about global patterns or colonial assimilation.

Serpent in the garden?

The essentially colonial characteristics of education in New Zealand have long attracted comment. The growth of modern schooling in Britain and the dissemination of its educational ideals and practices had a crucial impact on the character and structures of schooling in

New Zealand, the furthest outpost of the Empire, that continued into the twentieth century. The precedents of established institutions, the practices of schools and teachers, the traditions that underpinned and rationalised a wide variety of educational arrangements all had their sources in full or in part in what was widely regarded as 'Home'.

Equally to the point, such ideals and practices were continued or else adapted in subtle ways by teachers who themselves had in many cases been educated and trained in Britain, with textbooks that often came from Britain, for examinations based largely on British experience, values, and culture. A.E. Campbell, later Director-General of Education, suggested in 1941 that 'the education system of New Zealand as it stands today is incomprehensible unless one bears ever in mind that it originated and developed in a British colony in the nineteenth century'.[1] He emphasised the nostalgia of the colonists for their homeland which contributed to their desire to surround themselves 'with a barrier of familiar social institutions':

> If they could not surround themselves immediately with the flowers and trees and quiet hills of England, they could at least transplant the forms of social life with which they were familiar, and which they needed to assuage the homesickness that almost every colonist carries with him to the end. Just because they sought new worlds they did not necessarily seek a new way of life.[2]

For this reason, Campbell concluded, 'the historical principle of maintaining cultural continuity played a greater part in forming the education system of New Zealand than did the geographical principle of adaptation to a new environment'.[3] The school curriculum no less than the visible structures of the education system also bore unmistakable marks of the colonial past. According to J.L. Ewing, a prominent official and curriculum specialist, 'Trends in educational thought in Great Britain have naturally enough given the main leads to curriculum change in New Zealand. Sometimes it has taken a decade or more before new ideas and their implications for the classroom have filtered into the New Zealand system and become generally accepted; sometimes our response has been immediate.'[4]

This importation did not have uniform, linear or predictable results. The British connection was responsible for many ingrained traditions that proved highly resistant to change, but it also produced some of New Zealand's leading educational reformers of the twentieth century such as James Shelley, Peter Fraser and C.E. Beeby. Clearly, however, neither the origins nor the tradition of reform of New Zealand schooling is explicable without reference to its colonial context.

Often, too, there was an idealised and distinctly unreal quality about the images of England that were influential in New Zealand education. For example, F.B. Malim, visiting New Zealand in the 1940s, enthused over the English features of the leading independent schools. Of Christ's College in Christchurch, Malim remarked that 'Her grey walls and her elms suggest a civilisation more peaceful and stable than seems likely to be the portion of the New Zealand of today, and they remind us of an England with foundations still unshaken by the invention of the internal combustion engine.'[5] Malim's observations also highlighted something of the missionary zeal with which English educators had transported their own cultural baggage. He was especially glowing about Waitaki Boys' High School:

> The whole school is a museum devoted to the history of Britain. There is a special memorial to Captain Scott and those who died with him in the Antarctic icefields. The features of Nelson and Wellington, Roberts and Haig are familiar to every boy. There are reproductions of the historical cartoons in the Royal Exchange; fine railway posters of English Cathedrals; Medici prints, autograph letters of Queen Elizabeth. Every room and every passage is full of pictures, letters, caricatures, and most of them are intended to illustrate what Britain is and what Britain has done, to arouse pride and emulation in the heirs of this great heritage.[6]

This would appear to conform to J.A. Mangan's account of the 'imperial diffusion' of English traditions, for example in India where 'the British clung faithfully to the familiar educational blueprint which served their own upper classes so well'.[7] Mangan's work has placed particular emphasis upon the crucial role played by the 'public school administrator, missionary and educationist spread throughout the imperial world, more often than not imbued with a sense of moral commitment and muscular enthusiasm'.[8]

It is possible also to detect a rough equivalence in the kinds of educational reform developed in New Zealand and Britain at different stages of the twentieth century. In New Zealand as in Britain, the 1940s witnessed a wide-ranging attempt to extend secondary education to new groups, and to stress the role of education in augmenting citizenship. In the 1980s and 1990s, similarly, educational reforms often characterised as 'New Right' sought to emphasise the potential importance of the free market in education, while also reasserting state control in certain key areas.

The reforms of the first Labour government in New Zealand, from 1935 onwards, encouraged the ideal of equality of opportunity in education. This was articulated in particular by Peter Fraser as Minister of Education. Fraser abolished the Proficiency Examination in 1936, thus paving the way for free secondary education for all, and helped to establish a greater priority for schooling as a social service. The first sentence of his annual report as Minister of Education in 1939 was to become a basic tenet of schooling in New Zealand, its most often expressed official rationale, in favour of a 'free education of the type to which individual pupils were best fitted and to the fullest extent of their powers'.[9] Dr C.E. Beeby, Director of Education from 1940 until 1960, was also partly responsible for the growth of a system that envisaged both the 'education of the whole child' and the aspiration of equal opportunity for all. External examinations were altered to cater for the needs and abilities of a wider range of students, the curriculum was expanded in both primary and secondary schools, and special provisions were made for 'disadvantaged' students: 'country children, the Maori people, the handicapped, those with special difficulties in basic subjects, those with problems in the home and those in need of guidance'.[10]

In the late 1980s and early 1990s, too, the major reforms of the education system that were brought about in New Zealand were broadly similar to those that were being developed in Britain at the same time. Under David Lange's Labour government from 1987 onwards, educational administration was restructured to place a greater emphasis than hitherto on the initiative of individual learning institutions, as opposed to the authority of the State.[11] School zones were weakened, and eventually abolished, to assert the importance of consumer choice in a free market.[12] Such policies were extended further after the National Party (historically more conservative than Labour) was returned to power in 1990, although with increasing recourse to centralising measures such as the national curriculum introduced from 1992.[13]

It was not difficult to draw a clear distinction between a liberal-egalitarian tradition of New Zealand education policy, especially in relation to the reforms of the 1930s/1940s, and the general thrust of policies in the 1980s/1990s. Gerald Grace in particular has suggested that the New Zealand tradition of regarding education as a 'public good mediated through a publicly provided service' is 'currently under challenge from agencies which want to assert that education is a commodity in the market-place like any other'.[14] More specifically, Grace argues that while Fraser's statement of 1939 may be read as the 'founding charter of New Zealand's modern education policy', the Treasury briefing to the incoming Labour government in 1987 represented 'an attempt to displace that charter and to establish a new one in its place'.[15] Again, the historical framework established here seems reminiscent of that developed in Britain by critics who have compared the recent reforms unfavourably with those associated with the Education Act of 1944.

At the same time, there are many important specificities and differences in the New Zealand situation that cannot be merely 'read off' from the British case. In particular, the egalitarian impulse underlying New Zealand reforms in the twentieth century seems to have been on the whole markedly stronger, and more broadly influential, than similar aspirations in Britain. Reforms that took place in New Zealand in the 1960s seemed intended mainly to reaffirm the 'settlement' of the 1930s–1940s, rather than to revise it as tended to be the case in the British context.[16] While the reforms of the 1940s got under way 'earlier' in New Zealand than in Britain, those of the 1980s–1990s began 'later' and were arguably carried through more rapidly and more thoroughly. Geographical and political differences help to account for many of these discrepancies. In the 1940s, for example, liberal-egalitarian aspirations combined with the economics of small local communities to favour multilateral post-primary schools rather than the tripartite model that became established in Britain. In the 1980s, the centralised political structure and small elite network made it easier for free market ideologies to spread and gain an effective ascendancy.

It may be argued, indeed, that in many instances educational reform developed in New Zealand in explicit opposition to the trends identified as being associated with the 'Old Country'. The liberal-egalitarian thrust of New Zealand education policies could be contrasted with the class-based, differentiated and hierarchical structures of schooling in England. This worked in two ways: English traditions could be invoked by those discontented with the ideals of New Zealand education policies, while reformers such as Tawney could be drawn on in selective ways to support the dominant trends. It was common for those extolling the virtues of education in New Zealand to emphasise its advantages over that of class-divided England. According to the Director of Education T.B. Strong in 1928, for example:

> I am told that the teaching profession in England suffers even to the present day the humiliating effects of the old-time perfunctory provision for the education of the masses. There are still localities in England where the teacher has little or no social standing. In the Dominions, fortunately, the trend has been for the teacher to occupy an honoured position in society, and this fact has undoubtedly operated to the benefit of the schools. One cause, or it may be the effect of this, is the high social regard in which our 'public schools' are held.[17]

This flattering contrast allowed Strong to conclude stirringly: 'Wherever you may go you will find the children of rich and poor side by side, the child of the Cabinet Minister, of the Clergyman or the University Professor occupying the same public school bench as the child of the street sweeper or the casual labourer, and long may such democratic ideas flourish in the land.'[18] Meanwhile, conservatives tended to paint the ingrained social purposes and structural differentiation of the English education system in more complimentary colours to provide a respectable source of right-wing opinion, and to discredit the egalitarianism towards which New Zealand education policies tended to lean.

The egalitarian ideologies prominent in New Zealand education were in some senses akin to those of Scotland, which had also developed partly from opposition to English traditions and precepts. Robert Anderson notes an 'advanced and distinctive educational tradition' in Scotland that could be traced back to the Reformation, which nineteenth-century Scots considered to be 'both a point of superiority over England and a guarantee of Scotland's social and cultural autonomy within the Union'.[19] According to Anderson, the Scottish 'democratic myth' of education became a vital part 'both of the Scottish sense of nationhood and of the image which others have formed of the Scots'.[20] Underlying the 'myth' there were many unresolved problems and deep-seated inequalities that usually went unacknowledged,[21] while English-based structures and expectations increasingly encroached upon educational institutions north of the border to undermine the distinctive character and independence of the Scottish tradition. In New Zealand, the threat of such encroachment was more distant and yet at the same time more insidious. The English cultural origin of the New Zealand education system and its continued influence through the importa-

tion of the latest ideas, practices, teachers and texts posed a constant
threat to the integrity of New Zealand's egalitarian myth.

In many ways, therefore, New Zealand and Scotland faced a
common educational enemy. It was far from a coincidence that it
was a Scottish visitor, Dr William Boyd, who warned most clearly
of the dangers of the English influence at the New Education
Fellowship Conference held in New Zealand in July 1937. According to Boyd, 'With all the differences between the two national
systems there is so much common ground that we can help each
other to a fuller understanding of the big essential principles in
education and even, it may be, of some of their practical implications.'[22] The key problem facing New Zealand education, he
argued, was the influence of the English tradition, which had
already had a major impact at a structural level: 'the serpent in the
garden is the English influence in New Zealand education which
has demoralised your institutions.'[23] Rather than developing along
'good Scotch lines', Boyd continued, New Zealand education was
based on 'the English separation between primary and secondary
education'. This encouraged differentiation and selection at the
secondary school level: 'Your high schools, rather of the English
sort, were meant for an aristocracy, a selected group, and the old
primary schools for the common or ordinary people. This is the
English principle as opposed to the Scotch practice of having a
primary system which grows into a secondary system and forms a
satisfactory unity.'[24] To address this problem, Boyd strongly urged
that the secondary school curriculum should become less 'orientated
towards the university' and more a 'preparation for ordinary
living', and he advocated as a 'practical reform' towards this end
'the scrapping of matriculation – it simply perpetuates the hold of
the old dead culture on the schools of today'.[25]

The case of the Thomas Report

The Thomas Report on the post-primary curriculum, published in
1944, demonstrates the contested character of the English cultural
influence on the New Zealand educational reforms of the 1940s.
The committee responsible for the Report was established by C.E.
Beeby as Director of Education in November 1942. It was chaired
by William Thomas, ex-Rector of Timaru Boys' High School.
Thomas had already worked with Beeby in producing the book
Entrance to the University in 1939,[26] and they now joined forces
again to assert the general direction of post-primary education at a

crucial stage in its development. An increasing proportion of young people were entering post-primary schools following the abolition of the Proficiency Examination in 1936. As in England, this raised the issue of what sort of curriculum would be suitable for post-primary schools intended not only for the 'elite' but for the bulk of the population. Beeby anticipated that the School Certificate examination would soon become the measure of a completed post-primary school course, and therefore that 'In effect the control of the post-primary curriculum will pass over from the University to the Department and the change may well mark a turning point in post-primary education.'[27] The Thomas Committee was to stipulate both the choice of subjects and the content of these subjects for the School Certificate examination. It represented Beeby's chosen method for extending the control of the Education Department over post-primary education, and also for channelling post-primary education into a particular direction.

In these circumstances, the Thomas Committee aimed to define the character of a post-primary curriculum that would be appropriate for the whole age-range. Beeby insisted in his initial instructions to the committee members that 'the Government's definite policy is that the general interests of the pupils must not be sacrificed to the special needs of the few'. He added: 'The Department is anxious to maintain high academic standards for the scholarly but even this end must not be allowed to interfere with the schools' main function of giving a full and realistic education to the bulk of the population, culturally and economically, for the world of today. The Department would, however, welcome the Committee's advice on the best method of combining these two functions in the one institution.'[28] The committee's response was to recommend a core curriculum for post-primary schools. Unlike its equivalent in England, the Norwood Committee, it endorsed a multilateral arrangement for post-primary schools, and was also willing to prescribe and enforce a common curriculum. The Thomas Report announced a clear intention 'to ensure, as far as possible, that all post-primary pupils, irrespective of their varying abilities and their varying occupational ambitions, receive a generous and well balanced education' that would aim 'firstly, at the full development of the adolescent as a person; and secondly, at preparing him for an active place in our New Zealand society as worker, neighbour, homemaker, and citizen'.[29] It emphasised the need to 'cater for pupils of widely differing abilities and interests', but argued that this would not 'sacrifice the interests of the intellectually bright minority', since: 'We have in mind no "levelling down" process, but rather a state of affairs in which academic specialisation is a functional development from a broad and realistic course and not an impediment to balanced intellectual growth.'[30]

During 1943, as the committee was drafting its Report, some newspapers tried to promote popular opposition to its plans, and did so by emphasising the parallels and contrasts with the reforms that were being developed in Britain. The Auckland-based *New Zealand Herald* was especially active in this way, leading the Minister of Education, H.G.R. Mason, to note privately to Beeby that it was 'conducting a fairly persistent campaign against a syllabus it has not seen'.[31] The *New Zealand Herald* viewed the Thomas Committee as a dangerous and secretive elite group that was likely to take New Zealand further away from its English roots, and to emulate the 'lamentably ill-advised' features of education in the United States.[32] By contrast, it observed, 'It is a notable fact that the British White Paper on Educational Reconstruction which was published earlier this year proposes nothing revolutionary.'[33] Thus, the *New Zealand Herald* represented the proposals for reform in Britain as modest, conservative, and along established lines, and sought thereby to undermine the proposals that were being developed by the Thomas Committee. What it called the 'impenetrable veil of secrecy' around the Thomas Committee attracted similar criticisms: 'Vital aspects of the country's education system should not be transacted in hole-and-corner fashion. In Britain the Minister has laid the whole subject open for popular discussion in a White Paper . . . Mr Mason even yet could and should follow these free and democratic methods in the process of hammering out the heads of secondary school reform.'[34] Following the publication of the Thomas Report in February 1944, its ideas were compared unfavourably with the views expressed by the Norwood Report:

> Overseas authorities are treading away from the doctrines of self-expression. Sir Cyril Norwood's committee found that 'human personality contains many possibilities; some are worthy to be developed, some are not'. A need is seen for setting standards. Emphasis is being thrown less on individual right and sovereignty and more on citizenship and social duty. The committee's recommendations should be examined to discover the balance struck between the two objects and to determine whether it is a true and sound balance.[35]

Such criticisms did not, however, lead to any changes in the proposals, and Beeby quickly set about implementing the Report.[36]

William Anderson, Professor of Philosophy at Auckland University College, also made a strong attack on the principles of the Thomas Report in a widely circulated pamphlet entitled *The Flight from Reason in New Zealand Education*. Anderson protested against a 'growth of educational bureaucracy' and a likely decline in academic standards.[37] He also made a direct comparison between the New Zealand scheme and the educational reforms that were being developed in England: 'England preserves the grammar school; New Zealand liquidates it. According to England the fully academic course is essential for some; according to New Zealand it is good for nobody.'[38] This meant, he declared, that 'only those New Zealanders wealthy enough to send their children to Australia or England for their schooling will be able to obtain what has hitherto been the right of all, a grammar-school education'.[39] In general, he concluded, 'The Report represents the climax of a movement that has been going on for many years and has by now subverted well-nigh all the traditional standards of schooling in this country.'[40] Again, however, this critique had little effect on the Report or on general education policy in New Zealand.

The Thomas Report remained the basis for the secondary school curriculum in New Zealand into the 1990s, although it did not achieve all that its authors had anticipated. A.E. Campbell, who according to Beeby 'wrote most of the original Report',[41] noted in 1958 that 'we still have a great volume of dull factual teaching and the bad sort of authoritarianism, much neglect of individual differences, and so on'. Moreover, he suggested, 'the "core" rarely gets the flexible and imaginative treatment we had in mind and . . . at its worst it is a uniform "course"'.[42] The impact of the Report was limited by the failure of teachers to follow it through and by the social and economic pressures for such qualifications.[43] Also, in practice, the 'common core' subjects were open to different kinds of interpretation, allowing a more 'academic' treatment in some schools and a more 'multi-lateral' approach in others.[44] Even so, in spite of these major discrepancies between policy and practice, it was still possible to claim that the egalitarian ethos of the Thomas Report was the guiding spirit of the post-primary school curriculum, and Beeby himself was energetic in emphasising this. While in their general contours the reforms of the 1940s were closely related to those that were developed in Britain at the same time, they also encouraged a distinctive New Zealand educational tradition that was both more centralised and more egalitarian in its character.[45]

Education for citizenship?

Again as in the British example, the New Zealand reforms of the 1940s emphasised the notion of education for citizenship. On the other hand, this too was articulated in distinctive fashion, especially through the development of a new subject entitled 'Social Studies', despite the often central influence of ideas, resources and educators imported from Britain.

It was the British experience and model of change that provided the clearest influence on the reform of the New Zealand geography curriculum at this time. A widely circulated 'Memorandum on the Teaching of Geography', produced in Britain by the Incorporated Association of Assistant Masters in Secondary Schools, helped to inspire curriculum reformers at the other end of the world. This memorandum acknowledged that Geography had often been seen as the 'Cinderella of school subjects, despised and hated alike by those who had to learn it and by those who had to teach it against their will'.[46] However, its authors felt able to celebrate a 'revolutionary change' in the teaching of Geography through which 'New principles have been adopted, new ideas introduced, new teaching methods have replaced the old and are now established in the majority of schools.'[47] Thanks to these changes, it claimed, 'the position of Geography has been greatly advanced in schools of all types and in the universities throughout the country'.[48] The scope and rationale of the subject had been clarified, according to the memorandum, through the regional method developed at the beginning of the century by A.J. Herbertson. This had involved a shift in the focus of Geography from 'the consideration of the world as the theatre of natural phenomena', to 'that of the world as the home of man'.[49]

Herbertson's regional method was attractive as an alternative to what was often tagged the 'capes and bays' approach to Geography. This latter approach gave attention mainly to the physical environment, and tended to be based mainly on geology and topography. It was increasingly criticised as being responsible not only for the low status and unpopularity of the subject within schools, but also for the lack of a separate identity or institutional base at the university level. By contrast the regional approach promised a systematic and coherent course of study that was independent of other disciplines.[50] It could therefore help to justify an enhanced role for Geography in the school curriculum, and also stengthened the case for an independent place for Geography in the universities, separate from Geology and other established departments.

The kinds of criticism expressed in Britain also had resonance in New Zealand in the 1930s. Geography courses developed in the university colleges and teacher training colleges were based on geology and topography. There were frequent complaints also that school Geography was too superficial, based too much on a descriptive approach to the physical environment, and taught by teachers without any special training in geography. Such criticisms became increasingly articulate and potent when they could point to examples of successful reform overseas, especially in Britain, and when a subject teaching association based in New Zealand began to spread the word about a coherent alternative to 'capes-and-bays-topography'.[51]

Products of the 'new geography' in Britain were in an especially strong position to encourage similar developments in New Zealand. Kenneth Cumberland, probably the leading reformer of the Geography curriculum in the 1940s, derived much of his message from his background and experience in Britain. He had studied at University College, Nottingham, and graduated with honours in Geography at London in 1935. For the next three years he worked as an assistant lecturer in the Department of Geography at University College, London, before taking his Masters degree. He came to New Zealand in 1938 on being appointed to a lectureship in Geography at Canterbury University College.[52] Cumberland's criticisms of the school geography syllabus were strongly influenced by the reforms that had already taken place in the British Geography curriculum. 'The teaching of geography in New Zealand schools', he declared to a London publisher at the start of 1939, 'is in relation to English standards, relatively new and still rather primitive.'[53] School Geography, he argued, should no longer be seen as 'a cyclopaedic list of places and products'.[54] The Geography courses on offer at Canterbury were also revised and extended. Revised second- and third-year prescriptions were introduced in 1940, reflecting the influence of the 'new' regional approach to geography.[55] The following year a new MA honours course in Geography was put in place, largely based on that of the University of London. It is fair to add that as well as such obvious British influences, there were also links with 'progressive' elements in American geography, especially through journals like the *Geographical Review* and scholars such as Robert Bowman and Andrew Clark visiting Canterbury.

Of equal importance to these developments in the longer term were the efforts of a small group of enthusiasts based in Christchurch. A new grouping was advertised in 1939 as a Geographical Association in Christchurch that would constitute 'a Branch of the Geographical Association (Manchester)'.[56] The 'Memorandum on the teaching of Geography' published in London in 1935 had recommended local enthusiasts to adopt precisely this course of action,[57] and this advice had been heeded as far away as Canterbury. It was intended that this new Association would further the interests of geography through lectures, discussion classes, excursions and local surveys. It was also founded as a mediating body that sought to unite teachers in schools and universities behind a radical notion of the Geography curriculum. In March 1940, a further step was taken towards these aims through the Association's formation of a study group on Geography in schools. This group exemplified the mediating role of the subject association in that its members represented teachers in different types of educational institutions in the Christchurch area. It also extended the radicalising influence of its parent body by formulating a new Geography syllabus for all levels of the education system. These proposals attracted increasing attention as a new way of defining the subject. At the same time, the association came to assume a role in defending the interests of the subject especially in relation to the Thomas Report of 1944.

The reforming vision of the study group matched up with the social concerns that were becoming fashionable in wartime New Zealand, and this was especially important in putting its message across to a wider public. The emphasis on citizenship in the group's syllabuses was also prominent in the rhetoric surrounding the war effort against a totalitarian enemy. The urgent need for local planning and surveys and for resource conservation were further aspects that highlighted the relevance of geography. The study group was active in investigating land utilisation in its local area, and Cumberland's own research on agricultural land use had important practical implications. Geography could be presented as a means of taking control of 'a social and geographical laboratory in which its people have been trying out a series of unplanned and uncontrolled experiments in the modification and adaptation of natural resources'.[58] It also had clear relevance to an understanding of the war itself. The global dimensions of the conflict heightened the geographical awareness of the New Zealand public. The changing place of New Zealand itself in relation to the rest of the world was equally topical, first with the celebration of the centenary of the founding of the colony in 1840, and then with the developing fortunes of Britain and the United States as the war progressed.[59]

The activities of the study group established an effective point of reference for criticisms of the existing Geography syllabus, and a platform for demands for change. For example, they provided an important opportunity for the work of B.J. Garnier, a young Cambridge graduate in Geography, during the war years. Garnier had come to the attention of the Canterbury group in 1939. Cumberland was especially interested in his qualifications which emphasised the 'political and economic elements of geography' rather than cartography,[60] and Garnier's account of the problems and needs of school Geography strongly reflected the criticisms and prescriptions of the study group on Geography in schools. He emphasised the importance of regional geography, which he claimed led students to a sympathetic understanding of human groups in different parts of the world. According to Garnier, regional geography helped in reaching judgements on national and international affairs, provided a necessary background to the enjoyment of leisure, was consistent with modern trends in geography, and was suited to the mental development and interests of the average boy and girl. He also called for a greater place for Geography in the university colleges to prepare specialist Geography teachers. Overall, he declared:

> By accepting the concept of geography as a human study and by giving practical expression to the high aim which it embodies of seeing all men in a world perspective, teachers in New Zealand may justifiably claim that they are making a contribution, small perhaps, but none the less worthwhile, towards the creation of a world free from the jealousies, hates, angers, and misunderstandings which have, for so long, marred human progress.[61]

Garnier's book, *Geography for Post-Primary Pupils*, amounted to a manifesto for the new geography in New Zealand schools.

The idealism of Garnier's book, with its concern for citizenship and international co-operation, was equally evident in the Thomas Report on the post-primary school curriculum which was published in the same year (1944). The two documents reflected reforming activities that had been going on at quite different levels. Although they shared general aims and values in relation to the school curriculum, they parted company on how to achieve their desired goals. The Thomas Committee, which lacked a specialist geographer, sought a broad and integrated approach to the problem of how to educate pupils for future citizenship. It therefore recommended that History and Geography should be combined in the core curriculum to form the new subject of Social Studies. Garnier and his colleagues, by contrast, preferred to maintain the independence and integrity of Geography as a subject with its own identity. In response to the curriculum policies formulated by the State, Geography teachers looked to an alternative forum which would not only defend but also re-define their subject. The Thomas Committee's endorsement of a new and potentially rival subject that would usurp some of Geography's territory, effectively strengthened demands for a national organisation to pool the resources of the existing local branches and represent the interests of geography teachers. It was in this context that the New Zealand Geographical Society was formed in 1944, a subject association that continued to exist into the 1990s.

Hence, the character of 'education for citizenship' in the reforms of the 1940s was strongly contested between opposing groups. The Thomas Committee, unlike the Norwood Committee in Britain, supported the development of Social Studies for this purpose. The 'new geographers', taking their cue both from developments in their subject based in Britain and from the ideas of the Norwood Committee, strove to maintain the independence of Geography in the school curriculum. Again, therefore, a broad similarity in outlook concealed significant differences in strategy and outcomes in New Zealand and Britain, which served to reinforce notions of a distinctive educational ethos in the former colony despite the clear Antipodean echoes.

New directions

The historical framework that has been sketched out in this chapter asserts an important role for influences from overseas, in this case specifically from Britain. At the same time, it emphasises the specific local characteristics of the New Zealand situation. No less important, it also highlights the contestation involved within and between these spheres: conflicting images of the 'English tradition', for example, or debates over the distinctive ethos of New Zealand education, or the interplay and tensions between international and local influences.

Such considerations raise doubts over some ways in which recent and contemporary education policies have been depicted, and suggest possible new directions for their interpretation. In relation to the role of the 'New Right' in New Zealand education, it seems inadequate to subordinate the historical values, traditions and structures of New Zealand schooling to 'the prolonged economic crisis in Western Capitalism' within which some commentators have located 'New Right' theory.[62] On such a model, the key historical determinants and conditions for the rise to prominence of the 'New Right' are said to exist *outside* New Zealand, rather than within New Zealand's own historical experience. This view encourages a tendency to 'read off' the issues and policies of con-temporary New Zealand from what is happening elsewhere. It also tends to marginalise the history, to ignore its importance for an understanding of contemporary problems.

Nor does it seem appropriate to portray current developments in terms of hitherto unknown influences from overseas disrupting the steady improvement of educational provisions built up over the past century. Ivan Snook suggests a 'dialectic' between 'universal New Right theory' and 'local beliefs, values and institutions'.[63] In this version, a 'long-standing commitment to equality', a tradition of a strong welfare state, the co-existence of Maori and *pakeha* with a 'deep-seated belief in "one people" living in harmonious relations', and New Zealand's specific version of church–state relations in education, are contrasted with the foreign philosophy of the 'New Right'.[64] Such a view tends to idealise New Zealand's educational past, and fails to explain the kinds of criticism put forward for example by the *New Zealand Herald* in the 1940s, or the alternative models represented in the grammar schools of Auckland.[65] It also portrays the indigenous and imported traditions as fundamentally monolithic and unchanging. In other words, it fails to show the contested and changing character of the 'traditions' involved.

In going beyond these models towards a greater awareness of historical, international, and contested dimensions of New Zealand education, it seems very useful to relate the policies of the present to past attempts to define and articulate a distinctive educational tradition. This is clearly important when seeking to understand the policies that were put forward in the 1960s, especially in the Currie Report of 1962, which heavily underscored the precepts that had been developed in the 1930s and 1940s by Fraser and Beeby. Secure in these values and in their general acceptance, the Currie Commission saw the education system gradually evolving towards their practical realisation.[66]

It is possible also to read the education policies of the late 1980s, at least in part, in terms of an attempt to re-work the egalitarian aims of schooling that had provided a strong sense of purpose earlier in the century. 'Equality of opportunity' as envisaged by Fraser and the Currie Report appeared to be almost played out as a potent 'myth' motivating the development of schooling. The Picot Report and related policy developments of the late 1980s lent themselves instead to an emphasis on 'equity', or equality of results or of outcome. Under a new charter framework applied to every school in the country, 'equity objectives' were to 'underpin all activities' in schools, whose policies and practices would 'seek to achieve equitable outcomes for students of both sexes, for rural and urban students; for students from all religious, ethnic, cultural, social, family and class backgrounds, and for all students irrespective of their ability or disability'. This, it affirmed, would represent *genuine* equality of educational opportunity, to 'ensure equal opportunity for all students to participate and succeed in the full range of school activities'.[67]

The case-study of New Zealand may not be strictly applicable elsewhere, because of its particularly close historical relationship with Britain. Even so, it raises important issues that may be no less interesting when related to other national experiences. The relationship between 'cultural continuities' and 'global movements' is one such theme: how far were British influences directly responsible for the educational reforms that took place in many different countries in the 1940s, and how far were the influences truly international in nature? The nature of the influences involved is another key problem, as we seek to identify international networks and the ways in which these have interrelated with local individuals and groups. Lastly, disputes between opposing interests and values seem to have been crucial underlying factors in determining the kinds of echoes of British educational reconstruction that were heard especially loudly in the Antipodes. The processes involved in such contestation are again worthy of extended study, to find out how the reforms of the 1940s reverberated in their effects across space no less than through time.

NOTES

1. A.E. Campbell, *Educating New Zealand* (Wellington: Department of Internal Affairs, 1941), p.1.
2. Ibid., p.3.
3. Ibid., p.6.
4. J.L. Ewing, 'Curriculum development in New Zealand: an introductory survey', in *Education*, 17 (1968), p.10.

5. F.B. Malim, *Almae Matres: Recollections of Some Schools at Home and Abroad* (Cambridge: CUP, 1948), p.160.
6. Ibid., p.163.
7. J.A. Mangan, 'Eton in India: the imperial diffusion of a Victorian educational ethic', *History of Education*, 7/2 (1978), p.110.
8. J.A. Mangan, *The Games Ethic and Imperialism: Aspects of the Diffusion of an Ideal* (London: Viking, 1986), p.69.
9. Department of Education, *Annual Report*, 1939.
10. C.E. Beeby, 'The place of myth in educational change', *New Zealand Listener*, 8 November 1986.
11. See e.g. A. Jones, G. McCulloch, J. Marshall, G. Smith and L. Smith, *Myths and Realities: Schooling in New Zealand* (Palmerston North: Dunmore, 1990), and *Access*, vol.7 (1988), special issue, 'Picot and beyond'.
12. Gary McCulloch, 'School zoning, equity and freedom: the case of New Zealand', *Journal of Education Policy*, 6/2 (1991), pp.155–68.
13. Gary McCulloch (ed.), *The School Curriculum in New Zealand: History, Theory, Policy and Practice* (Palmerston North: Dunmore, 1992).
14. Gerald Grace, 'The New Zealand Treasury and the commodification of education', in Sue Middleton, John Codd and Alison Jones (eds.), *New Zealand Education Policy Today: Critical Perspectives* (Wellington: Allen & Unwin, 1990), p.27.
15. Gerald Grace, 'Labour and education: the crises and settlements of education policy', in Martin Holland and Jonathan Boston (eds.), *The Fourth Labour Government* (Auckland, 2nd edn, 1990), p.168.
16. On the significance of policy developments in the 1960s, such as the role of the Currie Commission on education in 1962, see Gary McCulloch, 'The ideology of educational reform: an historical perspective', in Middleton, Codd and Jones (eds.), *New Zealand Education Policy Today*, pp.53–67.
17. T.B. Strong, 'Present trend of education', in I. Davey (ed.), *Fifty Years of National Education in New Zealand, 1877–1928* (Wellington, 1928), p.145.
18. Ibid.
19. Robert Anderson, *Education and Opportunity in Victorian Scotland: Schools and Universities* (Oxford: OUP, 1983), p.1.
20. Ibid.
21. See e.g. Walter Hames and Hamish Paterson (eds.), *Scottish Culture and Scottish Education, 1800–1980* (Glasgow, 1983); Robert Anderson, 'In search of the "lad of parts": the mythical history of Scottish education', *History Workshop Journal*, 19 (1985), pp.82–104; Lindy Moore, 'Invisible scholars: girls learning Latin and mathematics in the elementary public schools of Scotland before 1872', *History of Education*, 13/2 (1984), pp.121–37; and James Roxburgh, *The School Board of Glasgow, 1873–1919* (London, 1971).
22. William Boyd, 'A Scotsman looks at New Zealand schools', in A.E. Campbell (ed.), *Modern Trends in Education* (Wellington: NZCER, 1938), p.470.
23. Ibid., pp.475–6.
24. Ibid., p.476.
25. Ibid., pp.484–5.
26. W. Thomas, C.E. Beeby and M.H. Oram, *Entrance to the University* (Wellington: NZCER, 1939).
27. C.E. Beeby to H.G.R. Mason (Minister of Education), 23 October 1942 (Wellington: Education Department papers, 34/1/23 Part 1).
28. C.E. Beeby, 'Memorandum for consultative committee on post-primary curriculum', 12 November 1942 (Education Department papers, 34/1/23 Part 1).
29. New Zealand Education Department, *The Post-Primary School Curriculum* (Wellington, 1944), Ch.2, Section 1.
30. Ibid., Ch.2, Section 2.
31. H.G.R. Mason, memo to C.E. Beeby, 21 October 1943 (Education Department papers, 34/1/23 Part 1).
32. *New Zealand Herald*, 9 October 1943, leading article, 'The New Education'.
33. Ibid.

34. *NZH*, 15 October 1943, leading article, 'Secondary education'.
35. *NZH*, 11 February 1944, leading article, 'Secondary education'.
36. C.E. Beeby to W. Thomas, 10 March 1944 (Education Department papers, 34/1/23 Part 1).
37. William Anderson, *The Flight from Reason in New Zealand Education* (Auckland, 1944), p.14.
38. Ibid., p.20.
39. Ibid., p.4.
40. Ibid.
41. C.E. Beeby, memo to Chief Inspector of Post-Primary Schools, 26 February 1958 (Education Department papers, 34/1/23 Part 1).
42. A.E. Campbell, memo to C.E. Beeby, 4 February 1958 (Education Department papers, 34/1/23 Part 1).
43. See Clive Whitehead, 'The Thomas report: a study in educational reform', *New Zealand Journal of Educational Studies*, 9/1 (1974), pp.52–64.
44. Chief Inspector of Post-Primary Schools, Wellington, memo to Director of Education, 8 January 1951 (Education Department papers, Auckland, 22/1/2).
45. E.g. Annual Report of Minister of Education, 1958: special report on post-primary curriculum, *Appendices to Journal of House of Representatives*, E1.
46. IAAM, *Memorandum on the Teaching of Geography* (London, 1935), p.2.
47. Ibid., p.v.
48. Ibid.
49. Ibid., p.9.
50. See e.g. *Geography*, 50/4 (1965), special issue on A.J. Herbertson.
51. New Zealand Geographical Society, 'Geography in New Zealand' (1945) (NZGS papers. I am grateful to the NZGS for allowing me access to these papers.)
52. Kenneth Cumberland to G.M. Wrigley (Editor of *Geographical Review*), 6 September 1939 (Cumberland papers. I am grateful to Professor Cumberland for allowing me access to his papers.)
53. Kenneth Cumberland to George C. Harrap, 7 February 1939 (Cumberland papers).
54. Kenneth Cumberland to A.W. Shrimpton, 25 July 1939 (Cumberland papers).
55. Kenneth Cumberland to Minister of Education, 16 November 1939; Kenneth Cumberland to Alan [Scott?], 17 July 1940 (Cumberland papers).
56. W.B. Harris, circular, 'To all interested in geography' (1939) (Cumberland papers).
57. 'Memorandum on the Teaching of Geography' (1935), Appendix 3.
58. C.B. Fawcett (University College, London) to Kenneth Cumberland, 20 November 1941 (Cumberland papers).
59. George Jobberns, 'Geography and national development', *New Zealand Geographer*, 1/1 (1945), p.6.
60. Kenneth Cumberland to George Jobberns, 6 November 1939 (Cumberland papers).
61. B.J. Garnier, *Geography for Post-Primary Pupils* (Wellington: NZCER, 1944).
62. Hugh Lauder, 'The New Right revolution and education in New Zealand', in Middleton *et al* (eds.), *New Zealand Education Policy Today*, p.3.
63. Ivan Snook, 'Educational reform in New Zealand: what *is* going on?', *Access*, 8/2 (1989), p.5.
64. Ibid.
65. See Gary McCulloch, '"Serpent in the garden": conservative protest, the "New Right", and New Zealand educational history', in *History of Education Review*, 20/1 (1991), pp.73–87. Also Gary McCulloch, 'Imperial and colonial designs: the case of Auckland Grammar School', *History of Education*, 17/4 (1988), pp.257–67.
66. See Jones *et al*, *Myths and Realities*, esp. pp.38–43.
67. Department of Education, *Charter Framework: Governing Schools* (Wellington, 1989).

10

Educational Reconstruction?

This book has ranged widely over some of the different kinds of significance that may be attached to the Education Act of 1944, and the cycle of reconstruction to which it belonged. The emphasis throughout has been on attempting to appreciate these reforms in a critical manner; that is, understanding something of the problems to which they gave rise, as well as the solutions that they offered and the hopes and aspirations that they encouraged. This has involved approaching the 1944 Act in five distinct but closely related ways: the interpretation has embraced the contestation that underlay it, the change and continuity that it represented, the wider contexts of which it was part, its longer term historical frameworks, and the impact and general influence that it made. So far as this last aspect is concerned, it may fairly be regarded as a defining moment, what might be described as a critical incident, for education in the twentieth century and probably also in the twenty-first, not only in Britain but also in other countries around the world.

Several themes have been examined in some depth, and these could well be multiplied further. This final chapter will content itself with raising three general questions. all unresolved and in need of further discussion but nevertheless key problems for us to address.

The first question that needs to be asked is why the general political consensus that facilitated the passage of the 1944 Act eventually broke down. Even though the Act itself remained in force for an unprecedented period, and indeed continued into the 1990s to be the master-Act to which new legislation referred, the potency of its appeal had begun to disintegrate certainly by the 1960s and perhaps even before. In an obvious sense, this process was part of the undermining of the post-war 'Welfare State'. Even more profoundly, it seemed to be bound up with criticisms that threatened the schooling project as a whole.

The national system of education had been rooted in Enlightenment philosophy and the aspirations and assumptions of the nineteenth century. It was conceived, albeit belatedly and grudgingly, as a social and economic investment for the nation. It was suffused with faith in education of the young as an instrument of social engineering, whether for established or for novel ends. It appealed on these grounds to a wide range of groups with different and even conflicting agendas, whether religious or scientific, for meritocracy or for hierarchy. The reforms of the 1940s strongly reflected these deeply rooted ends, and reconstructed them to appeal to the interests and ideals of mid-twentieth century society.

After the 1940s, it became increasingly difficult to re-fashion the schooling project in such a way as to achieve wide currency and appeal. As social engineering fell from grace, schooling began to look like another 'God that failed'. Rather than being seen as the solution to the social problems of the past, it was re-cast as part of the problem. In the process, it changed shape from salvation to scapegoat. Attempts to recover faith in the social possibilities of schooling in the late twentieth century had to contend with a growing burden of responsibility for the disappointments of the past, disappointments made all the greater by the inflated promises characteristic of educational reform.

A symptom of such fragmentation and decline, on this analysis, was the increasingly overt political divisions over the future of the education system from the 1950s onwards. Another was perhaps a narrowing and less well articulated notion of the purposes of schooling. It is noticeable from the late 1960s onwards that policy documents and public debates tended to be less explicit in their discussions of the social and political purposes of education than was the case in the nineteenth century. Indeed, the 1940s seem in retrospect to represent the last major upsurge of this kind of discussion. Even by the early 1960s, the central question, as it was described, of 'What kind of chaps do you wish the schools to turn out?' exposed disagreement on basic principles and tended to go unanswered.[1]

From this perspective, it is tempting to see the reform cycles of the 1960s and the 1980s/1990s as attempts to arrest the decline of the schooling project itself. The political conflicts that resulted, and the controversies to which they gave rise, might even be regarded as themselves constituting further symptoms of decay, rather than as signs of regeneration. The emphasis on the 'market' in the reforms of the 1980s and 1990s, celebrated in the White Paper *Choice and Diversity* in 1992 in the bald statement that 'parents know best', could be interpreted as representing a more advanced stage of the process of decline, in which responsibility for clear goals and objectives is abdicated or denied. Such a view is suggested in the work of historians such as Richard Johnson and Andy Green.[2] According to Green, indeed, there is a 'sad irony' in the possibility that 'the country which was last to create a national education system, and which never quite completed the job, should be the first to dismantle it'.[3] Considerations of the slow decline of the 'settlement' of 1944 therefore need to relate to this wider or more structural issue about the fortunes of schooling itself, taking a cue from the flawed but important work of the Centre for Contemporary Cultural Studies about the rise of what they term 'unpopular education'.[4]

The second general issue that deserves more extended reflection is the extent to which understanding the history assists the process of developing reforms. Historical debates are often treated as if they are irrelevant or incidental to contemporary problems.[5] The history of education as an area of study has also been severely undermined by recent changes in the teacher training curriculum. The analysis developed in this book, however, suggests that a great deal more attention needs to be given to the historical dimension of educational problems and policies. To put the matter another way, a general failure to pay attention to such issues may help to explain the problems that have afflicted recent educational reforms.

It seems by no means a coincidence that the reformers of the 1940s possessed by and large an acute awareness of historical frameworks and interpretations relating to the educational changes that they were seeking to encourage. These were closely associated with the philosophical and social goals of education. Thus Butler could discuss the importance of Plato with the socialist intellectuals G.D.H. Cole and Harold Laski. As Butler recorded:

> Mr Cole and I discussed in an amiable manner what Plato had attempted to discuss before us, namely, the best method of training the leaders of a community. He thought that the Public Schools should renounce their proud claim to constitute the method of training our leaders and should simply regard themselves as the boarding element in a national system of education.[6]

Chuter Ede, meanwhile, could invoke both the strengths and the limitations of previous educational reforms.[7]

It might be argued that a further consequence of such historical appreciation was that the reforms of the 1940s were designed with a view not only to the problems of the past, but also to those of the future. They built in a dimension of flexibility and a capacity to adapt to later demands, especially in the area of the school curriculum and on the actual structure of the local provision of education. In general, they did not make the mistake of assuming that theirs was the last word in reform, or that history had somehow come to an end. The 1944 settlement came under pressure earliest where it tried to prescribe matters in too much detail, for example with the local development plans that every LEA was supposed to prepare. As a rule, however, they were wise enough to avoid trying to set the reforms in concrete; their historical sense, we might say, warned them that political fashions and social trends would continue to change, and that educational reforms needed to accommodate themselves to these. By contrast, the 'tyranny of the present' tends to be not only ignorant about the past but also arrogant about the future, leading to attempts to cast the twenty-first century in its own image.

The third issue, closely related to these first two, concerns the prospects for the educational reforms that have been devised over the past decade. The tendency to seek a 'technical fix' to particular defined problems, combined with a lack of interest in broader historical, social, and philosophical goals, may be partly responsible for the lack of broad authority from which many of these recent reforms have suffered. A reliance on the market is perhaps an inadequate substitute for the civic ideology that lent weight to the reforms of the 1940s. At its worst, it can lead to policies based on the 'flavour of the month', contradicting those of the month before, policies that rise without trace, a frantic paperchase that subsides at last into exhaustion and disillusionment.

Education has been clearly signalled as a key area of social policy for the 1990s and beyond. And yet it will surely not respond well to a technical, 'Rubik's Cube' view of policy problems, in which cultural and historical issues are treated as fault lines that can be washed away through rational discussion or a show of force. A social vision for education in the twenty-first century has to be high on the agenda, and this will again entail a stronger sense of history and of theory. It would require a deeper understanding of the current context in terms of the problems involved in regenerating the project of schooling that is now over 150 years old. It would involve addressing how to revitalise an 'English tradition' of education that has lost much of its cohesion and broad support, and encouraging a public debate on the social goals of education, on what education is for. Only thus will we start on the long road to finding a worthy successor to the mission embarked on in the 1940s. 'Educational reconstruction' promises to be an even more ambitious and difficult venture in the twenty-first century than it appeared in 1944.

NOTES

1. R.A.R. Tricker, note to T.R. Weaver, 31 July 1961 (Ministry of Education papers, ED/147/794).
2. See e.g. Richard Johnson, 'Thatcherism and English education: breaking the mould, or confirming the pattern?', *History of Education*, 18/2 (1989), pp.91–121; and Andy Green, *Education and State Formation* (London: London, 1990).
3. Green, op. cit., p.316.
4. CCCS, *Unpopular Education: Schooling and Social Democracy in England Since 1944* (London: Hutchinson, 1981).
5. See e.g. Gary McCulloch, *The Secondary Technical School: A Usable Past?* (London: Falmer, 1989), Ch.2.
6. R.A. Butler, note of interview, 12 May 1942 (Board of Education papers, ED/136/599).
7. J. Chuter Ede, diary, 20 July 1943 (Chuter Ede diary manuscript, British Museum Add. Ms. 59696).

Appendix I

Board of Education White Paper *Educational Reconstruction*, Cmd. 6458, July 1943

INTRODUCTION

1. The Government's purpose in putting forward the reforms described in this Paper is to secure for children a happier childhood and a better start in life; to ensure a fuller measure of education and opportunity for young people and to provide means for all of developing the various talents with which they are endowed and so enriching the inheritance of the country whose citizens they are. The new educational opportunities must not, therefore, be of a single pattern. It is just as important to achieve diversity as it is to ensure equality of educational opportunity. But such diversity must not impair the social unity within the educational system which will open the way to a more closely knit society and give us strength to face the tasks ahead. The war has revealed afresh the resources and character of the British people – an enduring possession that will survive all the material losses inevitable in the present struggle. In the youth of the nation we have our greatest national asset. Even on a basis of mere expediency, we cannot afford not to develop this asset to the greatest advantage. It is the object of the present proposals to strengthen and inspire the younger generation. For it is as true to-day, as when it was first said, that 'the bulwarks of a city are its men'.

2. With these ends in view the Government propose to recast the national education service. The new layout is based on a recognition of the principle that education is a continuous process conducted in successive stages. For children below the compulsory school age of 5 there must be a sufficient supply of nursery schools. The period of compulsory school attendance will be extended to 15 without exemptions and with provision for its subsequent extension to 16 as soon as circumstances permit. The period from 5 to the leaving age will be divided into two stages, the first, to be known as primary, covering the years up to about 11. After 11 secondary education, of diversified types but on equal standing, will be provided for all children. At the primary stage the large classes and bad conditions which at present are a reproach to many elementary schools will be systematically eliminated; at the secondary stage the standard of accommodation and amenities will be steadily raised to the level of the best examples. The provision of school meals and milk will be made obligatory.

3. When the period of full-time compulsory schooling ends the young person will continue under educational influences up to 18 years of age either by remaining in full-time attendance at a secondary school, or by part-time day attendance at a young people's college. Throughout all the foregoing stages the benefits of medical inspection and treatment will be available without charge. Opportunities for technical and adult education will be increased.

4. Among other important features of the plan are an effective system of inspection and registration of schools outside the public system; new financial and administrative arrangements for the voluntary schools, and the recognition of the special place of religious instruction in school life. [. . .]

FULL-TIME SCHOOLING

PROPOSED REFORMS

General Provisions

22. It is intended that the raising of the school leaving age to 15, postponed in 1939, should be brought into effect as soon as possible after the war, but without the arrangements for exemptions made in the 1936 Act, and that provision should be made for a further extension to 16 at a later date.

23. It is proposed that the statutory system of public education shall cease to be severally administered for the purposes of elementary education and higher education respectively. It will be organised in three progressive stages to be known as primary education, secondary education, and further education, and a duty will be placed on each Local Education Authority to contribute towards the mental, moral, and physical development of the community by securing the provision of efficient education throughout those stages for all persons in the area capable of profiting thereby. For the fulfilment of the duties thus laid upon them Local Education Authorities will be required to make a comprehensive survey of the existing provision and the present and prospective needs of their areas and to prepare and submit to the Board development plans which will give a complete picture of the proposed layout of primary and secondary schools. In respect of all such schools, whether provided schools or non-provided schools (hereinafter called County and Auxiliary schools respectively), the plan will indicate the future organisation, the nature of the education to be given in the various types of secondary schools, and the alterations to the premises needed to bring the schools up to standards to be prescribed in Regulations of the Board. It will also contain information about the general arrangements to be made for the transport of pupils to and from school. Provision will be made for the Board, when they have approved the development plan, to make an education order for the area which will specify the steps which the

Authority are required to take by way, amongst other things, of maintaining existing schools, improving existing schools and providing new schools, and will contain a time-table to which the Authority will be required to conform in taking these steps.

24. The parent's duty will no longer be confined to causing his child to be efficiently instructed in the three R's; his duty will be to cause his child to receive efficient full-time education suitable to the child's age and aptitudes. [. . .]

Secondary Education

27. At about the age of 11 comes the change from the junior to the senior stage. At present all children of the appropriate age and standard enter for the Special Place examination and, from what has been said previously, it is clear that there is urgent need for reform. Accordingly, in the future, children at the age of about 11 should be classified, not on the results of a competitive test, but on an assessment of their individual aptitudes largely by such means as school records, supplemented, if necessary, by intelligence tests, due regard being had to their parents' wishes and the careers they have in mind. Even so, the choice of one type of secondary education rather than another for a particular pupil will not be finally determined at the age of 11, but will be subject to review as the child's special gifts and capacities develop. At the age of 13, or even later, there will be facilities for transfer to a different type of education, if the original choice proves to have been unsuitable. The keynote of the new system will be that the child is the centre of education and that, so far as is humanly possible, all children should receive the type of education for which they are best adapted.

28. If this choice is to be a real one, it is manifest that conditions in the different types of secondary schools must be broadly equivalent. Under present conditions the secondary school enjoys a prestige in the eyes of parents and the general public which completely overshadows all other types of school for children over 11. Inheriting as it does a distinguished tradition from the old English Grammar School it offers the advantages of superior premises and staffing and a longer school life for its pupils. Since 1902, when Local Education Authorities were first empowered to provide or aid secondary education, there has been a rapid expansion. In 1904 there were 86,000 pupils; to-day there are 514,000, of whom considerably more than half are in schools provided by Local Education Authorities. The success of the schools in dealing with this extension has been remarkable. The traditional curriculum has been widened and adapted to meet the ever-increasing variety of demands and, helped by the introduction in 1917 of the School Examinations system, an education has been evolved which in the main meets the needs of the more promising pupils. But in spite of this success, the schools are facing an impossible task. An academic training is ill-suited for many of the pupils who find themselves moving along a narrow educational path bounded by the

School Certificate and leading into a limited field of opportunity. Further, too many of the nation's abler children are attracted into a type of education which prepares primarily for the University and for the administrative and clerical professions; too few find their way into schools from which the design and craftsmanship sides of industry are recruited. If education is to serve the interests both of the child and of the nation, some means must be found of correcting this bias and of directing ability into the field where it will find its best realisation. [. . .]

35. But laws cannot build better human beings and it is not the machinery of education so much as its content that will count in the future. Already in one direction a start has been made. The curriculum of secondary schools, and especially that of the grammar schools, will be the subject of a report by the Norwood Committee. Public opinion will, undoubtedly, look for a new approach to the choice and treatment of school subjects after the war. In particular, consideration must be given to a closer relation of education in the countryside to the needs of agricultural and rural life and, more generally, to creating a better understanding between the people of the town and of the country. A new direction in the teaching of history and geography and modern languages will be needed to arouse and quicken in the pupils a livelier interest in the meaning and responsibilities of citizenship in this country, the Empire and of the world abroad. Education in the future must be a process of gradually widening horizons, from the family to the local community, from the community to the nation, and from the nation to the world. [. . .]

Appendix II

Board of Education – *Curriculum and Examinations in Secondary Schools: Report of the Committee of the Secondary School Examinations Council Appointed by the President Of The Board Of Education in 1941* (Norwood Report)

PART I
Chapter I

THE NATURE OF SECONDARY EDUCATION [. . .]

Variety of Capacity

One of the major problems of educational theory and organisation has always been, and always will be, to reconcile diversity of human endowment with practical schemes of administration and instruction. Even if it were shown that the differences between individuals are so marked as to call for as many curricula as there are individuals, it would be impossible to carry such a principle into practice; and school organisation and class instruction must assume that individuals have enough in common as regards capacities and interests to justify certain rough groupings. Such at any rate has been the point of view which has gradually taken shape from the experience accumulated during the development of secondary education in this country and in France and Germany and indeed in most European countries. The evolution of education has in fact thrown up certain groups, each of which can and must be treated in a way appropriate to itself. Whether such groupings are distinct on strictly psychological grounds, whether they represent types of mind, whether the differences are differences in kind or in degree, these are questions which it is not necessary to pursue. Our point is that rough groupings, whatever may be their ground, have in fact established themselves in general educational experience, and the recognition of such groupings in educational practice has been justified both during the period of education and in the after-careers of the pupils.

For example, English education has in practice recognised the pupil who is interested in learning for its own sake, who can grasp an argument or follow a piece of connected reasoning, who is interested in causes, whether on the level of human volition or in the material world, who cares to know how things came to be as well as how they are, who is sensitive to language as an expression of thought, to a proof as a precise demonstration, to a series of experiments justifying a principle: he is interested in the relatedness of related things, in development, in structure, in a coherent body of knowledge. He can take a long view and hold his mind in suspense; this may be revealed in his work or in his attitude to his career. He will have some capacity to enjoy, from an aesthetic point of view, the aptness of a phrase or the neatness of a proof. He may be good with his hands or he may not; he may or may not be a good 'mixer' or a leader or a prominent figure in activities, athletic or other.

Such pupils, educated by the curriculum commonly associated with the Grammar School, have entered the learned professions or have taken up higher administrative or business posts. Whether the curriculum was designed to produce men of this kind we need not enquire; but the assumption is now made, and with confidence, that for such callings a certain make-up of aptitudes and capacities is necessary, and such make-up may for educational purposes constitute a particular type of mind.

Again, the history of technical education has demonstrated the importance of recognising the needs of the pupil whose interests and abilities lie markedly in the field of applied science or applied art. The boy in this group has a strong interest in this direction and often the necessary qualities of mind to carry his interest through to make it his life-work at whatever level of achievement. He often has an uncanny insight into the intricacies of mechanism whereas the subtleties of language construction are too delicate for him. To justify itself to his mind, knowledge must be capable of immediate application, and the knowledge and its application which most appeal to him are concerned with the control of material things. He may have unusual or moderate intelligence: where intelligence is not great, a feeling of purpose and relevance may enable him to make the most of it. He may or may not be good at games or other activities. [. . .]

Again, there has of late years been recognition, expressed in the framing of curricula and otherwise, of still another grouping of pupils, and another grouping of occupations. The pupil in this group deals more easily with concrete things than with ideas. He may have much ability, but it will be in the realm of facts. He is interested in things as they are; he finds little attraction in the past or in the slow disentanglement of causes or movements. His mind must turn its knowledge or its curiosity to immediate test; and his test is essentially practical. He may see clearly along one line of study or interest and outstrip his generally abler fellows in that line; but he often fails to relate his knowledge or skill to other branches of activity. Because he is interested only in the moment he may be incapable of a long series of connected steps; relevance to present concerns is the only way of awakening interest, abstractions mean little to him. Thus it follows that he must have immediate returns for his effort, and for the same reason his career is often on his mind. His horizon is near and within a limited area his movement is generally slow, though it may be surprisingly rapid in seizing a particular point or in taking up a special line. Again, he may or may not be good with his hands or sensitive to Music or Art. [. . .]

Types of Curriculum

In a wise economy of secondary education pupils of a particular type of mind would receive the training best suited for them and that training would lead them to an occupation where their capacities would be suitably used; that a future occupation is already present to their minds while they are still at school has been suggested, though admittedly the degree to which it is present varies. Thus, to the three main types sketched above there would correspond three main types of curriculum, which we may again attempt to indicate.

First, there would be a curriculum of which the most characteristic feature is that it treats the various fields of knowledge as suitable for coherent and systematic study for their own sake apart from immediate considerations of occupation, though at a later stage grasp of the matter and experience of the methods belonging to those fields may determine the area of choice of employment and may contribute to success in the employment chosen.

The second type of curriculum would be closely, though not wholly, directed to the special data and skills associated with a particular kind of occupation; its outlook and its methods would always be bounded by a near horizon clearly envisaged. It would thus be closely related to industry, trades and commerce in all their diversity.

In the third type of curriculum a balanced training of mind and body and a correlated approach to humanities, Natural Science and the arts would provide an equipment varied enough to enable pupils to take up the work of life: its purpose would not be to prepare for a particular job or profession and its treatment would make a direct appeal to interests, which it would awaken by practical touch with affairs.

Of the first it may be said that it may or may not look forward to University work; if it does, that is because the Universities are traditionally concerned with the pursuit of knowledge as such. Of the second we would say that it may or may not look forward to the Universities, but that it should increasingly be directed to advanced studies in so far as the Universities extend their orbit in response to the demands of the technical branches of industry.

Purposes Common to Various Types of Curriculum

Hitherto we have treated secondary education as that phase of education in which differences between pupils receive the consideration due to them. But when the boy with special interest in Languages or Arts has been provided with an education which takes this interest into account, he still remains a boy. In other words, in spite of differences all pupils have common needs and a common destiny; physical and spiritual and moral ideals are of vital concern to all alike, and secondary education, whatever form it may take, must regard as its chief aim the satisfaction of all the needs of the child, both as a human being and as a member of a community. At the earliest stages there must be much that is common to the various types of secondary education, even as regards curriculum. For it would be

a mistake to regard transfer from the primary to the secondary stage as a
'break': rather it is a process, and the transfer must be eased by a
curriculum which carries over to some extent from the primary stage, and
later takes on a more pronounced colour according to the type of
secondary education chosen. Hence it would be reasonable that in the
various types of school offering secondary education there should always
be resemblances resulting from common purposes, but that in the early
stages the resemblances should be stronger.

To sum up, secondary education is the second stage in the growth of
the child. Healthy growth implies continuity, and, as we have said, the
change from primary education is a process. For this reason all schools
offering secondary education will have certain resemblances, but, since
the function of the secondary stage is to provide for special interests and
aptitudes, the differences between one type of curriculum and another
will progressively become more pronounced as the child grows older. If
secondary education as a whole is to do justice both to the individual pupil
and to the community, each type must strive for the achievement of those
aims which it shares with other types, while at the same time providing for
the special needs of those pupils to whom it offers its particular form of
education.

Secondary Education as it Exists in Fact

Under the existing organisation of secondary education in this country
the three kinds of curriculum which we have indicated have in fact been
provided in the Secondary Schools, in the various types of Junior Technical Schools and in the Senior Schools; within each type of school and
within individual schools various kinds of courses have been offered. In so
far as these schools assume, as they do, previously acquired skills and
habits exercised upon the elements of knowledge and on that assumption
go on to differentiate special aptitudes and interests and to cater for them,
the schools are in fact secondary in character, using the term secondary to
denote the second stage in education. Secondary education, as it exists in
fact, already shows the diversity which we regard as essential to its health.
The Junior Technical Schools, though inadequate in number and equipment, provide varied opportunities; the Senior Schools, though only in an
early stage of development, are showing enterprise in meeting the special
needs of particular localities. With Junior Technical Schools and with
Senior Schools we are not specifically concerned, except in so far as
consideration of them is necessary to the building of a single structure of
secondary education, and we shall make no attempt to describe them in
detail. The Secondary Schools show great variety as regards traditions,
the aim and destination of their pupils, the interests and abilities of pupils,
organisation and curriculum. Inheriting the tradition of the Grammar
School they have at the same time held to it and deviated from it: indeed
they now display a variety which some critics would say has reached the
point of confusion in aim and function. That there should be variety we
regard as essential; willingness to recognise needs and to make the

adaptation necessary to meet them is a sign of vitality in education. The question which concerns us, however, is whether, even amid the variety offered by Secondary Schools, the curriculum is really suited to all the pupils in them. Are the Secondary Schools, which have traditions and obligations of their own, attempting to satisfy needs which should be satisfied by other forms of education? [. . .]

Appendix III

Education Act, 1944: An Act to reform the law relating to education in England and Wales, 3rd August 1944.

PART I

CENTRAL ADMINISTRATION

1. (1) It shall be lawful for His Majesty to appoint a Minister (hereinafter referred to as 'the Minister'), whose duty it shall be to promote the education of the people of England and Wales and the progressive development of institutions devoted to that purpose, and to secure the effective execution by local authorities, under his control and direction, of the national policy for providing a varied and comprehensive educational service in every area.

(2) The Minister shall for all purposes be a corporation sole under the name of the Minister of Education, and the department of which he is in charge shall be known as the Ministry of Education. [. . .]

4. (1) There shall be two Central Advisory Councils for Education, one for England and the other for Wales and Monmouthshire, and it shall be the duty of those Councils to advise the Minister upon such matters connected with educational theory and practice as they think fit, and upon any questions referred to them by him.

(2) The members of each Council shall be appointed by the Minister, and the Minister shall appoint a member of each Council to be Chairman thereof and shall appoint an officer of the Ministry of Education to be secretary thereto.

(3) Each Council shall include persons who have had experience of the statutory system of public education as well as persons who have had experience of educational institutions not forming part of that system.

(4) The Minister shall by regulations make provision as to the term of office and conditions of retirement of the members of each Council, and regulations made by the Minister for either Council may provide for periodical or other meetings of the Council and as to the procedure thereof, but, subject to the provisions of any such regulations, the meetings and procedure of each Council shall be such as may be determined by them.

5. The Minister shall make to Parliament an annual report giving an account of the exercise and performance of the powers and duties

conferred and imposed upon him by this Act and of the composition and proceedings of the Central Advisory Councils for Education.

PART II
The Statutory System of Education

LOCAL ADMINISTRATION

6. (1) Subject to the provisions of Part I of the First Schedule to this Act, the local education authority for each county shall be the council of the county, and the local education authority for each county borough shall be the council of the county borough.[. . .]

THE THREE STAGES OF THE SYSTEM

7. The statutory system of public education shall be organised in three progressive stages to be known as primary education, secondary education, and further education; and it shall be the duty of the local education authority for every area, so far as their powers extend, to contribute towards the spiritual, moral, mental, and physical development of the community by securing that efficient education throughout these stages shall be available to meet the needs of the population of their area.

PRIMARY AND SECONDARY EDUCATION

Provision and Maintenance of Primary and Secondary Schools

8. (1) It shall be the duty of every local education authority to secure that there shall be available for their area sufficient schools –
   (a) for providing primary education, that is to say, full-time education suitable to the requirements of junior pupils; and
   (b) for providing secondary education, that is to say, full-time education suitable to the requirements of senior pupils, other than such full-time education as may be provided for senior pupils in pursuance of a scheme made under the provisions of this Act relating to further education;
   and the schools available for an area shall not be deemed to be sufficient unless they are sufficient in number, character, and equipment to afford for all pupils opportunities for education offering such variety of instruction and training as may be desirable in view of their different ages, abilities, and aptitudes, and of the different periods for which they may be expected to remain at school, including practical instruction and training appropriate to their respective needs. [. . .]

9. (1) For the purpose of fulfilling their duties under this Act, a local education authority shall have power to establish primary and secondary schools, to maintain such schools whether established by them or

otherwise, and, so far as may be authorised by arrangements approved by the Minister, to assist any such school which is not maintained by them. [. . .]

11. (1) As soon as may be after the date of the commencement of this Part of this Act, every local education authority shall estimate the immediate and prospective needs of their area, having regard to the provisions of this Act and of any regulations made thereunder and to the functions relating to primary and secondary education thereby conferred on them, and shall, within one year after that date or within such extended period as the Minister may in any particular case allow, prepare and submit to the Minister a plan (in this Act referred to as a 'development plan') in such form as the Minister may direct showing the action which the authority propose should be taken for securing that there shall be sufficient primary and secondary schools available for their area and the successive measures by which it is proposed to accomplish that purpose. [. . .]

15. (1) Voluntary schools shall be of three categories, that is to say, controlled schools, aided schools, and special agreement schools, and in schools of those several categories the management of the school, the secular instruction and religious education, and the appointment and dismissal of teachers, shall be regulated in accordance with the provisions hereinafter contained relating to those matters in controlled schools aided schools and special agreement schools respectively. [. . .]

Management of Primary Schools and Government of Secondary Schools

17. (1) For every county school and for every voluntary school there shall be an instrument providing for the constitution of the body of managers or governors of the school in accordance with the provisions of this Act, and the instrument providing for the constitution of the body of managers of a primary school is in this Act referred to as an instrument of management, and the instrument providing for the constitution of the body of governors of a secondary school is in this Act referred to as an instrument of government. [. . .]

Religious Education in County and Voluntary Schools

25. (1) Subject to the provisions of this section, the school day in every county school and in every voluntary school shall begin with collective worship on the part of all pupils in attendance at the school, and the arrangements made thereafter shall provide for a single act of worship attended by all such pupils unless, in the opinion of the local education authority or, in the case of a voluntary school, of the managers or governors thereof, the school premises are such as to make it impracticable to assemble them for that purpose. [. . .]

Primary and Secondary Education of pupils requiring
Special Educational Treatment

33. (1) The Minister shall make regulations defining the several categories of pupils requiring special educational treatment and making provision as to the special methods appropriate for the education of pupils of each category.
(2) The arrangements made by a local education authority for the special educational treatment of pupils of any such category shall, so far as is practicable, provide for the education of pupils in whose case the disability is serious in special schools appropriate for that category, but where that is impracticable, or where the disability is not serious, the arrangements may provide for the giving of such education in any school maintained or assisted by the local education authority. [. . .]

Compulsory Attendance at Primary and Secondary Schools

35. In this Act the expression 'compulsory school age' means any age between five years and fifteen years, and accordingly a person shall be deemed to be of compulsory school age if he has attained the age of five years and has not attained the age of fifteen years and a person shall be deemed to be over compulsory school age as soon as he has attained the age of fifteen. [. . .]

36. It shall be the duty of the parent of every child of compulsory school age to cause him to receive efficient full-time education suitable to his age, ability, and aptitude, either by regular attendance at school or otherwise. [. . .]

FURTHER EDUCATION

41. Subject as hereinafter provided, it shall be the duty of every local education authority to secure the provision for their area of adequate facilities for further education, that is to say:
(a) full-time and part-time education for persons over compulsory school age; and
(b) leisure-time occupation, in such organized cultural training and recreative activities as are suited to their requirements, for any persons over compulsory school age who are able and willing to profit by the facilities provided for that purpose;
Provided that the provisions of this section shall not empower or require local education authorities to secure the provision of facilities for further education otherwise than in accordance with schemes of further education or at county colleges. [. . .]

43. (1) On and after such date as His Majesty may by Order in Council determine, not later than three years after the date of the

commencement of this Part of the Act, it shall be the duty of every local education authority to establish and maintain county colleges, that is to say, centres approved by the Minister for providing for young persons who are not in full-time attendance at any school or other educational institution such further education, including physical practical and vocational training, as will enable them to develop their various aptitudes and capacities and will prepare them for the responsibility of citizenship. [. . .]

SUPPLEMENTARY PROVISIONS AS TO PRIMARY, SECONDARY AND FURTHER EDUCATION [. . .]

49. Regulations made by the Minister shall impose upon local education authorities the duty of providing milk, meals and other refreshment for pupils in attendance at schools and county colleges maintained by them; and such regulations shall make provision as to the manner in which and the persons by whom the expense of providing such milk, meals or refreshment is to be defrayed, as to the facilities to be afforded (including any buildings or equipment to be provided) and as to the services to be rendered by managers governors and teachers with respect to the provision of such milk, meals or refreshment, and as to such other consequential matters as the Minister considers expedient, so, however, that such regulations shall not impose upon teachers at any school or college duties upon days on which the school or college is not open for instruction, or duties in respect of meals other than the supervision of pupils, and shall not require the managers or governors of a voluntary school to incur expenditure. [. . .]

53. (1) It shall be the duty of every local education authority to secure that the facilities for primary secondary and further education provided for their area include adequate facilities for recreation and social and physical training, and for that purpose a local education authority, with the approval of the Minister, may establish maintain and manage, or assist the establishment, maintenance, and management of camps, holiday classes, playing fields, play centres, and other places (including playgrounds, gymnasiums, and swimming baths not appropriated to any school or college), at which facilities for recreation and for such training as aforesaid are available for persons for whom primary secondary or further education is provided by the authority, and may organise games, expeditions and other activities for such persons, and may defray or contribute towards the expenses thereof. [. . .]

Miscellaneous Provisions

61. (1) No fees shall be charged in respect of admission to any school maintained by a local education authority, or to any county college, or in respect of the education provided in any such school or college. [. . .]

PART IV
General

GENERAL PRINCIPLE TO BE OBSERVED BY MINISTER AND LOCAL EDUCATION AUTHORITIES

76. In the exercise and performance of all powers and duties conferred and imposed on them by this Act the Minister and local education authorities shall have regard to the general principle that, so far as is compatible with the provision of efficient instruction and training and the avoidance of unreasonable public expenditure, pupils are to be educated in accordance with the wishes of their parents. [. . .]

99. (1) If the Minister is satisfied, either upon complaint by any person interested or otherwise, that any local education authority, or the managers or governors of any county school or voluntary school, have failed to discharge any duty imposed upon them by or for the purposes of this Act, the Minister may make an order declaring the authority, or the managers or governors, as the case may be, to be in default in respect of that duty, and giving such directions for the purpose of enforcing the execution thereof as appear to the Minister to be expedient; and any such directions shall be enforceable, on an application made on behalf of the Minister, by mandamus. [. . .]

Select Bibliography

(1) Unpublished sources

Association of Heads of Secondary Technical Schools conference papers, correspondence, University of Leeds Special Collections

Board of Education records, Public Record Office, Kew

R.A. Butler diary, correspondence, Trinity College Cambridge

James Chuter Ede diary manuscript, British Museum, London

Kenneth Cumberland correspondence, papers, University of Auckland

Incorporated Association of Assistant Masters (IAAM), Institute of Education, London

McNair Committee on teachers and youth leaders papers and correspondence, University of Liverpool

Manchester Guardian archive, Manchester University Library

Ministry of Education records, Public Record Office, Kew

New Zealand Department of Education records, Wellington and Auckland Offices of the Department of Education

New Zealand Geographical Society, NZGS, University of Canterbury

Sir Ernest and Lady Simon correspondence, general papers, Manchester Central Library

John Strachey correspondence, private

R.H. Tawney correspondence, memos, Institute of Education, London; and British Library of Political and Economic Science

(2) Newspapers and periodicals

Journal of Education

Manchester Guardian

New Zealand Herald

The Independent

The Sunday Times

The Times

Times Educational Supplement (*TES*)

(3) Policy reports

BOARD OF EDUCATION (1926) *Report of the Consultative Committee on the Education of the Adolescent* (Hadow Report), HMSO, London

BOARD OF EDUCATION (1938) *Report of the Consultative Committee on Secondary Education with Special Reference to Grammar Schools and Technical High Schools* (Spens Report), HMSO, London

BOARD OF EDUCATION (1943) *Educational Reconstruction* (White Paper), HMSO, London

BOARD OF EDUCATION (1943) *Curriculum and Examinations in Secondary Schools* (Norwood Report) HMSO, London

BOARD OF EDUCATION (1943) *Education Bill: Explanatory Memorandum by the President of the Board of Education* (Cmd. 6492), HMSO, London

BOARD OF EDUCATION (1944) *The Supply, Recruitment and Training of Teachers and Youth Leaders* (McNair Report), HMSO, London

BOARD OF EDUCATION (1944) *The Public Schools and the General Educational System* (Fleming Report), HMSO, London

CENTRAL ADVISORY COUNCIL FOR EDUCATION (1967) *Children and their Primary Schools* (Plowden Report), HMSO, London

COMMITTEE ON HIGHER EDUCATION (1963) *Higher Education* (Robbins Report) HMSO, London

DEARING, R. (1993) *The National Curriculum and its Assessment: An Interim Report*, National Curriculum Council/School Examinations and Assessment Council, London

DEARING, R. (1994) *Final Report: The National Curriculum and its Assessment*, School Curriculum and Assessment Authority, London

DEPARTMENT FOR EDUCATION (1992) *Choice and Diversity*, HMSO, London

DEPARTMENT OF EDUCATION AND SCIENCE (1965) 'The organisation of secondary education' (Circular 10/65, 12 July)

DEPARTMENT OF EDUCATION AND SCIENCE (1991) *Education and Training for the 21st Century* (2 vols), HMSO, London

HOUSE OF COMMONS DEBATES

LONDON COUNTY COUNCIL (1947) *London School Plan*, LCC, London

MINISTRY OF EDUCATION (1947) *The New Secondary Education*, pamphlet no 9, HMSO, London

MINISTRY OF EDUCATION (1958) *Secondary Education for all: A New Drive* (Cmnd 604), HMSO, London

NATIONAL COMMISSION ON EDUCATION (1993) *Learning to Succeed: A Radical Look at Education Today and a Strategy for the Future*, Heinemann, London

NEW ZEALAND DEPARTMENT OF EDUCATION *Annual Reports*

NEW ZEALAND DEPARTMENT OF EDUCATION (1944) *The Post-Primary School Curriculum* (Thomas Report), Wellington

PUBLIC SCHOOLS COMMISSION (1968) *First Report*, HMSO, London

(4) Unpublished theses and dissertations

MORRIS, R. (1988) 'Education policy and legislation: a critical examination of the arguments for a new major Education Act to replace that of 1944', PhD thesis, University of Reading

SILTO, W. (1993) 'Compulsory day continuation schools: their origins, objectives and development, with special reference to H.A.L. Fisher's 1918 experiment', PhD thesis, University of London

(5) Secondary sources

a. *General background works*

ADLER, M., PETCH, A. and TWEEDIE, J. (1989) *Parental Choice and Educational Policy*, Edinburgh University Press, Edinburgh

ALDCROFT, D. (1992) *Education, Training and Economic Performance 1944 to 1990*, Manchester University Press, Manchester

ALDRICH, R. (1992) 'Educational legislation of the 1980s in England: an historical analysis', *History Of Education*, 21/1, pp. 57–69

ANDERSON, R.D. (1983) *Education And Opportunity in Victorian Scotland: Schools And Universities*, Edinburgh University Press, Edinburgh

ANDREWS, L. (1976) *The Education Act, 1918*, Routledge, London

BAILEY, B. (1987)'The development of technical education, 1934–1939', *History Of Education*, 16/1, pp.49–65

BAKER, K. (1993) *The Turbulent Years: My Life in Politics*, Faber & Faber, London

BALL, S. (ed.) (1984) *Comprehensive Schooling: A Reader*, Falmer, London

BALL, S. (1990) *Politics and Policy Making in Education: Explorations in Policy Sociology*, Routledge, London

BANKS, O. (1955) *Parity and Prestige in English Secondary Education*, Routledge & Kegan Paul, London

BARKER, R. (1972) *Education and Politics 1900–1951: A Study of the Labour Party*, Clarendon Press, Oxford

BARTON, L. and MEIGHAN, R. (eds) (1978) *Sociological Interpretations of Schooling and Classrooms*, Driffield, Nafferton

BENN, C. and SIMON, B. (1972) *Half Way There: Report on the British Comprehensive School Reform*, 2nd edn, Penguin, London

BENN, T. (1989) *Against the Tide: Diaries 1973–76*, Arrow Books, London

BOWE, R. and BALL, S. (1992) *Reforming Education and Changing Schools: Case Studies in Policy Sociology*, Routledge, London

BRENNAN, E.J.T. (ed.) *Education for National Efficiency: The Contribution of Sidney and Beatrice Webb*, Athlone Press, London

BROADFOOT, P. (1979) *Assessment, Schools and Society*, Routledge & Kegan Paul, London

BROADFOOT, P. (ed.) (1984) *Selection, Certification and Control: Social Issues in Educational Assessment*, Falmer, London

CENTRE FOR CONTEMPORARY CULTURAL STUDIES (1981) *Unpopular Education: Schooling and Social Democracy in England Since 1944*, Hutchinson, London

CHITTY, C. (1988) 'Central control of the school curriculum, 1944-87', *History Of Education*, 17/4, pp.321-34

CHITTY, C. (1989) *Towards a New Education System: The Victory of the New Right?*, Falmer, London

CHITTY, C. (1992) 'The changing role of the state in education provision', *History of Education*, 21/1, pp.1-14

CHITTY, C. and SIMON, B. (eds) (1992) *Education Answers Back: Critical Responses to Government Policy*, Lawrence & Wishart, London

CLARKE, F. (1923) *Essays in the Politics of Education*, Oxford University Press, Oxford

DALE, R. (1989) *The State and Education Policy*, Open University Press, Milton Keynes

DANCY, J. (1965) 'Technology in a liberal education', *Advancement of Science*, October, pp.379-87

DAVID, M. (1993) *Parents, Gender and Education Reform*, Polity Press, Cambridge

DEAN, D.W. (1992) 'Consensus or conflict? The Churchill government and educational policy, 1951-55', *History of Education*, 21/1 (1992), pp.15-35

DENT, H.C. (1971) 'To cover the country with good schools: a century's effort', *British Journal of Educational Studies*, 19/2, pp.125-38

ESDEN-TEMPSKA, C. (1990) 'Civic education in authoritarian Austria, 1934-38', *History of Education Quarterly*, 30/2, pp.187-211

FASS, P.S. (1989) *Outside In: Minorities and the Transformation of American Education*, OUP, Oxford

FLEMING, T. (1991) 'Canadian school policy in liberal and post-liberal eras: historical perspectives on the changing social context of schooling, 1846-1990', *Journal of Education Policy*, 6/2 (1991), pp.183-99

FLUDE, M. and HAMMER, M. (eds) (1990) *The Education Reform Act 1988: Its Origins and Implications*, Falmer, London

FRANKLIN, B.M. (1986) *Building the American Community: The School Curriculum and the Search for Social Control*, Falmer, London

FRASER, D. (1973) *The Evolution of the British Welfare State*, Macmillan, London

GOODSON, I. (1988) *The Making of Curriculum: Collected Essays*, Falmer, London

GOODSON, I. (1992) 'On curriculum form: notes toward a theory of curriculum', *Sociology of Education*, 65, pp.66-75

GORDON, P. (1980) *Selection for Secondary Education*, Woburn Press, London

GORDON, P. and WHITE, J. (1979) *Philosophers as Educational Reformers: The Influence of Idealism on British Educational Thought and Practice*, Routledge & Kegan Paul, London

GOSDEN, P. (1983) *The Education System Since 1944*, Martin Robertson, Oxford

GRACE, G. (ed.) (1984) *Education and the City: Theory, History and Contemporary Practice*, Routledge & Kegan Paul, London

GRAHAM, D. with TYTLER, D. (1992) *A Lesson for us All*, Routledge, London

GREEN, A. (1990) *Education and State Formation: The Rise of Education Systems in England, France and the USA*, Routledge, London

HAMILTON, D. (1989) *Towards a Theory of Schooling*, Falmer, London

HANSOT, E. and TYACK, D. (1982) 'A usable past: using history in educational policy', in A. Lieberman, M.W. McLaughlin (eds), *Policy-Making In Education*, National Society for the Study of Education, Chicago, pp.1–21

HARRIS, J. (1992) 'Political thought and the Welfare State 1870–1940: an intellectual framework for British social policy', *Past And Present*, 135, pp.116–41

HOBSBAWM, E. and RANGER, T. (eds) (1983) *The Invention Of Tradition*, Cambridge University Press, Cambridge

HUBBACK, E. and SIMON, E.D. (1934?) *Education For Citizenship*, Association for Education in Citizenship, London

HUNT, F. (1991) *Gender and Policy in English Education: Schooling for Girls 1902–1944*, Harvester, New York

JOHNSON, R. (1989) 'Thatcherism and English education: breaking the mould, or confirming the pattern?', *History of Education*, 18/2, pp.91–121

JONES, A., McCULLOCH, G., MARSHALL, J., SMITH, G. and SMITH, L. (1990) *Myths and Realities: Schooling in New Zealand*, Dunmore Press, Palmerston North

KATZ, M.B. (1987) *Reconstructing American Education*, Harvard University Press, London

KENNEDY, P. (1993) *Preparing for the Twenty-First Century*, Harper-Collins, London

KERR, J.F. (1968) *Changing the Curriculum*, University of London Press, London

LAUDER, H. and WYLIE, C. (eds) (1990) *Towards Successful Schooling*, Falmer, London

LAWN, M. and GRACE, G. (eds) (1987) *Teachers: The Culture and Politics of Work*, Falmer, London

LAWSON, J. and SILVER, H. (1973) *A Social History of Education in England*, Methuen, London

LOWE, R. (ed.) (1989) *The Changing Secondary School*, Falmer, London

McCULLOCH, G. (1984) 'Views of the Alternative Road: the Crowther concept', in D. Layton (ed.), *The Alternative Road: The Rehabilitation of the Practical*, University of Leeds, Leeds, pp.57–73

McCULLOCH, G. (1985) '"Teachers and missionaries": the Left Book Club as an educational agency', *History of Education*, 14/2, pp. 137–53

McCULLOCH, G. (1988) 'Imperial and colonial designs: the case of Auckland Grammar School', *History of Education*, 17/4, pp.257–67

McCULLOCH, G. (1989) *The Secondary Technical School: A Usable Past?*, Falmer, London

McCULLOCH, G. (1991) *Philosophers and Kings: Education for Leadership in Modern England*, Cambridge University Press, Cambridge

McCULLOCH, G. (1991) '"Serpent in the garden": conservative protest, the "New Right", and New Zealand educational history', *History of Education Review*, 20/1, pp.73–87

McCULLOCH, G. (1991) 'Usable past or inexcusable present? History and education policy', *Education Research And Perspectives*, 18/1, pp.3–13

McCULLOCH, G. (1991) 'School zoning, equity and freedom: the case of New Zealand', *Journal of Education Policy*, 6/2. pp.155–68

McCULLOCH, G. (ed.) (1992) *The School Curriculum in New Zealand: History, Theory, Policy and Practice*, Dunmore, Palmerston North

McCULLOCH, G., JENKINS, E., and L AYTON, D. (1985) *Technological Revolution? The Politics of School Science and Technology in England and Wales Since 1945*, Falmer, London

MacDONALD, B. and WALKER, R. (1976) *Changing the Curriculum*, Open Books, London

McPHERSON, A. and RAAB, C. (1988) *Governing Education: A Sociology of Policy Since 1945*, Edinburgh University Press, Edinburgh

MALIM, F.B. (1948) *Almae Matres: Recollections of Some Schools at Home and Abroad*, Cambridge University Press, Cambridge

MANGAN, J.A. (1978) 'Eton in India: the imperial diffusion of a Victorian educational ethic', *History Of Education*, 7/2, pp.105–18

MANGAN, J.A. (1986) *The Games Ethic and Imperialism: Aspects of the Diffusion of an Ideal*, Viking, London

MARSDEN, W.E. (1993) 'Recycling religious instruction? Historical perspectives on contemporary cross-curricular issues', *History of Education*, 22/4, pp.321–33

MATTHEWS, J.C. (1985) *Examinations: A Commentary*, George Allen & Unwin, London

MAYNES, M.J. (1985) *Schooling in Western Europe: A Social History*, State University of New York Press, Albany

MIDDLETON, S., CODD, J. and JONES, A. (eds) (1990) *New Zealand Education Policy Today: Critical Perspectives*, Allen & Unwin, Wellington

MILLER, P. (1989) 'Historiography of compulsory schooling: what is the problem?', *History Of Education*, 18/2 (1989), pp.123–44

MULLER, D., RINGER, F. and SIMON, B. (eds) (1987) *The Rise Of The Modern Educational System*, Cambridge University Press, Cambridge

MURPHY, J. (1972) *The Education Act 1870: Text and Commentary*, David and Charles, Newton Abbot

PERCY, E. (1958) *Some Memories*, Eyre & Spottiswoode, London

PETCH, J.A. (1953) *Fifty Years of Examining: The Joint Matriculation Board, 1903–1953*, Harrap, London

PIMLOTT, B. (1977) *Labour and the Left in the 1930s*, Cambridge University Press, Cambridge

RATTANSI, A. and REEDER, D. (eds) (1992) *Rethinking Radical Education*, Lawrence & Wishart, London

RICHTER, M. (1964) *The Politics of Conscience: T.H. Green and his Age*, Weidenfeld and Nicolson, London

ROACH, J. (1971) *Public Examinations in England, 1850–1900*, Cambridge University Press, Cambridge

SANDERSON, M. (1987) *Educational Opportunity and Social Change in England*, Faber, London

SAVAGE, G. (1983) 'Social class and social policy: the civil service and secondary education in England during the interwar period', *Journal of Contemporary History*, 18, pp.261–80

SCHLECHTY, P. (1990) *Schools for the Twenty-First Century*, Jossey-Bass, San Francisco

SELLECK, R.J.W. (1968) *The New Education, 1870–1914*, Pitman, London

SELLECK, R.J.W. (1972) *English Primary Education and the Progressives, 1914–1939*, Pitman, London

SHERINGTON, G. (1976) 'The 1918 Education Act: origins, aims and development', *British Journal of Educational Studies*, 24/1, pp.66–85

SHERINGTON, G. (1981) *English Education, Social Change and War, 1911–20*, Manchester University Press, Manchester

SILVER, H. (1990) *Education, Change and the Policy Process*, Falmer, London

SIMON, B. (1955) *The Common Secondary School*, Lawrence & Wishart, London

SIMON, B. (1965) *Education and the Labour Movement, 1870–1920*, Lawrence & Wishart, London

SIMON, B. (1974) *The Politics of Educational Reform, 1920–1940*, Lawrence & Wishart, London

SIMON, B. (1991) *Education and the Social Order, 1940–1990*, Lawrence & Wishart, London

SIMON, B. (1992) *What Future for Education?*, Lawrence & Wishart, London

SIMON, B. (1992) 'The politics of comprehensive reorganisation: a retrospective analysis', *History of Education*, 21/4, pp.355–62

SIMON, B. (1993) 'Education and citizenship in England', *Paedagogica Historica*, 29/3, pp.689–97

SIMON, J. (1977) 'The shaping of the Spens report on secondary education 1933–38: an inside view', Part I, *British Journal of Educational Studies*, 25/1, pp.63–80; Part II, *BJES*, 25/2, pp.170–85

SUMMERFIELD, P. and EVANS, E. (eds) (1990) *Technical Education and the State Since 1850: Historical And Contemporary Perspectives*, Manchester University Press, Manchester

SUTHERLAND, G. (1984) *Ability, Merit and Measurement: Mental Testing and English Education, 1880–1940*, Clarendon Press, Oxford

TAWNEY, R.H. (1935; 1964 edn) *Equality*, Unwin Books, London

TERRILL, R. (1973) *R.H. Tawney and his Times: Socialism as Fellowship*, Harvard UP, Harvard

THOMAS, A.A. (1919) *The Education Act, 1918*, P.S. King & Son, London

WALFORD, G. and MILLER, H. (1991) *City Technology College*, Open University Press, Milton Keynes

WIENER, M. (1981) *English Culture and the Decline of the Industrial Spirit, 1850–1980*, Cambridge University Press, Cambridge

WILLIAMS, M., DOUGHERTY, R. and BANKS, F. (eds) (1992) *Continuing the Education Debate*, Cassell, London

YONG, W.Y. and MARSDEN, W.E. (1993) 'Continuity and change in geography's contribution to citizenship education in England in the 19th and 20th century', *Paedagogica Historica*, 29/2, pp.483–502

YOUNG, M. (1958; 1963 edn) *The Rise of the Meritocracy, 1870–2033*, Penguin, London

b. *Works specifically on the 1944 Education Act and the reforms of the 1940s*

ADDISON, P. (1975) *The Road to 1945: British Politics in the Second World War*, Jonathan Cape, London

AKENSON, D.H. (1971) 'Patterns of English educational change: the Fisher and the Butler Acts', *History of Education Quarterly*, 11 (1971), pp.143–56

ALDRICH, R. and LEIGHTON, P. (1985) *Education: Time for a New Act?*, Institute of Education, University of London

ALEXANDER, Sir W. (1969) *Towards a New Educa*
Education Press, London

ANDERSON, W. (1944) *The Flight from Re*
Auckland

BARNETT, C. (1986) *The Audit of*
as a Great Nation, Macmillan

BRERETON, J.L. (1944) *
Place in Education*
Cambridge

BROOKE, S
World W

BUT

D
on
Histo

DENT,
Impact o)
Paul, Lond

DENT, H. (1
some Problems

DENT, H.C. (195
University of Lond

DENT, H.C. (1954) *G*
& Kegan Paul, London

EVANS, B.J. (1982) 'Furt
continued and technical ec
pp.45–55

FISHER, P. (1982) *External Exa*
and Wales, 1944–1964, Universi

GARNIER, B.J. (1944) *Geography*
Council for Educational Research,

GILES, G.C.T. (1946) *The New Schoo*

GOSDEN, P. (1976) *Education In The*
Policy and Administration, Methuen, Lon

198

EDUCATIONAL RECONSTRUCTION

SIMON, B. (1986) 'The 1944 Education Act: a Conservative measure?',
History of Education, 15/1, pp.31–43

SIMON, J. (1989) 'Promoting educational reform on the home front: The
TES and *The Times* 1940–1944', *History of Education*, 18/3, pp.195–211

SMITH, F. (1943) 'Curriculum and examinations in secondary schools',
British Journal of Educational Psychology, 13/3, pp.159–62

SMITH, H. (ed.) (1986) *War and Social Change: British Society in the
Second World War*, Manchester University Press, Manchester

TAWNEY, R.H. (1941) *Why Britain Fights*, Macmillan war pamphlet n
13, London

THOM, D. (1986) 'The 1944 Education Act: the "art of the possible"?'
Smith (ed.), *War And Social Change*, pp.101–28.

WALLACE, R.G. (1981) 'The origins and authorship of the 1944 Educ
Act', *History Of Education*, 10/4, pp.283–90

WHITEHEAD, C. (1974) 'The Thomas report: a study in educ
reform', *New Zealand Journal of Educational Studies*, 9/1, pp.52

Index